Agriculture in Rigveda

Seeds of India's Civilizational Prosperity

D. K. Srivastava

2022
Gurugram and Mangalore
India

Copyright @ D. K. Srivastava

No part of this book and its future editions in print and electronic formats should be reproduced without permission from the Author.

Contact email: dkscloud@gmail.com

Published by D. K. Srivastava *Arthabodh*

Year: 2022

The place of the Vedas for mankind is acknowledged by Sri Krishna himself as representing his own presence. The Vedas represent divine knowledge showered upon mankind for their benefit. From Srimad Bhagvad Gita: Chapter 9, Shloka 17

"I am the Rigveda, Samveda, and the Yajurveda"

G 1 Srimad Bhagvad Gita: Chapter 9, Shloka 17

पिताहमस्य जगतो माता धाता पितामहः ।
वेद्यं पवित्रमोङ्कार ऋक्साम यजुरेव च ॥ 9-17

This translates to: 'Of this universe, I am the Father; I am also the Mother, the Sustainer, and the Grandsire. I am the purifier, the goal of knowledge, the sacred syllable Om. **I am the Rigveda, Samaveda, and the Yajurveda**'.

[Translation by Swami Mukundananda [https://www.holy-bhagavad-gita.org/chapter/9]

Rigveda (Mandal 7, Sukta 73, Richa1) suggests that it is the vehicle to reach knowledge and cross the (river of) darkness of ignorance.

Crossing to the opposite shore of darkness (ignorance), being guided by the Rigveda:

R 1 Richa 7/73/1 मैत्रावरुणिर्वसिष्ठः, अश्विनौ, त्रिष्टुप्

अतारिष्म तमसस्पारमस्य प्रति स्तोमं देवयन्तो दधानाः ।
पुरुदंसां पुरुतमां पुराजाऽमर्त्या हवते अश्विना गीः ॥7/73/1

This Richa translates to: 'Devoted to the Devtas, and extolling their praise, we have crossed to the opposite shore of this (state of) darkness. This worshipper invokes the Ashwins, the doers of many deeds, the most-mighty, the first-born, and the immortal'.

This Richa conveys the conviction of Rishi Vashishtha who visualized this Richa that the Rigvaidic Mantras can enable mankind to cross the river of darkness and thereby reach its opposite shore, that is of knowledge.

Thus, in this Volume, we endeavour to understand and acknowledge the true nature of Agriculture with the help of Rigvaidic Richas.

Preface

The universe of the Rigveda is the universe itself. Messages from the Rigveda have an appeal and relevance, which is universal and time independent. Rigveda encompasses in its vast canvas, men, Devtas, and the Creator himself. Its subject matter ranges from routine and earthly affairs of men to the celebrated deeds of the Devtas. In it, not only the deep mysteries concerning the creation of universe are addressed, but practical matters such as the ploughing of land, sowing, nursing and reaping of crops, weaving of cloth, driving of vehicles including different kinds of chariots, and making and sailing of boats are discussed with equal emphasis and detail. It is concerned with the past, present and future of mankind. It deals with not only terrestrial matters but also heavenly affairs. It is earthly and practical on the one hand, and mystic and universal, on the other. It contains a vast ocean of knowledge, which is mankind's common and universal inheritance.

Rigveda informs us of our ancient past. It constructs the picture of a land, abounding in huge mountains, mighty rivers running down to massive oceans, and large forests covering a vast landmass. In the Rigvaidic description, the whole landmass of India, that is Bharat or Jambudweep, an area much larger than the present-day India, was covered by a network of rivers. Ninety rivers have been mentioned in Rigveda indicating their extremely large number. The mightiest and the most ancient of the Rigvaidic rivers is Saraswati. Sindhu and Ganga rose to prominence later. Accomplished Rishis set up their Ashrams deep in the mysterious forests, close to or on the banks of the rivers described in Rigveda that often assumed a divine status. These Rishis conversed with the Devtas, performed Yajnas, and provided instructions to guide mankind. The Rishis and their disciples set up an extensive system of education and learning and ensured inter-generational transmission of this knowledge.

The economy of this vast and growing population was agriculture-centric but supported by developed industrial tools and technologies as well as a vast network of trade and finance. This economy prospered by using agriculture, taking advantage of the rich soil, lying across riverbanks, and the ample and good quality water that flowed downstream from the network of rivers originating in the great Himalayas and elsewhere in India. The rivers also brought with them, in their downward journeys, through the plains, vast quantities of rich minerals, drawn from their mountainous origins, making the agricultural lands in the plains, highly rich and fertile. These rivers also facilitated development of towns and cities and laid the foundation of a prosperous civilization.

Our Rishis ensured that the rich body of knowledge contained in the Vedas would be passed on from generation to generation for the benefit of mankind. It was preserved for thousands of years by word of mouth through a well- established tradition of teachers and disciples, a tradition known in India as the Guru-Shishya Parampara. It was transcribed into written form much later. But the written form by itself should be considered as remaining incomplete unless the Richas or Mantras are also visualized, recited and heard at the same time. In fact, Richas in the Rigveda need to be seen, read, visualised, heard, and meditated upon in order to comprehend their true meaning and importance.

Vedas are supposed to be received knowledge, the residue of information that got transmitted from the e]arlier to later creation cycles of the universe. These cycles are the repetitive cycles of creation and destruction described in an elaborate way in the ancient Sanskrit literature. The present set of Vedas consisting of Rigveda, Samveda, Atharvaveda, and Yajurveda is what we have inherited from the earlier rounds of creation for the benefit of the present one. Of these, the Rigveda is the most prominent and the other three Vedas derive their Mantras often linked to those of Rigveda.

Rigveda is a compilation of Vaidic Richas containing and conveying ancient Indian thought emanating from the Rishis who are known to have

Agriculture in Rigveda: Seeds of India's Civilizational Prosperity

drawn this knowledge from the universe itself by visualizing the individual Richas which were later compiled in the form of different Vedas. While the commonplace view has been that Rigveda provides the foundation of Indian philosophical and religious thought, which is also true, it is generally not recognized that in the Rigveda, there is also an extensive representation of the Indian thought on substantive and critical economic subjects. The importance of prosperity and material wellbeing finds a central position in the Rigvaidic Richas. In fact, Rigveda provides a holistic view of "Artha" as integrally linked to the wholesome pursuit of the four-fold endeavours of human life namely, *Dharma, Artha, Kama, and Moksha*. These are called the four *Purusharthas*. Of these, Artha (economic pursuits) and Kama (desires) may be considered as directly dealing with the subject matter of Economics.

The task that I had embarked upon while undertaking this work was to trace the roots of Indian economic thought from its ancient literature. Usually, many analysts pick up the thread from Kautilya's *Arthasastra*. But I wanted to find roots of economic activities and economic thought from the most ancient inheritance of India's philosophic and scientific thinking namely, the Rigveda. In Rigveda, there are detailed references to subjects like agriculture, industry, trade, technology and services like health and education, as also to the concepts and importance of wealth and welfare. Not only economic activities and practices but also economic thought and philosophy have been propounded, which have significant implications for modern times covering different aspects of Economics ranging from micro to macro, from individual welfare to social welfare, and from policy matters to the endeavours of an individual. The role of government through the enunciation of the duties of the king or leaders of the society is also discussed at length. The subject of taxation also finds mention in Rigveda and other Vaidic texts.

In this Volume, I have endeavoured to link the development of agriculture through its Vaidic roots, seeded in the areas under river Saraswati's sway as well as numerous other rivers including Ganga, Yamuna, and Sindhu to India's civilizational prosperity, which refers not only to economic prosperity but also to India's riches in terms of cultural and philosophical underpinnings of economic pursuits.

In becoming acquainted with the messages that our ancient Rishis left for practical matters such as agriculture, industry and technology, I have realized that it is not only in terms of history of economic ideas but also in terms of the related practices, that their messages have considerable significance for contemporary times. There are a number of modern endeavours to practice agriculture according to the Vaidic principles. The enunciation of agricultural practices in Rigveda places agriculture on a divine platform, organized around Yajnas. Every activity, every input, and every output are associated in the Vedas, with a Devta. From that high pedestal, agriculture has arrived to modern times through a downward and persistently degenerative route. Most of this descent has gathered momentum rather recently. With the intensive use of chemicals, fertilizers and other polluting agents, accompanied by erosion of soil fertility, modern agriculture has become more a vehicle of disease rather than that of nourishment. Plants draw into themselves, polluted and poisonous water and dangerous chemicals from the soil. Further, the air around them is equally polluted. Mechanization and commercialization have distorted the relationship between man, agriculture, and nature. Genetically modified seeds used in modern times, are also accompanied by irreversible damage to the long-term growth of agriculture.

A number of works have traced the practice of agriculture in Rigvaidic times. One useful reference is that of Majumdar (1927) which was a thesis on the subject of 'Vanaspati-Plants and Plant-Life as in Indian Treatises and Traditions' which was awarded the Griffith Memorial Prize Essay for 1925.

The benefit of the practice of agriculture, I had occasion to witness first-hand, when for a number of years, I saw my own Guru, Swami Bimalananada, put in practice these principles, although on a small scale in his Ashrams at Allahabad and Pahalgam and saw and tasted the difference in the quality and volume of output. This convinced me that linking back to our roots in our endeavours would yield great benefits in modern economic systems. In the Allahabad Ashram, Swamiji also ran a Goshala. He cultivated a variety of vegetables and flowers, which were far more nourishing and beautiful to look at than similar products available from the market. The vegetables tasted divinely superior. I have described some part of Swamiji's demonstration of how these productive activities are to be undertaken in our commemorative Volume entitled 'Guru Smriti: Swami Bimalananda and His Yoga Teaching' [D. K. Srivastava (edited), 2018)].

Most of the present work took shape in Mangalore, as we were cornered by a Corona-coerced confinement in our 20th storey flat in Brigade Pinnacle in Derabail. This gave me enough time and opportunity to develop this work during 2020 and 2021. During these days, my wife was the only constant companion. She looked at the manuscript from time to time as it developed and made valuable suggestions. My colleagues, Muralikrishna, Tarrung, and Ragini went through the manuscript in considerable detail and richly contributed to the overall outcome. I had informed my children, daughter Mrinmayee and son, Mrinal Kanti as to the progress of the work. Eventually, when the first draft was complete, I shared it with them and benefitted from their feedback. One advantage, compared to Covid's many disadvantages, has been that contact with my brothers, sisters and close family members, telephonically or by other online modes, had increased in its frequency. I kept them posted about the progress of this work and I was constantly encouraged by their good wishes.

Mangalore **D. K. Srivastava**

Sanskrit text on the cover page of the Volume is sourced from:
https://wijsheidsweb.nl/wijsheid/indra-and-vritra-the-dragon-in-the-rig-veda/

Contents

Preface vii

Contents xii

List of Figures xvii

List of Tables xvii

List of cited Shlokas from Srimad Bhagavad Gita xviii

List of cited Richas from Rigveda xix

List of cited Atharvaveda Mantras xxv

Glossary of non-translatable Sanskrit words used in this Volume ... 1

Notes on Rigveda Translations 7

Chapter 1 Rigveda: A Brief Introduction 11

   On Vaidic Chandas (Metres) 14

   On Sanskrit and Vaidic Sanskrit 16

   Some Well-known Rigveda Suktas 19

   Richas and their Subject Matter: Self-sameness 23

   Structure of Rigveda 24

   Age of Rigveda 26

   Rishis in Rigveda 31

   Devtas in Rigveda 32

   Summary and Key Points 36

Chapter 2 Vaidic Roots of Agriculture 39

   Agriculture: Gift from Devtas to Mankind 42

Agriculture: Conceptualized as Yajna 45

Summary and Key Points 50

Chapter 3 Kshetra and Kshetrapati 53

Krishi Sukta in Rigveda: Mandal 4, Sukta 57 53

Krishi Sukta in Atharvaveda: Kanda 3, Sukta 17 64

Kshetra as Human Body 71

Summary and Key Points 72

Chapter 4 Earth and Sources of Water 77

Earth as Devta: A Water Planet 77

Rivers and River-beds 85

The Saraswati Sukta: Mandal 6 Sukta 61 93

The Nadi Sukta: Mandal 10 Sukta 75 106

Mention of 90/ 99 rivers 114

Mandal 7 Suktas 95 and 96: Saraswati, Saraswan, and Nationhood 117

Mandal 7 Sukta 95 117

Mandal 7 Sukta 96 123

Mandal 10 Sukta 125: The Mysterious Rastri Sukta 127

Historicity of River Saraswati 135

   1. Course of Saraswati 136

   2. Major Epochs 138

   3. Age of Saraswati: results from archaeological studies 142

   4. Revival of Saraswati 145

Summary and Key Points 147

Chapter 5 Rainfall and Rain-Devtas 151

Parjanya Sukta: Mandal 5 Sukta 83 151

Seasons in Indian Agriculture 164

Yajna of Creation: Place of Foodgrains and Rainfall 166

Summary and Key Points 168

Chapter 6 Forms of Agri-wealth: Food grains, Cattle, and Land .. 171

Food grains, Cattle, Fertile Land as Forms of Wealth 171

Famous Go-Sukta 10/169/1-4 179

Summary and Key Points 189

Chapter 7 Rigveda's Aushadhi Sukta: praising medicinal plants . 191

Mandal 10 Sukta 97 Aushadhi Sukta 193

Summary and Key Points 213

Chapter 8 Agriculture and Industry 215

Mandal 10 Sukta 101: Agriculture-Industry Interface 215

Summary and Key Points 226

About the author 229

References 233

Appendix 1: Notes on Krishi Parashar and other Ancient Indian Texts on Agriculture and related aspects 239

A.1 Notes on Krishi Parashar 240

A.2 Notes on Kaashyap Krishi Sukti 251

A.3 Notes on Vrikshayurveda 254

A.4 Notes on other ancient texts pertaining to agricultural implements, land categories, and practices 258

Appendix 2: Vaidic Agriculture in Modern Times 260

Appendix 3: Notes on medicinal plants 266

Appendix 4: Notes on India's Erstwhile Prosperity 272

Appendix 5: More on the Historicity of River Saraswati 275

Index 282

List of Figures

Figure 1: Rupa Bhaty's timeline of India's civilizational evolution 29

Figure 2: Course of river Saraswati 137

Figure 3: Distribution of Harappan settlements 141

Figure 4 and 5: Continuity of Civilization 142

Figure 6: River Saraswati and habitation clusters 143

Figure 7: Yajna of Creation 167

Figure 8A1.1: Images of plough and yoke 248

Figure 9A4.1: India's share in world GDP 273

Figure 10A5.1: Paleochannels recognised in the Ghaggar-Hakara-Nara 277

Figure 11A5.2: Phases of fluvial activity 279

List of Tables

Table 1: Metre Structure in Rigveda 15

Table 2: Notes on Seven Main Chandas 15

Table 3: Structure of Rigveda 25

Table 4: Reference to Saraswati in Rigveda 86

Table 5: Ground water ages of samples collected along the paleo channels in Jaisalmer and Ganganagar districts, Rajasthan* 144

Table A1.1: Predicted quantity of rainfall based on astronomical considerations by Muni Parashar 243

Table A3.1: list of medicinal plants 266

Table A4.1: India's share in world GDP: a long history 273

List of cited Shlokas from Srimad Bhagavad Gita

G 1 Srimad Bhagvad Gita: Chapter 9, Shloka 17 v

G 2 Srimad Bhagvad Gita: Chapter 4, Shloka 33 3

G 3 Srimad Bhagvad Gita: Chapter 4, Shloka 29 3

G 4 Srimad Bhagvad Gita: Chapter 4, Shloka 30 4

G 5 Srimad Bhagvad Gita: Chapter 4, Shloka 23 4

G 6 Srimad Bhagvad Gita: Chapter 15, Shloka 1 19

G 7 Srimad Bhagvad Gita: Chapter 3, Shloka 11 35

G 8 Srimad Bhagvad Gita: Chapter 13, Shloka 2 71

G 9 Srimad Bhagvad Gita: Chapter 3, Shloka 14 166

G 10 Srimad Bhagvad Gita: Chapter 3, Shloka 15 166

G 11 Srimad Bhagvad Gita: Chapter 3, Shloka 16 166

G 12 Srimad Bhagvad Gita: Chapter 10, Shloka 26 197

List of cited Richas from Rigveda

R 1 Richa 7/73/1 मैत्रावरुणिर्वसिष्ठः, अश्विनौ, त्रिष्टुप्...................................vi
R 2 Richa 8/22/6 मधुच्छन्दा वैश्वामित्रः, अग्निः, गायत्री....................................31
R 3 Richa 8/22/6 सोभरिः काण्वः, अश्विनौ, प्रगाथः = (विषमा बृहती , समा सतोबृहती)...................42
R 4 Richa 6/56/1 बार्हस्पत्यो भरद्वाजः, पूषा, गायत्री..45
R 5 Richa 10/22/10 ऐन्द्रो विमदः प्राजापत्यो वा, वासुक्रो वसुक्रद्वा, इन्द्रः, पुरस्ताद्बृहती.......46
R 6 Richa 1/117/21 कक्षीवान् दैर्घतमस औशिजः, अश्विनौ, त्रिष्टुप्................................47
R 7 Richa 1/174/9 अगस्त्यो मैत्रावरुणिः, इन्द्रः, त्रिष्टुप्..............................47
R 8 Richa 8/28/1 मनुर्वैवस्वतः, विश्वे देवाः, गायत्री....................................48
R 9 Richa 8/30/2 मनुर्वैवस्वतः, विश्वे देवाः, पुरउष्णिक्...............................49
R 10 Richa 4/57/1 वामदेवो गौतमः, क्षेत्रपतिः, अनुष्टुप्.................................53
R 11 Richa 4/57/2 वामदेवो गौतमः, क्षेत्रपतिः, त्रिष्टुप्................................54
R 12 Richa 4/57/3 वामदेवो गौतमः, क्षेत्रपतिः, त्रिष्टुप्................................55
R 13 Richa 4/57/4 वामदेवो गौतमः, शुनः, अनुष्टुप्.....................................56
R 14 Richa 4/57/5 वामदेवो गौतमः, शुनासीरौ, पुर उष्णिक्................................57
R 15 Richa 4/57/6 वामदेवो गौतमः, सीता, अनुष्टुप्......................................58
R 16 Richa 4/57/7 वामदेवो गौतमः, सीता, अनुष्टुप्......................................59
R 17 Richa 4/57/8 वामदेवो गौतमः, शुनासीरौ, त्रिष्टुप्..................................60
R 18 Richa 10/94/13 अर्बुदः काद्रवेयः सर्पः, ग्रावाणः, जगती..........................61
R 19 Richa 10/33/6 शबरः काक्षीवतः, गावः, त्रिष्टुप्...................................62
R 20 Richa 10/34/13 कवष ऐलूषः, अक्षो मौजवान् वा, ऋषिः................................63
R 21 Richa 6/70/1 बार्हस्पत्यो भरद्वाजः, द्यावापृथिवी, जगती............................77
R 22 Richa 6/70/4 बार्हस्पत्यो भरद्वाजः, द्यावापृथिवी, जगती............................78
R 23 Richa 6/70/5 बार्हस्पत्यो भरद्वाजः, द्यावापृथिवी, जगती............................79
R 25 Richa 6/70/6 बार्हस्पत्यो भरद्वाजः, द्यावापृथिवी, जगती............................80
R 24 Richa 7/49/2 मैत्रावरुणिर्वसिष्ठः, आपः, त्रिष्टुप्................................83

R 27 Richa 8/69/12 प्रियमेध आङ्गिरसः, वरुणः, अनुष्टुप्........................84

R 28 Richa 2/41/16 गृत्समद (आङ्गिरसः शौनहोत्रः पश्चाद्) भार्गवः शौनकः, सरस्वती, अनुष्टुप्.....88

R 29 Richa 2/41/17 गृत्समद (आङ्गिरसः शौनहोत्रः पश्चाद्) भार्गवः शौनकः, सरस्वती, अनुष्टुप्.....89

R 30 Richa 2/41/18 गृत्समद (आङ्गिरसः शौनहोत्रः पश्चाद्) भार्गवः शौनकः, सरस्वती, बृहती........90

R 31 Richa 7/2/8 ऋजिश्वा भारद्वाजः, विश्वे देवाः, त्रिष्टुप्.........................90

R 32 Richa 7/2/9 ऋजिश्वा भारद्वाजः, विश्वे देवाः, त्रिष्टुप्.........................91

R 33 Richa 6/49/7 ऋजिश्वा भारद्वाजः, विश्वे देवाः, त्रिष्टुप्........................92

R 34 Richa 6/52/6 ऋजिश्वा भारद्वाजः, विश्वे देवाः, त्रिष्टुप्........................93

R 35 Richa 6/61/1 बाहस्पत्यो भरद्वाजः, सरस्वती, निचृत् जगती........................94

R 36 Richa 6/61/2 बाहस्पत्यो भरद्वाजः, सरस्वती, जगती........................95

R 37 Richa 6/61/3 बाहस्पत्यो भरद्वाजः, सरस्वती, निचृत् जगती........................96

R 38 Richa 6/61/4 बाहस्पत्यो भरद्वाजः, सरस्वती, निचृत् गायत्री........................97

R 39 Richa 6/61/5 बाहस्पत्यो भरद्वाजः, सरस्वती, विराट गायत्री........................97

R 40 Richa 6/61/6 बाहस्पत्यो भरद्वाजः, सरस्वती, विराट गायत्री........................98

R 41 Richa 6/61/7 बाहस्पत्यो भरद्वाजः, सरस्वती, गायत्री........................99

R 42 Richa 6/61/8 बाहस्पत्यो भरद्वाजः, सरस्वती, गायत्री........................99

R 43 Richa 6/61/9 बाहस्पत्यो भरद्वाजः, सरस्वती, निचृत् गायत्री........................100

R 44 Richa 6/61/10 बाहस्पत्यो भरद्वाजः, सरस्वती, विराट गायत्री........................101

R 45 Richa 6/61/11 बाहस्पत्यो भरद्वाजः, सरस्वती, निचृत् गायत्री........................101

R 46 Richa 6/61/12 बाहस्पत्यो भरद्वाजः, सरस्वती, निचृत् गायत्री........................102

R 47 Richa 6/61/13 बाहस्पत्यो भरद्वाजः, सरस्वती, निचृत् जगती........................103

R 48 Richa 6/61/14 बाहस्पत्यो भरद्वाजः, सरस्वती, पंक्ति........................103

R 49 Richa 1/3/10 मधुच्छन्दा वैश्वामित्रः, सरस्वती, गायत्री........................104

R 50 Richa 1/3/11 मधुच्छन्दा वैश्वामित्रः, सरस्वती, गायत्री........................105

R 51 Richa 1/3/12 मधुच्छन्दा वैश्वामित्रः, सरस्वती, गायत्री........................105

R 52 Richa 10/75/1 सिन्धुक्षित् प्रैयमेधः, नद्यः, जगती........................106

R 53 Richa 10/75/2 सिन्धुक्षित् प्रैयमेधः, नद्यः, जगती........................107

R 54 Richa 10/75/3 सिन्धुक्षित् प्रैयमेधः, नद्यः, जगती 108

R 55 Richa 10/75/4 सिन्धुक्षित् प्रैयमेधः, नद्यः, जगती 108

R 56 Richa 10/75/5 सिन्धुक्षित् प्रैयमेधः, नद्यः, जगती 109

R 57 Richa 10/75/6 सिन्धुक्षित् प्रैयमेधः, नद्यः, जगती 110

R 58 Richa 10/75/7 सिन्धुक्षित् प्रैयमेधः, नद्यः, जगती 110

R 59 Richa 10/75/8 सिन्धुक्षित् प्रैयमेधः, नद्यः, जगती 111

R 60 Richa 10/75/9 सिन्धुक्षित् प्रैयमेधः, नद्यः, जगती 112

R 61 Richa 10/43/3 कृष्ण आङ्गिरसः, इन्द्रः, जगती 114

R 62 Richa 1/121/13 कक्षीवान् दैर्घतमस औशिजः, इन्द्रो विश्वे देवा वा, त्रिष्टुप् 115

R 63 Richa 1/191/13 अगस्त्यो मैत्रावरुणिः, अप् त्रिण सूर्याः, महाबृहती 116

R 64 Richa 7/95/1 मैत्रावरुणिर्वसिष्ठ:, सरस्वती, त्रिष्टुप् 117

R 65 Richa 7/95/2 मैत्रावरुणिर्वसिष्ठ:, सरस्वती, त्रिष्टुप् 118

R 66 Richa 7/95/3 मैत्रावरुणिर्वसिष्ठ:, सरस्वान्, त्रिष्टुप् 120

R 67 Richa 7/95/4 मैत्रावरुणिर्वसिष्ठ:, सरस्वती , त्रिष्टुप् 121

R 68 Richa 7/95/5 मैत्रावरुणिर्वसिष्ठ:, सरस्वती , त्रिष्टुप् 121

R 69 Richa 7/95/6 मैत्रावरुणिर्वसिष्ठ:, सरस्वती , त्रिष्टुप् 122

R 70 Richa 7/96/1 मैत्रावरुणिर्वसिष्ठ:, सरस्वती, बृहती 123

R 71 Richa 7/96/2 मैत्रावरुणिर्वसिष्ठ:, सरस्वती, सतोबृहती 124

R 72 Richa 7/96/3, मैत्रावरुणिर्वसिष्ठ:, सरस्वती, प्रस्तारपंक्तिः 125

R 73 Richa 7/96/4 मैत्रावरुणिर्वसिष्ठ:, सरस्वती, गायत्री 125

R 74 Richa 7/96/5 मैत्रावरुणिर्वसिष्ठ:, सरस्वती, गायत्री 126

R 75 Richa 7/96/6 मैत्रावरुणिर्वसिष्ठ:, सरस्वती, गायत्री 127

R 76 Richa 10/125/1 वागाम्भृणी, आत्मा, त्रिष्टुप् 128

R 77 Richa 10/125/2 वागाम्भृणी, आत्मा, त्रिष्टुप् 129

R 78 Richa 10/125/3 वागाम्भृणी, आत्मा, त्रिष्टुप् 130

R 79 Richa 10/125/4 वागाम्भृणी, आत्मा, त्रिष्टुप् 132

R 80 Richa 10/125/5 वागाम्भृणी, आत्मा, त्रिष्टुप् 132

R 81 Richa 10/125/6 वागाम्भृणी, आत्मा, त्रिष्टुप्	133
R 82 Richa 10/125/7 वागाम्भृणी, आत्मा, त्रिष्टुप्	134
R 83 Richa 10/125/8 वागाम्भृणी, आत्मा, त्रिष्टुप्	134
R 84 Richa 5/83/1 भौमोऽत्रिः, पर्जन्यः, त्रिष्टुप्	151
R 85 Richa 5/83/2 भौमोऽत्रिः, पर्जन्यः, जगती	152
R 86 Richa 5/83/3 भौमोऽत्रिः, पर्जन्यः, जगती	152
R 87 Richa 5/83/4 भौमोऽत्रिः, पर्जन्यः, जगती	153
R 88 Richa 5/83/5 भौमोऽत्रिः, पर्जन्यः, त्रिष्टुप्	154
R 89 Richa 5/83/6 भौमोऽत्रिः, पर्जन्यः, त्रिष्टुप्	155
R 90 Richa 5/87/7 भौमोऽत्रिः, पर्जन्यः, त्रिष्टुप्	155
R 91 Richa 5/83/8 भौमोऽत्रिः, पर्जन्यः, त्रिष्टुप्	157
R 92 Richa 5/83/9 भौमोऽत्रिः, पर्जन्यः,अनुष्टुप्	157
R 93 Richa 5/83/10 भौमोऽत्रिः, पर्जन्यः, त्रिष्टुप्	158
R 94 Richa 5/84/3 भौमोऽत्रिः, पृथिवी, अनुष्टुप्	159
R 95 Richa 5/85/3 भौमोऽत्रिः, वरुण, त्रिष्टुप्	159
R 96 Richa 5/86/6 भौमोऽत्रिः, इन्द्राग्नी, विराट् पूर्वा	160
R 97 Richa 1/25/15 आजीगर्तिः शुनः शेपः स कृत्रिमो वैश्वामित्रो देवरातः, वरुणः, गायत्री	161
R 98 Richa 1/2/4 मधुच्छन्दा वैश्वामित्रः, इन्द्र-वायु, गायत्री	162
R 99 Richa 7/22/6 मैत्रावरुणिर्वसिष्ठः, इन्द्रः, विराट्	163
R 100 Richa 5/70/4 उरुचक्रिरात्रेयः, मित्रावरुणौ, गायत्री	171
R 101 Richa 6/25/4 बार्हस्पत्यो भरद्वाजः, इन्द्रः, त्रिष्टुप्	172
R 102 Richa 1/23/15 मेधातिथिः काण्वः, पूषा, गायत्री	173
R 103 Richa 1/127/6 परुच्छेपो दैवोदासिः, अग्निः, अतिधृतिः	174
R 104 Richa 1/100/18 वार्षगिराः ऋज्रा श्वाऽम्बरीष-सहदेव-भयमान-सुराधसः, इन्द्रः, त्रिष्टुप्	175
R 105 Richa 8/21/3 सोभरिः काण्वः, इन्द्रः, ककुप्	176
R 106 Richa 3/45/4 गाथिनो विश्वामित्रः, इन्द्रः, बृहती	178
R 107 Richa 10/169/1 शबरः काक्षीवतः, गावः, त्रिष्टुप्	179

R 108 Richa 10/169/2 शबरः काक्षीवतः, गावः, त्रिष्टुप्	180
R 109 Richa 10/169/3 शबरः काक्षीवतः, गावः, त्रिष्टुप्	180
R 110 Richa 10/169/4 शबरः काक्षीवतः, गावः, त्रिष्टुप्	181
R 111 Richa 10/68/3 अयास्य आंगिरसः, बृहस्पतिः, त्रिष्टुप्	182
R 112 Richa 1/29/4 आजीगर्तिः शुनःशेप स कृत्रिमो वैश्वामित्रो देवरातः, इन्द्रः, पंक्ति	183
R 113 Richa 6/47/20 गर्गो भारद्वाजः, इंद्रः, देव–भूमि-बृहस्पतीन्द्रा, त्रिष्टुप्	184
R 114 Richa 3/45/3 गाथिनो विश्वामित्रः, इन्द्रः, बृहती	185
R 115 Richa 1/36/8 कण्वो घौरः, अग्निः, प्रगाथः	186
R 116 Richa 6/39/5 बार्हस्पत्यो भरद्वाजः, इन्द्रः , त्रिष्टुप्	187
R 117 Richa 6/63/10 बार्हस्पत्यो भरद्वाजः, अश्विनौ , त्रिष्टुप्	187
R 118 Richa 7/18/1 मैत्रावरुणिर्वसिष्ठः, इन्द्रः, त्रिष्टुप्	188
R 119 Richa 7/27/5 मैत्रावरुणिर्वसिष्ठः, इन्द्रः, त्रिष्टुप्	189
R 120 Richa 10/97/1 आथर्वणो भिषग्, ओषधयः, अनुष्टुप्	193
R 121 Richa 10/97/2 आथर्वणो भिषग्, ओषधयः, अनुष्टुप्	193
R 122 Richa 10/97/3 आथर्वणो भिषग्, ओषधयः, अनुष्टुप्	194
R 123 Richa 10/97/4 आथर्वणो भिषग्, ओषधयः, अनुष्टुप्	195
R 124 Richa 10/97/5 आथर्वणो भिषग्, ओषधयः, अनुष्टुप्	196
R 125 Richa 10/97/6 आथर्वणो भिषग्, ओषधयः, अनुष्टुप्	199
R 126 Richa 10/97/7 आथर्वणो भिषग्, ओषधयः, अनुष्टुप्	200
R 127 Richa 10/97/8 आथर्वणो भिषग्, ओषधयः, अनुष्टुप्	201
R 128 Richa 10/97/9 आथर्वणो भिषग्, ओषधयः, अनुष्टुप्	201
R 129 Richa 10/97/10 आथर्वणो भिषग्, ओषधयः, अनुष्टुप्	202
R 130 Richa 10/97/11 आथर्वणो भिषग्, ओषधयः, अनुष्टुप्	203
R 131 Richa 10/97/12 आथर्वणो भिषग्, ओषधयः, अनुष्टुप्	204
R 132 Richa 10/97/13 आथर्वणो भिषग्, ओषधयः, अनुष्टुप्	204
R 133 Richa 10/97/14 आथर्वणो भिषग्, ओषधयः, अनुष्टुप्	205
R 134 Richa 10/97/15 आथर्वणो भिषग्, ओषधयः, अनुष्टुप्	206

R 135 Richa 10/97/16 आथर्वणो भिषग्, ओषधयः, अनुष्टुप्..........................207

R 136 Richa 10/97/17 आथर्वणो भिषग्, ओषधयः, अनुष्टुप्..........................207

R 137 Richa 10/97/18 आथर्वणो भिषग्, ओषधयः, अनुष्टुप्..........................208

R 138 Richa 10/97/19 आथर्वणो भिषग्, ओषधयः, अनुष्टुप्..........................209

R 139 Richa 10/97/20 आथर्वणो भिषग्, ओषधयः, अनुष्टुप्..........................210

R 140 Richa 10/97/21 आथर्वणो भिषग्, ओषधयः, अनुष्टुप्..........................210

R 141 Richa 10/97/22 आथर्वणो भिषग्, ओषधयः, अनुष्टुप्..........................211

R 142 Richa 10/97/23 आथर्वणो भिषग्, ओषधयः, अनुष्टुप्..........................212

R 143 Richa 10/101/1 बुधः सौम्यः, विश्वे देवा ऋत्विजो वा, त्रिष्टुप्..........................215

R 144 Richa 10/101/2 बुधः सौम्यः, विश्वे देवा ऋत्विजो वा, त्रिष्टुप्..........................216

R 145 Richa 10/101/3 बुधः सौम्यः, विश्वे देवा ऋत्विजो वा, त्रिष्टुप्..........................217

R 146 Richa 10/101/4 बुधः सौम्यः, विश्वे देवा ऋत्विजो वा, त्रिष्टुप्..........................217

R 147 Richa 10/101/5 बुधः सौम्यः, विश्वे देवा ऋत्विजो वा, बृहती..........................218

R 148 Richa 10/101/6 बुधः सौम्यः, विश्वे देवा ऋत्विजो वा, गायत्री..........................219

R 149 Richa 10/101/7 बुधः सौम्यः, विश्वे देवा ऋत्विजो वा, त्रिष्टुप्..........................219

R 150 Richa 10/101/8 बुधः सौम्यः, विश्वे देवा ऋत्विजो वा, त्रिष्टुप्..........................220

R 151 Richa 10/101/9 बुधः सौम्यः, विश्वे देवा ऋत्विजो वा, त्रिष्टुप्..........................221

R 152 Richa 10/101/10 बुधः सौम्यः, विश्वे देवा ऋत्विजो वा, त्रिष्टुप्..........................222

R 153 Richa 10/101/11 बुधः सौम्यः, विश्वे देवा ऋत्विजो वा, त्रिष्टुप्..........................223

R 154 Richa 10/101/12 बुधः सौम्यः, विश्वे देवा ऋत्विजो वा, जगती..........................224

R 155 Richa 10/48/7 वैकुण्ठ इन्द्रः, इन्द्रः, त्रिष्टुप्..........................225

R 156 Richa 10/71/2 बृहस्पतिरांगिरसः, ज्ञानम्, त्रिष्टुप्..........................226

List of cited Atharvaveda Mantras

M 1 Atharvaveda Mantra 12/1/42 अथर्वा, भूमिः, स्वराडनुष्टुप्..44

M 2 Atharvaveda Mantra 3/17/1 विश्वामित्रः, सीता, आर्षी गायत्री..64

M 3 Atharvaveda Mantra 3/17/2 विश्वामित्रः, सीता, त्रिष्टुप्..65

M 4 Atharvaveda Mantra 3/17/3 विश्वामित्रः, सीता, पथ्यापङ्क्तिः..66

M 5 Atharvaveda Mantra 3/17/4 विश्वामित्रः, सीता, अनुष्टुप्..67

M 6 Atharvaveda Mantra 3/17/5 विश्वामित्रः, सीता, त्रिष्टुप्..67

M 7 Atharvaveda Mantra 3/17/6 विश्वामित्रः, सीता, अनुष्टुप्..68

M 8 Atharvaveda Mantra 3/17/7 विश्वामित्रः, सीता, विराट् पुर उष्णिक्..69

M 9 Atharvaveda Mantra 3/17/8 विश्वामित्रः, सीता, निचृत्..69

M 10 Atharvaveda Mantra 3/17/9 विश्वामित्रः, सीता, त्रिष्टुप्..70

M 11 Atharvaveda Mantra 12/1/55 अथर्वा, भूमिः, त्रिष्टुप्..82

M 12 Atharvaveda Mantra 12/1/36, अथर्वन्, भूमि, विपरीतपादलक्ष्मापंक्तिः..164

M 13 Atharvaveda Mantra 12/1/42 अथर्वन्, भूमि, स्वरादनुष्टुप..165

M 14 Atharvaveda Mantra 3/6/3 जगद्द्वीजं पुरुषः, वानस्पत्योऽश्वत्थः, अनुष्टुप्..197

M 15 Atharvaveda Mantra 3/6/8 जगद्द्वीजं पुरुषः, वानस्पत्योऽश्वत्थः, अनुष्टुप्..198

Glossary of non-translatable Sanskrit words used in this Volume

In this Volume, we have used certain Sanskrit words as they are, since there are no appropriate corresponding words or expressions in English that would capture or convey their proper meaning. These have been appropriately referred to as Sanskrit 'non-translatables' [see, Rajiv Malhotra and Satyanarayan Dasa Babaji] (Malhotra, 2020).

The vocabulary of Sanskrit is very large since in Sanskrit, words are formed from root letters. They can take many forms emanating from one root. In fact, many other languages derived from Sanskrit, and a large number of Sanskrit words have already been taken into other languages.

Some of the frequently Sanskrit words which are referred to as they are, are briefly given below

Sukta

Sukta, although ordinarily translated as a hymn, is better referred to as Sukta itself. A Sukta is a specific aggregation of Richas, which have defined forms described as Chandas of Metres, and has associational link with one or more Rishi(s) and Devta(s).

Richa

Richa is based on the root word 'Rik' or 'Rk', which means received knowledge or truth. Rigveda-Samhita is a compilation of verses of specific forms or construction, known as Rik. Rik refers to those Mantras which are meant for the praise of the Devtas. For each Richa, the Rishi who visualized the Richa is specified along with the Richa. The Metre or Chanda in which the Richa is to be recited is also indicated along with the name of one or more Devta(s) in whose praise or whose accomplishments are described in the Richa. The collection (Samhita) of Richas is known as Rigveda-Samhita. R1, R2......etc., refer to the sequence in which the Richas appear in this volume.

Rishi

Rishi is often translated as a sage. In Hindi and Sanskrit, there are words like Muni and Sant, which are also used to denote a sage. But the word 'Rishi' has a more specific meaning and connotation. Rishi is the receiver or seer of the Rik. As such, the Rishis are not ordinary sages. They have received or meditated upon the Riks, that is knowledge or truth. They have visualised and organised this knowledge in the form of Chandas, so that these can be recited or chanted.

More exalted levels of Rishis are referred to as Devarshi, Brahmarshi, and Maharshi. Devarshi refers to Rishis having access to or status of Devtas. Rishis contemplating on the Brahman are Brahmarshis. Rishis who have attained an eminent status among the group of Rishis are referred to as Maharshis.

Veda

Veda is the received body of knowledge containing both spiritual as well as earthly knowledge. Four Vedas that are known today are: Rigveda, Samveda, Yajurveda, and Atharvaveda. Rigveda is recognized as the earliest, the most ancient, and also the most comprehensive. In fact, in Samveda and Yajurveda, many of the Richas are the same or comparable as in Rigveda. Some eminent scholars consider that all the Vedas were received from 'Brahma' simultaneously.

In Gita, Sri Krishna says in Chapter 9 (Rajvidya Rajguhya Yoga, that is the science of Royal Knowledge and Royal Mysteries) that He himself is the Rigveda, Samveda, and Yajurveda. This Shloka is given on Page 2 of this Volume. These Vedas, thus, consist of knowledge as emanating from the Creator himself. In fact, the Creator identifies his own self with the knowledge contained in these Vedas.

Yajna

Yajnas can be interpreted in physical as well as more abstract ways. In a physical sense, Yajna is the performance of a sacrificial rite according to prescribed methods, sanctified by Mantras, which involve sacrificing material such as ghee (clarified butter) and grains while chanting Mantras in praise of or offering to Devtas. Both the ghee (clarified butter) and the grains produced from agriculture are gifts from the Devtas. Yajnas are in fact an acknowledgment of the contribution of the Devtas to the development and growth of mankind. Through the Yajnas, symbolically the gifts from the Devtas such as grains and the products from cow's milk are returned back as offering to the Devtas. The recitation of the Mantras creates positive vibrations. The burning of the sacrificial material helps clean up the environment. Yajnas also take a more subtle and abstract form. Yajnas pertaining to those of Pranas and Knowledge are described in Srimad Bhagvad Gita as superior forms of Yajnas. In Srimad Bhagvad Gita, a distinction is made between Yajnas that make use of physical material for the sacrifice in a physical fire vis.-a-vis. Yajnas in which only knowledge is involved and Yajnas in which different layers of breath are involved. Thus,

G 2 Srimad Bhagvad Gita: Chapter 4, Shloka 33

श्रेयान्द्रव्यमयाद्यज्ञाज्ज्ञानयज्ञः परन्तप ।
सर्वं कर्माखिलं पार्थ ज्ञाने परिसमाप्यते ॥ 4-33

In this Shloka, Sri Krishna says that the knowledge Yajna leads to greater welfare than Yajnas based on physical material. He asserts that all actions eventually result only in the creation of knowledge. Thus, the process of conversion of actions into knowledge can be considered as Yajna. Similarly, in the context of breaths which are distinguished in Vaidic literature as Prana Vayu, Apana Vayu, Samana Vayu, and so on, the process of Yogic Yajna is described.

G 3 Srimad Bhagvad Gita: Chapter 4, Shloka 29

अपाने जुह्वति प्राणं प्राणेऽपानं तथापरे ।
प्राणापानगती रुद्ध्वा प्राणायामपरायणाः ॥ 4-29

G 4 Srimad Bhagvad Gita: Chapter 4, Shloka 30

> अपरे नियताहाराः प्राणान्प्राणेषु जुह्वति ।
> सर्वेऽप्येते यज्ञविदो यज्ञक्षपितकल्मषाः ॥ 4-30

These Shlokas are translated by Swami Mukundananda as: "Still others offer as sacrifice the outgoing breath in the incoming breath, while some offer the incoming breath into the outgoing breath. Some arduously practice pranayam and restrain the incoming and outgoing breaths, purely absorbed in the regulation of the life-energy. Yet others curtail their food intake and offer the breath into the life-energy as sacrifice. All these knowers of sacrifice are cleansed of their impurities as a result of such performances." (The Bhagwad Gita – commentary by Swami Mukundananda, 2014)

In these Shlokas, the process of Yajnas is described where one breath is sacrificed into the fire of same kind of breath or another kind of breath. Another form of Yajna is where the subject domain of the knowledge senses is sacrificed into the sense itself. Thus, the domain of ears is sound and that of eyes is the visual domain. The entire external universe is described in terms of words for the comprehension of mind. In all these cases, the content of the domain of the knowledge senses are to be sacrificed in the fire of control or regulated consumption.

G 5 Srimad Bhagvad Gita: Chapter 4, Shloka 23

> श्रोत्रादीनीन्द्रियाण्यन्ये संयमाग्निषु जुह्वति ।
> शब्दादीन्विषयानन्य इन्द्रियाग्निषु जुह्वति ॥ 4-23

This Shloka is translated by Swami Mukundananda as: "They are released from the bondage of material attachments and their intellect is established in divine knowledge. Since they perform all actions as a sacrifice (to Devtas), they are freed from all karmic reactions." (The Bhagwad Gita – commentary by Swami Mukundananda, 2014)

Devta

Devta is often translated as a god or deity. However, the term Devta as used in the Rigveda has specific connotations. Devtas have been described as travelling on chariots, as coming from another planet, as travelling through space, and as being fond of Somaras. Devtas participated in agricultural activities, teaching our ancestors, the art of agriculture. Devtas fought for their devotees in order to establish a society which followed the prescribed dharmic rules including the performance of Yajnas. Later in this volume a more detailed discussion is taken up on Devtas.

Dyulok

Dyulok refers to planet of the Devtas in space. It is often translated as heaven, but it may be best to use the word Dyulok directly to refer to the abode of Devtas. Dyulok literally means the planet or land of light. Dyulok is in many ways similar to Earth. It has considerable amount of water and many rivers. It has trees and forests. It is rich in resources. In Rigveda, Dyulok and Prithvi, that is Earth, are often used together and referred to as Dyava-Prithvi.

Mantra

Mantra is a specific composition of Aksharas (Sanskrit alphabet that is supposed to be immutable). Mantras are addressed to a Devta. Each Mantra is meant to be accomplished up to a certain level when it starts yielding benefits. In Sanskrit, this stage is called reaching a stage of Siddhi of a Mantra. Mantras are meant to be recited repetitively so as to reach this stage of Siddhi.

Literally, Mantra means that which saves or achieves a certain objective through mental powers. It is defined as 'Mananat trayate iti mantrah' *(see, for example, Parthasarathi, Srinidhi K., 2020)*. This means sustained repetition of that which protects. Mantra delivers, saves, protects, or purifies, through the power of the mind. M1, M2......etc., refer to the sequence in which the Atharvaveda Mantras appear in this volume.

Similarly, G1, G2.....etc., refer to the sequence in which the Shlokas from Srimad Bhagavad Gita are cited in this volume.

Mandal

Mandal refers to a chapter in Rigveda. There are ten Mandals in Rigveda. In fact, in Rigveda, each Mandal is a compilation of Suktas, which contains a set of Richas visualized by Rishis and their descendants. There are some Mandals however, where Richas compiled by a number of Rishis have been brought together. Chapters are referred to by different names in the other Vedas namely, Samaveda, Yajurveda and Atharvaveda. In Yajurveda, chapters are referred to as Adhyaya. In Samaveda and Atharvaveda, these are referred to as Kandas.

Notes on Rigveda Translations

In preparing this Volume, the main translation of Rigveda, which has been referred to, is by Sayan, which is itself in Sanskrit. Sayan is the most consulted translation by translators who have endeavoured to render the Rigveda text into other languages. Sayan usually provides an interpretation of a Richa in three ways or at three levels referred to as Adhibhautic, Adhidaivik, and Adhyatmik. These levels of interpretations may apply to the same Richa and may be considered relevant depending on the context. Adhibhautic refers to the external or physical world. Adhidaivik refers to Devtas who have dominance over defined aspects of nature. Adhyatmik refers to the inner self of a person or the spiritual aspects of his existence.

Amongst Hindi translations, I have referred to Maharshi Dayanand's Satyartha Prakash and his translation of Rigveda, Richa by Richa, which is available in a Volume edited and compiled by Satyavir Shastri. This compilation consists of translations by Maharshi Dayanand for Mandals 1 to 6, and by his disciples, for Mandals 7 to 10. These translations are themselves drawn from the commentaries by Sripad Damodar Satvelkar and Sayan. This Volume was published under the title "Rigveda" by D.P.B. Publications, Delhi-6. The second edition of this work was published in 2018. Another important Hindi translation is by Pandit Ram Govind Trivedi who published his work under the title "Hindi Rigveda". The publisher is Indian Press Ltd, Prayag (Allahabad). It was published in 1954.

For a deeper interpretation, the guidance available in the interpretations given by Mahidas in Aitereya Brahman and Yaska in Nirukta are very valuable. Aitereya Brahman provides a deeper understanding of the Rigvaidic Richas while Yaska has focused on etymological interpretations of each word/phrase such that the link with its root alphabet (akshar) becomes clear. Further, Yagyavalkya's Shatpath Brahman is immensely valuable in exploring the deeper and spiritual meanings of the Rigvaidic

Richas. Acharya Agnivrat has used these extensively to develop his interpretation of Physics through his Rashmi theory of creation of the universe. I have consulted Acharya Agnivrat's valuable works published in four Volumes under the title 'Veda Vigyan Alok: A Vaidic Theory of Universe', published in 2017 by Shri Vaidic Swasti Pantha Nyas, Jalore, Rajasthan. I have made reference to some of the concepts used in Acharya Agnivrat's works to some extent in the context of Economics. Acharya's interpretations and enunciation of the Vaidic Rashmi theory of Physics are largely inspired by the Aitereya Brahman by Maharshi Mahidas.

The main English translations that I have referred to are the following three. Griffith has translated the Rigveda in the form of verses. Wilson, whose elaborate work was published in six volumes, has followed mainly the translation by Sayan. The latest translation in English is by Jamison and Brereton (2014) published by the Oxford University Press.

I have relied extensively on a rich website (Vedic Heritage), developed by the Indira Gandhi National Centre for the Arts, Ministry of Culture, Government of India. This website gives Sanskrit texts as well as Hindi and English translations. In writing the Sanskrit text of the Richas, I have utilized the material pertaining to Rigveda and Atharvaveda contained in this website.

While I have consulted different translations to understand the meaning of a Richa, I have endeavoured to convey my own understanding and interpretation of a Richa, particularly since I have been looking for the economic implications of a Richa apart from its wider meaning. For each Richa referred to in this Volume, I first provide the literal meaning of individual words or combination of words, and then its literal or near-literal translation. Finally, I endeavour to provide its wider interpretation and attempt to place it in its relevant context. In this process, I have realized that the meaning of the Vaidic words slowly reveals itself, the more one dwells upon these words and the more one consults the interpretations by the eminent authorities. As such, all that I have endeavoured to write here in these pages should be considered as an intermediate step, which is meant to be revised from time to time as the deeper meaning of the concepts become clearer through continued devotion and reflection.

Chapter 1 Rigveda: A Brief Introduction

Rigveda, as also the other Vedas are the common inheritance of mankind. The universe of Rigveda encompasses the entire creation including its beginning, its rationale, its cyclical repetitive courses and the place of mankind in its deep mysteries. In its vast canvas, Rigveda covers all beings including men, Rishis, Devtas, Asuras, all life forms, all aspects of Nature, and the Creator himself. Its subject matter ranges from routine affairs of men to the celebrated deeds of the Devtas. In it, not only the deep mysteries concerning the creation of the universe are explored, but practical and livelihood matters such as the ploughing of land, sowing of seeds, watering of plants, nursing and reaping of crops are discussed with equal emphasis. All of these activities are interpreted as Yajnas. Vedas deal with the past, present and future of mankind. Its subject matter covers not only earthly matters but also matters pertaining to Dyulok which is the abode of Devtas. Apart from its spiritual underpinnings, Rigveda is also quite practical. It contains a vast ocean of knowledge gathered by our Rishis through meditation and Yajnas. Our Rishis ensured that this body of knowledge would be passed on from generation to generation for the benefit of mankind. As discussed earlier, this knowledge was preserved for thousands of years by word of mouth through a well-established tradition of teachers and disciples, a unique tradition developed and perfected in India. This tradition, which came to be known as the Guru-Shishya Parampara, ensured not only the continuity of the transmission of knowledge but also its understanding and comprehension, which depend on repeated recitation with correct and prescribed pronunciation. Rigvaidic Richas were transcribed into written form relatively recently. But the written form by itself should be considered incomplete unless the Richas or Mantras are also recited and heard at the same time. In fact, Richas in the Rigveda need to be read, visualised, heard, and meditated upon in order to understand their true meaning.

Vedas denote received knowledge, the residue of the reservoir of information and knowledge that got transmitted from the earlier to later creation cycles of the universe (concept referred to as Manvantaras where each Manvantara consists of four Yugas), in the repetitive cycles of creation and destruction of the physical construct of the universe. The present set of Vedas consisting of Rigveda, Samaveda, Atharvaveda, and Yajurveda constitute what we have inherited from the preceding round of creation for the benefit and welfare of the present one.

There are two ways in which we can consider the order of creation of the four Vedas. In one way, we can consider that all the Vedas emanated from the four mouths of Brahma simultaneously. This would imply that all the Vedas were created at the same time. However, subsequently, their Mantras may have been visualized and compiled by the Rishis over time where their sequence may have been different. In the context of this latter interpretation, Rigveda may be considered as the first compilation of the Vaidic Mantras containing a comprehensive body of knowledge emanating from the Rishis who are known to have drawn this knowledge from the universe by visualizing the Mantras contained in the Vaidic Richas. The commonplace view is that Rigveda lays the foundation of Indian philosophical and religious thought. Its matter has been supplemented by the other three Vedas. It is also important to recognize that the Rigveda and other Vedas also contain a discussion of substantive and foundational economic subjects. The importance of prosperity and material well-being find a central position in the Rigvaidic Richas. In fact, Rigveda provides a holistic view of "Artha" as integrally linked to the wholesome endeavour for the four-fold pursuits of human life namely, Dharma, Artha, Kama, and Moksha. These are called the four Purusharthas. Of these, Artha (economic pursuits) and Kama (desires) may be considered as directly dealing with the subject matter of Economics.

Rigveda deals with agriculture, industry, trade, technology, and publicly provided services like education and health in extensive detail. The Rigvaidic Richas mention barley, rice and porridge in Richas such as 6/56,

Agriculture in Rigveda: Seeds of India's Civilizational Prosperity

8/22, 8/70, 8/77 and 8/83. Metals are also mentioned. The term "Ayas" (metal) occurs in the Rigveda. Richa 5/63 mentions "metal cloaked in gold", suggesting that working with metals including their use in making of weapons, instruments and houses had developed extensively in the Vaidic times.

Considerably detailed references are made to industrial products and advanced technologies for manufacture or fabrication. Various skills for making products and different inputs for industrial processes are also described. The importance of specialization in different skills is also elaborated upon. Products that are described encompass, among others, wheels, chariots, armour, bows and arrows, plough, whip, houses, boats, ships, clothes and weaving, wooden instruments, needles, and metals. Even though there is an extensive discussion with respect to worldly goods and services, the related discourse almost always takes off to attain philosophical and divine heights.

Rigveda provides a detailed description of the interface between mankind and nature. The role of sun and the planetary system as also of the stars and the galaxies for human life is described with great understanding and reverence. Earth itself is placed on a high pedestal, emphasising again and again, that its resources should not be overexploited. Plant life is understood as integrally critical to the welfare of different life forms including mankind. The subject of agriculture is placed in this broader context. The interlinkages between crops, clouds, sunrays, wind, water, rivers, and soil are captured in detail.

This Volume is focused on agriculture. It may be considered as part of a more comprehensive Volume on Economics in Rigveda. In that Volume, it may be possible to consider some key aspects of Economics as conceptualized in the Rigveda. These topics would cover subjects like importance of equilibrium and stability of systems, importance of maintaining harmony in society, the concept and the importance of wealth and prosperity and of autonomy and sovereignty of the self and that of a nation. Rigveda also makes reference to the subject of taxation and desirability of the willingness of the subjects to pay taxes to the king for their protection and welfare. Rigveda also discusses the capacity and importance of maintaining education and health facilities in the society. Rigveda also highlights behavioural norms in the society. While these aspects may be covered in a comprehensive Volume on Economics in Rigveda, for the present work, we may recognize that these aspects are also important for agriculture.

On Vaidic Chandas (Metres)

Sanskrit prosody or Chandas refer to the study of poetic Metres and verses in Sanskrit. The Vaidic Chandas are organized around seven major Metres supplemented by a number of other Metres. Each Metre has its own rhythm, movements and aesthetics. These Metres include those based on a fixed number of syllables per verse, and those based on fixed number of morae (intonations) per verse.

Ancient manuals on Chandas include Pingala's *Chandasutra*, while an example of a medieval Sanskrit prosody manual is Kedara Bhatta's Vrittaratnakara. The most exhaustive compilation of Sanskrit prosody describes over 600 Metres. Pingala's *Chandasutra*, also called Pingala Sutras, is the oldest known Sanskrit prosody text. The Pingala text provides distilled information in the form of aphorisms.

The Metre structure with respect to the seven most frequently used Metres in Rigveda is summarized in Table 1.

The shortest and the most sacred of Vaidic Metres is the Gayatri Metre. In the Gayatri Metre, a verse consists of three octosyllabic sections (pada). This is the second most frequently used Metre after Trishtup. Seven Metres namely, Trishtup, Gayatri, Anushtup, Jagati, Ushnith, Pankti, and Brihati have been used in nearly 92 per cent of the Rigvaidic Richas. There are however, quite a number of other special Metres, which account for the remaining 8 per cent of the Richas.

Table 1: Metre Structure in Rigveda

Metre	Syllable Structure	Number of Verses	% Share in no. of Richas in Rigveda
Gayatri	8 8 8	2447	23.2
Ushnith	8 8 12	341	3.2
Anushtup	8 8 8 8	855	8.1
Brihati	8 8 12 8	181	1.7
Pankti	8 8 8+ 8	312	3.0
Trishtup	11 11 11 11	4253	40.3
Jagati	12 12 12 12	1318	12.5
Sum		**9707**	**92.0**
Others		845	8.0
Total		**10552**	**100.0**

Source: https://en.wikipedia.org/wiki/Vaidic_meter#:~:text=Vedic%20meter%20refers%20to%20the,of%20the%20six%20Vedanga%20disciplines.

Table 2: Notes on Seven Main Chandas

Name	Colour	No. of letters (pada)	Gotra	Devta	Recitation/ Singing (Swar)
Gayatri	White-like the colour of Moon	24	Aagniveshya	Agni	'Sa' Sadaj
Ushnik	Multi-coloured (saarang)	28	Kashyap	Savita also Pusha (in Maitrayani Samhita)	'Ra' Rishabh
Anushtup	Brown with a tinge of red	32	Gautam	Som	Gandhar
Brihati	Black	36	Angiras	Brihaspati	Makar (Madhyam)
Pankti	Blue	40	Bhas hargava	Mitra-Varuna	Pancham
Trishtup	Red	44	Kaushik	Indra	Dhaivat
Jagati	Fair-white	48	Vashistha	Viswedeva	Nishad

Based on Naishthik, Acharya Agnivrat (2017), Ved Vigyan Alok, A Vaidic Theory of Universe, published by Vaidic Swasti Pantha Nyas, Jodhpur

Note: Each Chanda Rashmi has eight forms: Arshi, Daivi, Asuri, Prajapatya, Yajushi, Saamni, Archi, Brahmi. The number of letters or padas given above are with reference to class or group called Arshi, that is, pertaining to the Rishis.

In Table 2, we describe the main characteristics of these seven Chandas in terms of their associated Devta, Colour, Gotra and Property. In a recent work relating to Physics, Acharya Agnivrat (2017) has proposed the Rashmi theory of the creation of the Universe in which the vibrations associated with each of these Chandas have a specific role to play in the process of creation.

The work/property of the different Chandas relating to different Metres are given below:

1. **Gayatri:** They cover prana Rashmis like skin.
2. **Ushnik:** Wrap from outside Gayatri Rashmis; join together; speed up.
3. **Anushtup:** Holds or supports other Rashmis; adopts to their form; acts like Mother Rashmi.
4. **Brihati:** Propagates itself surrounding other Rashmis; builds periphery or outer boundaries.
5. **Pankti:** While expanding linearly give rise to various activities.
6. **Trishtup:** Work as the centre for other Rashmis; Hold other Rashmis in three ways.
7. **Jagati:** Travel farthest; encompass the whole universe.

This discussion is based on the elaboration of the properties of different Rashmis (waves/rays) as given in Acharya Agnivrat's Naishthik.

On Sanskrit and Vaidic Sanskrit

Vaidic Sanskrit is an ancient form of Sanskrit, expressed by the Rishis. In later times, Sanskrit became more refined. The grammar rules were defined more rigorously. Vaidic use of Sanskrit is validated as 'Arsha Prayog', that is use or application by the Rishis who had the flexibility to modify the expressions or deviate from strict grammatical rules, which were defined and coded later. They were expressing Mantras, which carry deep and divine meaning and are not subject to any man-made rules of grammar. Also, the Richas are expressed in Metric form, that is, in the form of Chandas and sometimes the words are required to be modified in order to fit into the required Metric form.

Sanskrit as a language has been designed more to serve as a language to store knowledge rather than as a transactional language for routine conversations. Drawing a metaphor from Economics, all languages may be considered as similar to money. Money serves two purposes: as a means of exchange and as a store of value. Similarly, a language serves two purposes: as a means of exchanging thoughts, particularly transactional expressions, and as a means of storing knowledge.

Sanskrit was developed as a means of storing accumulated knowledge, which can be passed on from generation to generation while avoiding any corruption of the content which usually happens in frequent transactional usage of a language. The knowledge expressed in the Mantras could be passed on orally from generation to generation without the need for writing. For this purpose, in the Sanskrit language, conjoining of words, that is 'Sandhi' was given considerable importance. This provided compactness to the expression. It also ensured that by hanging together, the expressions could not be corrupted as the Mantras were passed on from generation to generation. The Vaidic Mantras were recited in a prescribed way. The words were conjoined together very tightly in integrally poetic and recitable formats called 'Chandas'. This is how this great and received knowledge has survived in India even before these could be written. While the written words and documents could be destroyed in various invasions, the knowledge carried forward from generation to generation through this oral strategy of inter-generational transfer of knowledge, could survive these challenging intermediate times without any degeneration.

In praising this oral tradition, Witzel (1995, updated 2001) has appropriately written:

"The Vedic texts have been composed orally; and, what is more, to this day are also largely transmitted in this fashion. ... generally, all manuscripts remain inferior to the orally transmitted version, which has been extremely faithful, contrary to the norm (as exhibited by the transmission of the Epics, for example). Right from the beginning, in Rigvedic times, elaborate steps were taken to insure the exact reproduction of the words of the ancient poets. As a result, the Rigveda still has the exact same wording in such distant regions as Kashmir, Kerala and Orissa, and even the long-extinct musical accents have been preserved. Vedic transmission is thus superior to that of the Hebrew or Greek Bible, or the Greek, Latin and Chinese classics. We can actually regard present-day Rigveda-recitation as a tape recording of what was first composed and recited.... In addition, unlike the constantly reformulated Epics and Puranas, the Vedic texts contain contemporary materials. They can serve as snapshots of the political and cultural situation of the particular period and area in which they were composed..." *Witzel (1995, updated 2001) [Note: in this citation, I have skipped references to the timelines, since the timelines are subject to considerable controversies].*

Sanskrit, among languages, is like gold is among moneys. It is the root of all languages like gold is, or used to be, behind different forms of money. Since it is used predominantly for storing knowledge, it is best to preserve it like gold rather than let its pristineness erode through frequent transactional use. In fact, even with frequent usage, Sanskrit, like gold, does not get corrupted. Most languages that derive from Sanskrit have suffered transactional erosion and mutation while Sanskrit has preserved its pristine form.

In Chapter 15 of the Srimad Bhagvad Gita, Vedas are referred to as an inverted tree of knowledge whose roots are at the top and the Richas that are composed in the form of Chandas are like leaves hanging down so that they can be easily accessed.

Agriculture in Rigveda: Seeds of India's Civilizational Prosperity

G 6 Srimad Bhagvad Gita: Chapter 15, Shloka 1

> ऊर्ध्वमूलमधःशाखमश्वत्थं प्राहुरव्ययम् ।
> छन्दांसि यस्य पर्णानि यस्तं वेद स वेदवित् ॥ 15-1

This Shloka is translated as: "The Supreme Divine Personality said: They speak of an eternal Ashwattha tree with its roots above and branches below. Its leaves are the Vaidic hymns, and one who knows the secret of this tree is the knower of the Vedas." *(Translation by Swami Mukundananda, 2014) [Note: Ashwattha tree refers to a Peepal tree]*

The oral tradition of reciting the Vaidic Richas and Mantras of Rigveda as well as other Vedas has continued without break in modern times. There are a number of institutions in India in various states including Uttar Pradesh, Karnataka, Kerala, Tamil Nadu and Andhra Pradesh where scholars devote a lifetime pursuing the study of Vedas through this tradition of oral recitation. In this context, the contribution of the Sri Kanchi Kamakoti Peetham requires to be acknowledged.

Some Well-known Rigveda Suktas

Some of the well-known Suktas are now known by their names. These Suktas are devoted to one single theme or Devta, and accordingly they have been named or described. A few of these Suktas that are often quoted and discussed are mentioned below.

1. **Nasadiya Sukta 10/ 129 (1-7):** The name Nasadiya derives from the first word of the first Mantra of this Sukta namely, Nasad. This means that when there was nothing in the universe or when there was only darkness to begin with. This is one of the most mysterious Suktas of Rigveda where Universe as it existed before the process of creation started, has been described.

2. **Krishi Sukta 4/57 (1-8):** Krishi Sukta is devoted entirely to the activity of agriculture. Similar Suktas are available in Yajurveda and Atharvaveda that are devoted to agriculture. It is this Sukta which is the main focus of discussion of the present Volume.

3. **Saraswati Sukta 7/95 (1-6):** There are many Richas devoted to the praise of Saraswati, which may have the connotation of a river, of a Devta presiding over knowledge, and of a mother that is, mother of the Universe. In Mandal 7 of the Rigveda, there is one Sukta where each Richa is devoted entirely to Saraswati.

4. **Nadi Sukta 10/75 (1-9):** The Nadi Sukta which occurs in Mandal 10 of Rigveda describes not only Saraswati but a number of other rivers especially Ganga, Yamuna and Sindhu.

5. **Go Sukta 10/169 (1-4):** The Go Sukta is devoted to the special status given to cows in the ancient Indian literature especially in the Vaidic literature. In this Sukta, the interdependence of cows with the human civilization and how they are useful to each other is described.

6. **Purush Sukta 10/90 (1-16):** This Sukta also describes the process of creation of the Universe. 'Purush' refers to the Creator himself and all beings emanate from this original Purush. This Sukta emphasizes the organic and integral view of Brahman who emanates from the head of the Purush, Kshatriya who emanates from the arms of the Purush, Vaishya who emanates from the stomach of the Purush and Shudra who derives from the legs of the Purush. These limbs cannot be imagined as separate from each other. As they exist integrally in the body of the Purush, similarly, they must be viewed integrally and organically interlinked as members of the society. In fact, in each human body, the Brahman aspect, the Kshatriya aspect, the Vaishya aspect and the Shudra aspect co-exist, together and interdependent.

7. **Vivaha Sukta 10/85 (1-47):** This Sukta describes the wedding of Surya, the daughter of Sun with the Ashwini Kumars. It describes the process of wedding as approved by the Devtas. The same

values and steps of marriages are also to be followed by the society of men for receiving the blessings of Devtas.

8. **Shristi-Sukta 10/130 (1-14):** This Sukta is most directly related to the process of creation of the Universe and the arrival of Devtas, Rishis and men in the Universe. The Devta of this Sukta is Brahma himself.

9. **Yam-Yami Sukta 10/10 (1-14):** The Yam-Yami Sukta describes a dialogue between a brother and a sister, and it provides the basis as to why in a society, marriages should not take place between brothers and sisters.

10. **Dashrajna Yudhha Sukta 7/18 (1-25):** The Dashrajna Yudhha Sukta is one of the most important Suktas in the Rigveda which has a historical significance in the context of the out of India theory of migration. This Sukta describes the battle between the Aryan king Sudas with a number of Aryan and non-Aryan kings on or on the banks of river Parushni which is known in modern times, as river Ravi. In this battle, the Aryan king wins and the other kings, whether Aryan or non-Aryan, move out of India towards the west, spreading out throughout the globe.

11. **Ayudh Sukta 7/75 (1-19):** This Sukta describes the various weapons used in battles that occurred in the Rigvaidic times. It also describes the valour of the warriors of those days and the technological advances which the warring communities were able to utilize for the fabrication and invocation of their Mantras.

12. **Hiranyagarbha Sukta 10/121 (1-10):** This Sukta is also an essential part of the narration of the process of the creation of the Universe as described in Rigveda. It makes reference to the stage where the Universe appeared like a golden egg. This corresponds closely to the modern-day Physics where after the Big Bang, the first stage that is reached is that of a highly dense egg-like object.

13. **Rastri-Sukta 10/125 (1-8):** This Sukta is devoted to the making of a nation. It describes the meaning of sovereignty. In fact, the Rishi of the Sukta is Vagambharni which also refers to the goddess of speech that is Saraswati.

14. **Aushadhi Sukta 10/97 (1-23):** This Sukta considers medicinal plants and trees as the Devta. It provides the seeds for the medicinal science of Ayurveda.

15. **Shraddha Sukta 10/ 151 (1-5):** In this Sukta, the Devi is Shraddha and the Rishi is also named Shraddha from the family of Kama. The Richas in this Sukta highlight the importance of Shraddha which may be only roughly translated to faith or conviction in belief. This Sukta has only five Richas. The fifth Richa says that we must remain firm in the conviction in our belief (in the Devtas) at all times and places.

16. **Vrishti Sukta 7/101 (1-6):** This Sukta is devoted entirely to the subject of rainfall. The Devta in this Sukta is Parjanya. This Sukta emphasises the critical role played by rainfall in the natural and human activities. It emphasises the interdependence between agriculture, water, crops and their maturity, clouds and rainfall.

In this Volume, our focus is on the understanding of agriculture in India's past as contained in the Rigveda. Agriculture is the key to the evolution of the Indian civilization and its prosperity which was sustained over a long period of time. Agriculture spread out on the banks and in the vicinity of India's major rivers namely, Saraswati, Sindhu, and Ganga, and their numerous tributaries and distributaries. These rivers provided water to the crops over land and underground, making land extremely fertile. The fertility of land, particularly the topsoil was enriched by the ample minerals that these rivers carried with them from the higher reaches of the Himalayan ranges. The productive land resulted in the generation of surpluses, facilitating growth and sustenance of population, which spread throughout India along the riverbanks and basins. The rivers ran their course from the Himalayas to the ocean on both sides of the Indian peninsula.

There was an organic relationship between agriculture and animal husbandry based on cows, oxen, and horses. Cows were worshipped for their divine origin and as a source of all forms of wealth. They produced abundant surplus of milk over and above the needs of their calves. This laid the foundation of a major dairy based economy. Oxen were used in the agricultural fields and with the carts, grains could be transported to the granaries and markets. Horses were used to draw vehicles, particularly the chariots. Similarly, there was a special relationship between man and nature. Most aspects of nature such as land, soil, rainfall, plants, mountains, forests and rivers are visualized in the Rigveda as having a divine quality.

The generation of surpluses from farm activities and from animal husbandry gave rise to population growth, industrial activities, urbanization of population, and development of cities, which became centres of trade and commerce as also of generation and dispersal of knowledge. Around these economic activities, guided by the Rigvaidic Mantras, India's civilizational prosperity took roots.

India's ancient economic universe was characterised by economic activities including agriculture where every facet of the activities had a spiritual underpinning. Every activity had a presiding Devta. Rigveda's agriculture presents a symbiotic relationship between farm activities, nature, water, the animal world, the food economy, industrial activities, and activities of trade and commerce.

Richas and their Subject Matter: Self-sameness

Sometimes observers find that the same Mantra or part of Mantra is taken up or contained in a different Mantra. This may not be considered as a repetition. This should be taken as evidence of 'self-sameness'. In the modern theory of *Chaos*, it is often shown that the underlying dynamics or relationship that gives rise to creation is the same although the visible part appears different depending on which part of the unfolding truth one sees. Once, starting from any point, different or similar, when the examination goes deeper, one lands up with the same underlying reality. Many of the Rishis saw the same Mantra, or a common part of the Mantra, and internalized it and taught it to their disciples.

Different Rishis often praised the same Devtas and referred to the same events. Their praises may have differed in the choice of words and Metres in which the Richa was visualised or composed but they would often be seen as covering the same ground.

Structure of Rigveda

Two compilations of Rigveda namely, Shaakal Samhita and Ashvalayan Samhita are known. It is the Shaakal Samhita that is generally used. The Rigveda Samhita contains about 10,552 Mantras, classified into ten books called Mandals. Each Mandal is divided into several sections called Anuvakas. Each Anuvaka consists of a number of hymns called Suktas and each Sukta is made up of a number of verses called Riks. This division of the Rigveda is the most popular and systematic.

A Sukta is a group of Mantras. The number of Mantras in a Sukta is not fixed. Some Suktas have a small number of Mantras while others have a large number of Mantras. It is important to note that every Sukta is associated with a Rishi and is devoted to one or more Devata(s). It is also constructed according to one or more prescribed Metre(s) i.e., Chanda(s). As mentioned, the Samhita of the Rigveda comprises 10 Mandals, 85 Anuvakas, 1,028 Suktas and 10,552 Mantras. Usually, Anuvaka is not mentioned for the reference of a Mantra of the Rigveda. Any Richa can be identified by three coordinates namely, Mandal, Sukta, and the sequence number of the Richa in the Sukta.

In Table 3, the structure of Rigveda in terms of Mandals, Sukta, and number of Richas is summarised.

Agriculture in Rigveda: Seeds of India's Civilizational Prosperity

Table 3: Structure of Rigveda

Mandala	Suktas	Mantras	Average no. of Suktas	Name of Rishis
1	191	2006	10.5	Madhuchanda, Medhatithi, Gotama and others
2	43	429	10	Gritasamada and family
3	62	617	10	Vishvamitra and family
4	58	589	10.2	Vamadeva and family
5	87	727	8.4	Atri and family
6	75	765	10.2	Bharadwaja and family
7	104	841	8.1	Vashishtha and family
8	103	1716	16.7	Kanva, Angira and their families
9	114	1108	9.7	Soma Devta but different Rishis
10	191	1754	9.2	Vimada, Indra, Shachi and others
All	1028	10552	10.3	

Source: Compiled

Out of the ten Mandals, two Mandals namely, Mandal 1 and Mandal 10, containing 191 Suktas each, are considered to be the 'younger' Mandals, while Mandals 2 to 9 are considered older Mandals. The younger Mandals are so called as the Rishis who visualized the Mantras in these Mandals are considered to be relatively more recent compared to the Rishis in Mandals 2 to 9. A reference to more recent and more ancient Rishis is made in the Rigveda itself. Mandal literally means a 'circle', an entity which completes or brings together a comprehensive theme. Out of these, Mandals 2 to 7 are referred to as 'family' books implying that these pertain to one main Rishi and his lineage consisting of sons, daughters, and disciples. Mandal 9 is devoted exclusively to the theme of 'Somaras'. Mantras in this Mandal are visualized by different Rishis from different traditions.

The first Mandal is the largest, with 191 Suktas and 2006 Richas. It is said that it was added to the text after Books 2 through 9. The last, or the 10th Book, also has 191 Suktas containing 1754 Richas, making it the second largest. Language analytics suggests that the 10th Book, chronologically, was composed and added last[1]. The content of the 10th Book also suggests that the authors knew and relied on the contents of the first nine books.

The Rigvaidic Suktas may all have been formulated at different times. Thus, when one considers the time of writing or compilation of Rigveda, it is best to take it as a range covering possibly thousands of years.

From out of the two compilations of Rigveda namely, Shaakal Samhita and Ashvalayan Samhita, our references are to the Shaakal Samhita. The structure of Rigveda can be described as being organised in two ways: arranged according to Mandals (10) or arranged according to parts (8). Our references are to the Mandal-wise arrangements.

Rigvaidic Rishis draw similes and metaphors extensively from nature as well as human behaviour. Many Mantras express a profound thought where an appropriate comparison with some natural phenomenon makes it easy to understand.

The methodology of investigation that the Rishis follow is to look inwardly and to meditate, look outwardly and examine features of the external world, and look at human interactions. They are supposed to have visualised the Mantras as these manifested in front of them, a remnant of knowledge from times long gone but whose information content has not been lost.

Age of Rigveda

The Rigveda Samhita is the oldest compilation of human wisdom. This Samhita is unique in the sense that it is not a book by one author or a set of co authors. Instead, it is a compilation consisting of several

---

[1] James Hastings, Encyclopaedia of Religion and Ethics at Google Books, Vol. 7, Harvard Divinity School, TT Clark, pp. 51–56 (published in 1908 and digitized in 2007)

independent compilations by Rishis and their schools which were developed over a long period of time. Thus, Rigveda consists of older and newer contributions, which are all, for our purposes, quite ancient.

There are two major debates in the context of India's civilizational ancestry. One debate pertains to whether Aryans migrated from out of India or whether they came to India from outside. These versions are referred to as 'Out of India' theory (OIT) or 'Indigenous Aryan' theory (IAT) on the one hand, and 'Aryan Invasion' theory (AIT) or 'Aryan Migration' theory (AMT) on the other. The other debate refers to the age of India's ancient civilization and literature including that of Rigveda. In recent years, many Indian scholars have joined this debate largely arguing in favour of the OIT and significantly ancient ancestry of India's civilization and literature. While we do not take a view on this subject, given recent evidence particularly based on astronomical references in texts such as Rigveda, Ramayana and Mahabharat, this debate is likely to be eventually settled in favour of the Indian scholars.

In regard to the issue of age of Rigveda, there are two aspects. First, there is the issue of the age of the beginning of Rigveda and second, there is the issue with respect to the period over which the Richas were visualized and compiled. Most western scholars consider the beginning of the Rigveda to be relatively recent, that is, around 1500 BCE to 2000 BCE. According to Jamison and Brereton (2014), the dating of this text "has been and is likely to remain a matter of contention and reconsideration".

Most Indian scholars consider it to be far older. Many Indian scholars particularly the more recent ones such as Nilesh Oak[2] and Raj Vedam[3] date the Rigveda and the Rigvaidic times as going back to 17,000 BCE to 24,000 BCE or earlier. More recently, Rupa Bhaty has contended that there are references in Rigveda especially of King Brihadratha of the

---

[2] https://nileshoak.wordpress.com/2021/09/09/comprehending-antiquity-of-indian-civilization/

[3] https://www.youtube.com/watch?v=RGyjvyXEKdc

Ikshvaku dynasty that would take its antiquity back to about 34,000 BCE[4]. In fact, Rupa Bhaty has prepared a detailed chart describing major landmarks in India's ancient history which goes back to 74,000 BCE or earlier. In Figure 1, Rupa Bhaty's timelines of India's civilizational evolution in ancient times are reproduced with her permission. She has triangulated the dates using astronomical references in Rigveda with other complementary evidence. She refers to 60,000 BCE as the probable time of agriculture based on references to the constellations or the Shuna-Sira in Rigveda.

Pandit Ram Govind Trivedi, in his Hindi translation of Rigveda, makes reference to a Richa where an unstable situation of Earth is described. He writes that according to geologists, such a situation existed about 25,000 to 50,000 years before present. This situation is described by the sages who might have seen it. There are quite a number of Rigveda Mantras that describe astronomical and geological phenomena that can be given only by somebody who witnessed these. Based on such references, Trivedi, writing in 1954, in his *Hindi Rigveda*, asserts that the creation of Rigveda would be during 18,000 years to 50,000 years before present. A few Richas referred to by Trivedi in this context may be mentioned as follows:

1. Mandal 10, Sukta 85, Richa 13
2. Mandal 10, Sukta 136, Richa 6

---

[4] https://www.youtube.com/watch?v=fRhO-y9NgjI

Agriculture in Rigveda: Seeds of India's Civilizational Prosperity

Figure 1: Rupa Bhaty's timeline of India's civilizational evolution

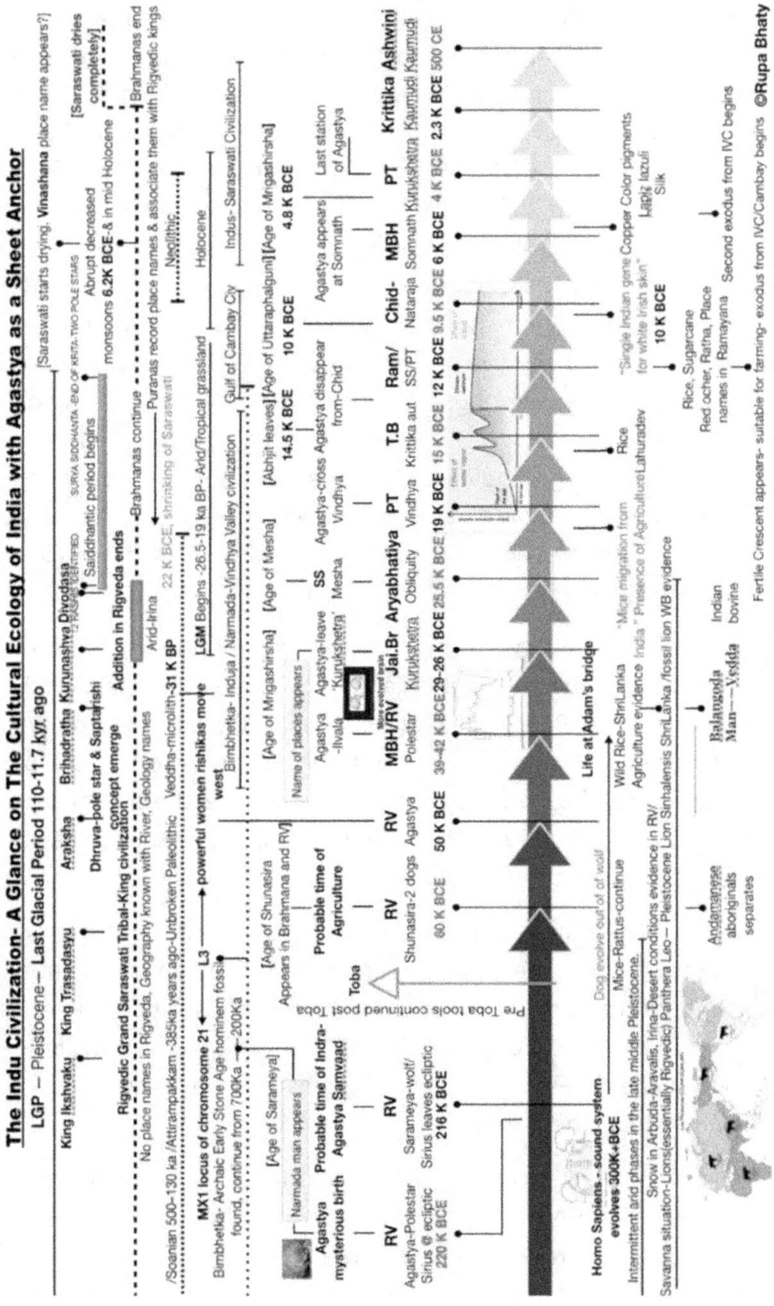

The Indu Civilization- A Glance on The Cultural Ecology of India with Agastya as a Sheet Anchor

Both Nilesh Oak and Raj Vedam and several other Indian scholars have been using internal astronomical references in the ancient Indian texts to date them. Thus, Nilesh Oak has used this methodology of linking textual references in Rigveda to indicate that the beginning of Rigveda may be considered as 22,000 BCE or earlier and the compilation may have continued up to 2000 BCE. Nilesh Oak has also used this methodology of linking references to astronomical phenomena in Valmiki's Ramayana and Vedvyas's Mahabharata to identify the dates for the Ram-Ravana war and the Parinirvan of Bhishmapitamah. Accordingly, he identifies 12,209 BCE for the Lanka war and 5561 BCE for the Mahabharata war. There is a debate amongst Indian scholars about the dating of Ramayana and Mahabharata. Different authors have used astronomical, archeological, geological, and other evidence to justify their claims. Eventually, this debate may settle down. My sense is that in most of these debates, it is the relatively earlier dates which may prove to be the most reliable estimates.

In fact, just as the Rishis ensured the continuity of the Vedas by establishing an oral tradition and Sanskrit was an ideal language for this purpose, the Rishis also ensured that the age of the Vedas could eventually be confirmed by references to astronomical phenomena. Accordingly, based on astronomical evidence, the beginning of Rigveda may be 22,000 BCE or older and the compilation may have continued up to 2000 BCE.

As discussed later in this Volume, the age and duration of Rigveda is coincident with the development of the Saraswati civilization. Saraswati civilization also got initiated in the vicinity of about 22,000 BCE. It reached its peak during 10,000 BCE to 6000 BCE. This civilization slowly migrated out of the Saraswati valley and plains to areas covered by Sindhu and Ganga and other rivers.

Over time, it is becoming clearer that the time spans resultant from the western dating efforts are so short that they cannot accommodate a meaningful narration of the various generations of Indian Kings and dynasties that have been described in the Vedas, Puranas, and Itihaasas (Valmiki Ramayana and Vedvyas Mahabharat) among other Indian texts.

This is also clear by the nature of the construction of the Richas as coming from successive generations of Rishis. Thus, starting from the Adi-Rishis, the contributions continued through many generations of their descendants including children and disciples. This process may have continued over several centuries or even millennia. It is also useful to recognize that within the Rigveda, a distinction is made between older or original Rishis and newer or later generations of Rishis.

In the first Mandal, the very first Richa of the Rigveda, is by Rishi Madhuchanda, who is a descendant of Rishi Vishwamitra, whose contributions are compiled in a later Mandal, that is Mandal 3. In the second Richa of Sukta 1 in Mandal 1, Rishi Madhuchanda recognizes the distinction between old and new Rishis.

R 2 Richa 8/22/6 मधुच्छन्दा वैश्वामित्रः, अग्निः, गायत्री

अ॒ग्निः पूर्वेभि॑र्ऋषिभि॒रीड्यो॒ नूत॑नैरुत।
स दे॒वाँ एह व॑क्षति ॥ 1/1/2

This translates to: "May that Agni, who is celebrated by both ancient and contemporary Rishis, conduct the Devtas towards us". Of course, what was contemporary for Rishi Madhuchanda, is now quite ancient for us.

The Rigveda is also the largest amongst all the four Vedas. It contains the roots of India's philosophical and material thoughts and activities which evolved over the centuries. The value of the Rigveda at all times has been its universal relevance and relevance that transcends time and space.

Rishis in Rigveda

Different Richas in Rigveda have emanated from different Rishis. Mandals 2 to 9 are considered the family Mandals in as much as each one of those pertain to a family of Rishis descending from one main Rishi. Mandals 1 and 10, which are the largest Mandals containing 191 Suktas each, include Suktas from a long list of Rishis. Some of the prominent

Rishis are Vashishtha, Vishwamitra, Vamadev, Bharadwaj, and Kanva. Sometimes, Devtas themselves become the Rishis for some Richas.

There are also a number of female Rishis who are sometimes referred to as 'Rishikas'. However, in Vaidic references, both female Rishis and female Devtas are referred to as Rishis and Devtas only. Some of the notable names of Rishikas are: Ajeyi Apala (8/91), Yami (10/10), Indrasnusha (10/28), Ghosha Kakshivati (10/39 and 10/40), Aditi (10/72), Surya (10/85), Indrani (10/86 and 10/145), Urvashi (10/95), and Godha (10/134). These Rishikas were also seers of Mantras just like their male counterparts.

Devtas in Rigveda

Associated with each Richa is one or more Devta(s). A Richa is constructed in praise of the Devta for that Richa. It would usually contain a request or an appeal to that Devta by or on behalf of the performer of Yajna, for bestowing the performer with knowledge, riches, progeny, a house, protection, and victory over enemies. In the Yajna, the Richa or Mantra is recited according to the prescribed Chanda underlying the Richa.

Worship of Agni is age-old in India. Agni in Rigveda is recognized not only as a Devta but also as the gateway, an ambassador, a conduit, and a messenger to all the other Devtas. Rigveda's first Richa is addressed to Agni.

It is possible to make a distinction between two categories of Devtas who have been referred to. For one group of Devtas, the reference is to beings who may have come from another planet. There are quite a number of references to these Devtas as being thirty-three in number. It is also said in many Richas that they are residents of another planet. These Devtas may have physical forms similar to men or they may have the capacity to adopt different forms. These Devtas perform many physical actions such as engaging in war, travelling in chariots, conducting surgical procedures, and engaging in agriculture. Important among these Devtas are Indra, Mitra, Varuna, Aryama, Vishnu, Rudra, Vayu, Surya, and Ashwini Kumars.

There is another group of Devtas, who do not have a recognizable physical form but who are the underlying divine spirits in physical matter as well as animals. Planetary positions and other astronomical phenomena are also referred to as Devtas. Thus, in different Richas, references are made, for example, to Heaven and Earth (Dyawa-Prithvi), "Shuna-Seerau", "Sita" (referring to fertility of soil), "Vastoshapati", meaning Devta of the science of construction. The defining feature of Rigveda and, in fact, the ancient Indic tradition, is to recognize an underlying divinity in all beings and in nature, whether live or apparently inert.

There are a number of important female Devtas associated with different Rigvaidic Richas. Some of their names are: Dadhrika (4/38, 4/39 and 4/40), Usha (4/51 and 4/52), Savita (4/53), and Dyava Prithvi (4/56).

It is not only male or female Devtas but sometimes, animals are also given the status of Devtas. Thus, Indra's two horses are praised as Devtas (10/96). Cows are also praised as Devtas and full Suktas are devoted to them (10/169). Tarkshaya (Garuda) is also referred to as a Devta in one of the Suktas (10/178). Even medicinal plants or herbs are referred to as Devtas (10/97).

Another way in which Devtas are recognized is to visualize them as residing within the (human) body. According to the Taitariya Samhita of Yajurveda, Devtas reside in different parts of the human body. This is detailed below. This description is taken from Taitariya Samhita *(श्री कृष्णयजुर्वेदीय तैत्तिरीय संहितायां चतुर्थकाण्डेसप्तमः प्रपाठकः)*.

ॐ प्रजननेब्रह्मा तिष्ठतु: Brahma resides in all procreative limbs and energies for inter-generational and intra-body creation. The human body is a colony of millions of cells. At any instant, many new cells are created replacing many that die out. The procreator ensures transmission of evolutionary information from one cell to another just as from one generation to another through the RNAs and DNAs. The process of bifurcation of the DNAs is a procreative strategy to transmit information.

पादयोर्विष्णुस्तिष्ठतु: Vishnu resides in the legs, providing the foundational support to existence, in His appearance as Vaman avatar, he encompassed the three Universes in two steps.

हस्तयोर्हरस्तिष्ठतु: Hara (Shiva) resides in the palms, extending human reach for his endeavours.

बाह्वोरिन्द्रस्तिष्ठतु: Indra resides in the arms, providing strength to the human body to undertake physical action.

जठरेऽग्निस्तिष्ठतु: Agni resides in the stomach as fire and source of energy in which Yajna or sacrifices are to be made so that the offerings can be provided to the Devtas according to their due share. Thus, Agni is visualized as a doorway to all other Devtas.

हृदयेशिवस्तिष्ठतु: Shiva resides in the heart which is the centre of existence.

कण्ठेवसवस्तिष्ठन्तु: Vasus reside in the throat.

वक्त्रे सरस्वती तिष्ठतु: Saraswati resides on the tongue, she is the Devi of expression whereby all internal intelligence find expression through speech.

नासिकयोर्वायुस्तिष्ठतु: Vayu (winds) reside in the nostrils, presiding Devta of the endogenized airs or Paranas that ensures all the bodily movements, balance, and functions.

नयनयोश्चन्द्रादित्यौ तिष्ठेताम्: Sun and moon reside in the eyes.

कर्णयोरश्विनौतिष्ठेताम्: The Ashwini Kumars reside in the ears.

ललाटेरुद्रास्तिष्ठन्तु: Rudras reside on the forehead.

मूर्ध्यादित्यास्तिष्ठन्तु: Aditya (Sun) resides on the top of the head.

शिरसि महादेवस्तिष्ठतु: Mahadev resides in the head.

शिखायां वामदेवस्तिष्ठतु: Vamadev resides on the plait on the crest.

पृष्ठेपिनाकी तिष्ठतु: Pinaki, Shiva's bow, resides on the back.

पुरतः शूली तिष्ठतु: Shiva's trishul resides in the entire body.

पार्श्वयोः शिवाशङ्करौतिष्ठेताम्: Shiva (Parvati) and Shankar reside on the two sides of the body.

सर्वतोवायुस्तिष्ठतु: Vayu resides in the entire body.

ततोबहिः सर्वतोऽग्निज्र्वालामाला परिवृतस्तिष्ठतु: On the outer layer of the body, a circle of energy emanating from Agni surrounds the entire body.

सर्वेष्वङ्गेषुसर्वा देवता यथास्थानं तिष्ठन्तु: All the Devtas reside in their appropriate places in all the limbs and senses of the entire body.

मा रक्षन्तु: May all the Devtas protect us.

सर्वान् महाजनान् रक्षन्तु: May all the great beings protect us.

The physically visible Yajna is an externalized version of an intra-body Yajna, where food is sacrificed in the fire of the digestive process, and the released nourishment is distributed among the Devtas, who are the presiding deities of different limbs and energies in the body with their share from out of the sacrificed food in the Yajna. This gets distributed among them according to an in-built algorithm so that each Devta receives his due share. The Vaidic Richas that praise the Devtas address both the Devtas in the external universe and in the internal universe, invoking their properties in both universes.

This is the reason why in Srimad Bhagwad Gita, Sri Krishna says that men and Devtas should take care of each other's welfare. This Shloka is in Chapter 3 as given below.

G 7 Srimad Bhagvad Gita: Chapter 3, Shloka 11

देवान्भावयतानेन ते देवा भावयन्तु वः ।
परस्परं भावयन्तः श्रेयः परमवाप्स्यथ ॥ 3-11

This Shloka is translated as: "By your sacrifices, the celestial gods will be pleased, and by cooperation between humans and the celestial gods, great prosperity will reign for all" *(Translation by Swami Mukundananda, 2014)*.

Summary and Key Points

The universe of Rigveda is the universe itself. Its relevance is also universal, transcending time and space. Rigvaidic Richas contain true knowledge about the creation and the purpose of the universe and the place of mankind in it. Associated with each Richa is a Rishi who received the Mantra of the Richa, visualised it, meditated upon it, recited it, and ensured that it is passed on from generation to generation in its original form. Apart from the universal wisdom to guide mankind, Rigveda provides essentials of Economics including practical productive activities such as agriculture. Some of the key points of this Chapter are summarized below.

➢ Rigveda is earthly and practical on the one hand, and mystic and universal, on the other.

➢ India's Rishis ensured that this body of knowledge would be passed on from generation to generation, undiluted for the benefit of mankind by a teacher-disciple tradition that relied on repeated recitation.

➢ Rigveda is commonly understood to contain the roots of both sciences and philosophy. Although not generally recognized, Rigveda contains the roots and essence of the subject called Economics or Arthashastra.

➢ A Vaidic Richa is associated with one or more Devta(s), one or more Rishi(s), and a specific Chanda or Metric structure. The substantive meaning of the words of the Mantra as well as the sound or sound waves created by the recitation of the Mantra are equally important.

➢ Seven Metres namely, Trishtup, Gayatri, Anushtup, Jagati, Ushnith, Pankti, and Brihati have been used in nearly 92 per cent of the Rigvaidic Richas.

Agriculture in Rigveda: Seeds of India's Civilizational Prosperity

- ➤ Rigveda, according to the Shaakal Samhita, consists of 10 Mandals or chapters, consisting of Suktas that are groups of Mantras.
- ➤ The first and the tenth Mandals are the longest, consisting of 191 Suktas each. The total number of Suktas is 1,028 and the total number of Mantras is 10,552. These numbers may marginally differ according to compilations.

Chapter 2 Vaidic Roots of Agriculture

Agriculture is an economic activity. It is the first activity that distinguished humans from other animals, making it possible to survive without the necessity to feed on other creatures. There are quite a number of Suktas in Rigveda in which agricultural and related activities are described in detail. In Rigveda, it is acknowledged that agriculture was taught to mankind by the Devtas. Devtas also gifted to mankind, the seed of the first grain, namely barley which is referred to as Yava in Rigveda. It is called 'Jau' in northern India, which appears to be derived from Yava. Since the original seeds were received from the Devtas, that may be the reason why barley and other grains are offered to the Devtas in the Yajnas, symbolizing offerings to the Devtas as an act of acknowledgement.

Agriculture is concerned with sowing, nursing, and finally harvesting the crops. There is a central role of water and sunlight in the growth of the crop. Water is to be sourced from underground sources, rivers, streams and water falls as also through rainfall. Riverbeds and rainfall have an important position in Rigveda in bringing out the fertility, productivity, and life-force that emanates from the Earth. In agriculture, there is an important and organic relationship between humans and animals, particularly cattle and horses. Rigveda prescribes a harmonious and happy relationship between the two. In Rigveda, various industrial products and technological implements used in agriculture in the Vaidic times are also mentioned. Many of these instruments are used even today. For the successful completion of the agricultural cycle, a harmonious relationship between forces of nature and activities of men, their relationship with the animal world, knowledge about the land where tilling is to be done are all important aspects. Food grains, vegetation, and herbs that constitute the output of the agricultural activity are crucial for the sustenance, strength, and growth of the population. Food grains, referred to as 'Dhaanya' are an important form of wealth and storing of food grains according to seasonal requirements is mentioned in detail in

Rigveda. Understanding of the different seasons is also quite important for sowing and reaping different types of crops.

Sources of water, fertile land, and cattle are cited as salient causes of disputes among different groups of Vaidic people indicating that all of these were considered as important forms of assets. These disputes often turned into major wars among the Kings and Chieftains of those times.

Agriculture heralds the beginning of a culture, transitioning out from a nomadic culture, where the human population attempts to settle down in specific geographic locations. Agriculture binds the society to a specific location. If a crop is sown, one must wait there, for it to mature so that it can be reaped. Thus, Vaidic agriculture provided mankind a culture based on drawing sustenance from land and milk and milk products from cows. It provided the possibility of sustenance based on an entirely vegetarian diet moving away from the life of daily hunting and surviving involved in a nomadic way of life. Agriculture produced a surplus over and above what is required for next year's sowing. Hence the tradition of 'Daan' and 'offering' in Yajnas. It offered mankind spare time for developing instruments and technologies and getting involved in other industrial, educational, and cultural activities.

The essential role of water led the society to settle around the riverbeds made fertile by the downstream flow of water from mountainous ranges. The Indian civilization followed the path of river Saraswati, the most abundant in water, flowing down from the mountains to plains with a massive width, and carrying with it, rich minerals. Land around both banks of Saraswati and its tributaries became fertile with alluvial soil thereby facilitating human settlement. Since Saraswati was fed with powerful streams of water by a number of tributaries, land around these rivers also got habitations. These lands were suitable for agriculture and raising cattle. There is also considerable internal evidence within Rigveda of a number of industrial activities and technological developments. There are direct references to cities and townships and trade amongst them. Areas where population density increased, evolved into towns and

Agriculture in Rigveda: Seeds of India's Civilizational Prosperity

cities. Port towns where from ships and boats for trade may have been launched also became large cities. Thus, human settlements may have spread from mountains to plains stretching down further to river deltas and coastal areas.

Agriculture was the major economic force of India and almost every major Indian festival was related to agricultural activities. In ancient times, Indians used to perform Yajnas before farming which helped them to obtain nutrient-rich and nourishing crops. One important example of this kind of farming is based on the Agnihotra Yajna which can bring critical changes to contemporary farming.

In Vaidic times, for the timely occurrence of rains that nourish the crops, people would perform Yajnas so as to please the Devta of rains. The main ingredients of such a sacrifice were ghee (clarified butter) and firewood, which are provided by Mother Cow and Mother Nature respectively.

Two of the prominent Suktas in Rigveda that are devoted almost fully to agriculture are Sukta 57 in Mandal 4, and Sukta 101 of Mandal 10. In Mandal 5, Sukta 83 is devoted almost entirely to rainfall and its role for cultivation and vegetation. Some other important references to agriculture are in Richa 15 of Sukta 23 in Mandal 1, Richa 15 of Sukta 25 in Mandal 1, Richa 4 of Sukta 70 in Mandal 5, Richa 4 of Sukta 25 in Mandal 6, and Richa 6 of Sukta 22 in Mandal 8. This is by no means an exhaustive list. All the Richas referred to in this Volume are listed in the List of Richas, given after the Preface.

This Volume is devoted to the discussion of agriculture primarily in Rigveda. Subsequently, agriculture has been discussed in a number of other works by our Rishis. There are a number of references in Atharvaveda and Brahmanas. I have made a limited set of cross-references to the description of agriculture in Atharvaveda.

In this and the subsequent chapters, I take up specific Rigvaidic Richas that relate to some specific dimension of agriculture. In interpreting each Richa, it is useful first to consider the literal meaning of the words or combination of words. After that, the translation of the Richa is taken up, followed by considering the implicit meaning or interpretation of the Richa particularly in the context of agriculture. Each Richa is referred to by first mentioning the number of the Mandal, then the Sukta, and then the serial number of the Richa in the Sukta.

We start with the Richa in Rigveda where an acknowledgement is made that Ashwini Kumars, the twin Devtas, who taught Manu how to cultivate the soil using a plough, gave the barley seeds, and bestowed rainfall, which has a divine origin.

Agriculture: Gift from Devtas to Mankind

This acknowledgement is contained in Richa 6 of Sukta 22 in Mandal 8.

R 3 Richa 8/22/6 सोभरि: काण्व:, अश्विनौ, प्रगाथ: = (विषमा बृहती, समा सतोबृहती)

For this Richa, the Rishi is Sobharih Kanvah, that is Sobhari who is descended from Rishi Kanva. The Devtas are Ashwini Kumars. The Richa is given below. Since this is an even-numbered Richa, the applicable Chanda is Satobrihati.

> दुश॒स्यन्ता॒ मन॑वे पू॒र्व्यं दि॒वि य॒वं वृ॒केण॑ कर्षथः ।
> ता वा॒मद्य सु॒मति॑भिः शुभस्पती॒ अश्विना॒ प्र स्तु॑वीमहि ॥ (8/22/6)

Meaning of words/combination of words

शुभस्पती (Shubhaspati) means doers of auspicious things मन॑वे (Manve) for Manu, पू॒र्व्यं (Purvayam) in earlier times or ancient times, दि॒वि (Divi) in the abode of Devtas, य॒वं (Yavam) refers to the grain called barley. In Hindi, it is referred to as Java or Jau, वृ॒केण (Vrikena) refers to that implement which is curved, meaning a plough, दुश॒स्यन्ता॒ (Dashasyanta) refers to the act of giving, कर्षथः (Karshathah) indicates the act of pulling or drawing with some friction *[This may be the root word from which the term Krishi is derived which refers to agriculture in Hindi or Sanskrit]*. Thus, agriculture stands for the art or practice of pulling or drawing the plough on Earth. The basic role of the plough is to turn over the topsoil thereby retaining the fertility of the soil. This art was taught to mankind by the

Agriculture in Rigveda: Seeds of India's Civilizational Prosperity

Devtas who also gave the first seeds of barley. अश्विना (Ashwina), that is the Ashwini Kumars, ता वाम् (Taa Vaam) means pertaining to the two of you, अद्य (Adya) indicates 'in the present', प्र स्तुवीमहि means 'we praise' and सुमतिभिः (Sumatibhih) means with a favourable predisposition.

Thus, this Richa means: 'Bestowing upon Manu, the ancient (rain) which was located in the land of the Devtas, you taught him (and through him, all mankind) to cultivate the (soil) with the plough and grow the barley. Now, therefore we praise the two of you, Ashwini Kumars, with a happy disposition.'

Barley (known as Yava in both Vaidic and classical Sanskrit) is mentioned many times in Rigveda and other Indian scriptures as one of the principal grains in ancient India. Yava is used as the offering in Yajnas as 'Samidha', which is sacrificed in the auspicious fire as acknowledgement to the Devtas saying that: 'You gave these grain seeds to us, which have multiplied manifold and are now available to us in abundance.'

Barley is one of the earliest crops accessed by mankind. According to Rigveda, it is the very first crop. In this Richa, there is an acknowledgement that the seed of barley, the art of ploughing, and the rains are all divine gifts.

Traces of barley cultivation have been found in post-Neolithic Bronze Age Harappan civilization 5700–3300 years before present[5]. It could be older.

---

[5] https://en.wikipedia.org/wiki/Barley
Tibetan barley has been a staple food in Tibetan cuisine since the fifth century CE. This grain, along with a cool climate that permitted storage, produced a civilization that was able to raise great armies. It is made into a flour product called tsampa that is still a staple in Tibet.[42] The flour is roasted and mixed with butter and butter tea to form a stiff dough that is eaten in small balls.

In Atharvaveda, apart from Yava, rice was also mentioned as one of the main agricultural crops. This occurs in one of the very well-known Suktas devoted Earth that is referred to as the Bhumi Sukta by Rishi Atharva.

References to Atharvaveda Mantras indicate the Kanda (Chapter), Sukta and the sequence of the Mantra in the Sukta. For each Mantra, first the Rishi, followed by the Devta of the Mantra and finally the Chanda used in the Mantra are given in this sequence.

M 1 Atharvaveda Mantra 12/1/42 अथर्वा, भूमिः, स्वराडनुष्टुप्

For this Mantra, the Rishi is Atharva. Devta is Bhumi. Metre is Swarat Anushtup.

> यस्यामन्नं व्रीहियवौ यस्यां इमाः पञ्चं कृष्टयंः ।
> भूम्यै पर्जन्यंपत्न्यै नमोंऽस्तु वर्षमेंदसे ॥ 12/1/42

Meaning of words/combination of words

यस्यामन्नं Whose grains are व्रीहियवौ rice and barley यस्यां इमाः पञ्चं कृष्टयंः on these grains, these five peoples thrive भूम्यै पर्जन्यंपत्न्यै for this Earth, who is the wife of Devta Parjanya नमोंऽस्तु I bow with reverence वर्षमेंदसे that is saturated with rains.

This Mantra translates to: 'We bow with reverence to this Earth, who is the wife of Devta Parjanya and who is saturated with rains, who bestows us with foods such as rice and barley, upon whom our five peoples thrive.'

The purport is that the Earth is blessed by ample rain which enables it to produce food grains such as rice and barley which are consumed by our five peoples. These grains are produced in ample quantity because of the abundant rain and the agricultural practices that these five peoples have adopted. Elsewhere, these peoples have been recognized in Rigveda as Puru, Yadu, Turvasa, Anu, and Druhyu, along with their descendants, who are all sons of Yayati.

Agriculture: Conceptualized as Yajna

In Rigveda, agriculture is conceptualized as a Yajna. Associated with Yajna, there is a Devta, a Rishi, a Mantra or Strotra. The process involves offering of Havi along with the praise in acknowledgement of the contribution of the Devta, while praying for blessings in the form of food grains, wealth, knowledge, and progeny. All these elements are present in agriculture. Every aspect of agriculture, every activity of agriculture in Rigveda is guided by Devtas. That is why, in acknowledgement, men are supposed to offer symbolically, the output of agriculture, that is grains, to the Devtas. That is why, in Mandal 6, Sukta 56, Richa 1, it is said that once the offering of Yava is made in the Yajna to Pushan Devta, no more offerings are required.

R 4 Richa 6/56/1 बाहस्पत्यो भरद्वाजः, पूषा, गायत्री

For this Richa, the Rishi is Bharadwaj, from the lineage of Brihaspati. The Devta for the Richa is Pushan. The Chanda is Gayatri.

> य एनमादिदेंशति करम्भादितिं पूषणम् ।
> न तेनं देव आदिशें ॥ 6/56/1

Meaning of words/combination of words

य एनमादिदेंशति The one who offers करम्भादितिं Karambha (Dahi, that is curd, mixed with flour of Yava) initially पूषणम् refers to 'Pusha', न तेनं देव आदिशें for Pushan, no other offering is needed. No (other) Devta is needed to be worshipped by him who declares the offering of Yava mixed with ghee (clarified butter) to be intended for Pushan.

This Richa translates to: 'Once the offering of Karambha is made for Pushan, no other Devta is to be worshipped and no other offering is needed.'

The connotation is that the offering of Yava and the offering to the Devta named as Pushan can be considered as a symbolic offering representing all grains and all Devtas. Thus, for Devtas, the most pleasing offering is that emanating from some preparation of Yava (barley).

R 5 Richa 10/22/10 ऐन्द्रो विमदः प्राजापत्यो वा, वासुक्रो वसुकृद्वा, इन्द्रः, पुरस्ताद्बृहती

For this Richa, the Rishi is Vimada. The Devta is Indra. The Chanda is Purastad-brihati.

> त्वं तान्वृंत्रहत्यें चोदयो॒ नृन्कांर्पा॒णे शूंर वज्रिवः ।
> गुहा॒ यदीं॑ कवी॑नां विंशां नक्षं॑त्रशवसाम् ॥10/22/10

Meaning of words/combination of words

शूंर वज्रिवः O great warrior, wielder of the Vajra त्वं you तान्वृंत्रहत्यें for destroying Vritra चोदयो॒ persuade or animate नृन्कांर्पा॒णे the warriors (reference is to Maruts) गुहा॒ यदीं॑ कवी॑नां विंशां नक्षं॑त्रशवसाम् when you hear the praises of the sages for the Devtas, who are residents of the other planet.

This Richa translates to: 'O Indra, the great warrior, the wielder of the Vajra, you persuade the warriors (Maruts) for the destruction of the Vritra, when you hear the praises sung by the Rishis for the Devtas, who are residents of the other planet, that is other than Earth.'

This Richa indicates that there is the recognition in Rigveda that the Devtas hailed from another planet where they reside. In many Richas, Devtas are known to travel frequently on spaceships traversing as well as descending from the interstellar space. Both the Earth and the planet of the Devtas are characterized by abundance of water, which is recognized and praised in many Rigvaidic Richas. Indra, the chief Devta, is also a visitor from the Devta's planet namely, Dyulok. Reading Richas R1 and R2 together, it is indicated that the Yava seeds came from another planet, that is, the Devta's planet, and these were brought by them for initiating agriculture on Earth. Devtas are 33 in number according to Rigveda as given in Richas (8/28/1) and (8/30/2).

Agriculture in Rigveda: Seeds of India's Civilizational Prosperity

R 6 Richa 1/117/21 कक्षीवान् दैर्घतमस औशिजः, अश्विनौ, त्रिष्टुप्

For this Richa, the Rishi is Kakshiwan. The Devtas are the Ashwini Kumars. The Metre is Trishtup.

यवं वृकेणाश्विना वपन्तेषं दुहन्ता मनुषाय दस्रा ।
अभि दस्युं बकुरेणा धमन्तोरु ज्योतिश्चक्रथुरार्याय ॥1/117/21

Meaning of words/combination of words

यवं वृकेणाश्विना वपन्तेषं Sowing barley by using the plough, O Ashwini Kumars दुहन्ता drawing water (from the clouds) मनुषाय for the sake of Manu and his descendants दस्रा O Dasras (Ashwini Kumars) अभि दस्युं बकुरेणा destroying Dasyus with their sharp weapon धमन्तोरु ज्योतिश्चक्रथुरार्याय and providing a well-lit place for the Aryas, the cultured ones.

This Richa translates to: 'O Ashwins, you have caused the barley to be sown in fields prepared by the plough, drawing rain from the clouds for the sake of Manu and his descendants, destroying the Dasyus with a sharp weapon, you have provided a well-lit place for the Aryas.'

This Richa also acknowledges that the cultivation of Yava was initiated by the Ashwins for Manu and his descendants. They also procured rain from the skies and gifted Manu with water, and his descendants with a well-lit land, implying a land where abundant sunshine is available.

R 7 Richa 1/174/9 अगस्त्यो मैत्रावरुणिः, इन्द्रः, त्रिष्टुप्

For this Richa, the Rishi is Agastya from the lineage of Devtas Mitra and Varuna. The Devta for the Richa is Indra. The Chanda is Trishtup.

त्वं धुनिरिन्द्र धुनिमतीर्ऋणोरपः सीरा न स्रवन्तीः ।
प्र यत् समुद्रमति शूर पर्षि पारयां तुर्वशं यदुं स्वस्ति ॥1/174/9

Meaning of words/combination of words

त्वं धुनिरिन्द्र Indra, you are the terrifier of your enemies धुनिमतीर्क्रिणोरुपः those that overflow their banks सीरा न सवन्तीः you make the water of Seera flow प्र यत् संमुद्रमर्ति when you fill up the oceans शूर fully पर्षि पारयां making them cross the ocean तुर्वशं यदुं स्वस्ति for the wellbeing of Turvasu and Yadu.

This Richa translates to: 'Indra, you are the terrifier of your foes. You have made the trembling waters of Seera overflow the Earth like flowing rivers. When you filled up the oceans, you have protected the wellbeing of Turvasu and Yadu by making them cross the ocean.'

Dyulok, the planet of Devtas, has a divine river named Seera, according to the Rigvaidic Richa (1/174/9). Indra is responsible for bringing divine waters to the Earth through the overflowing rivers that break through their banks. These rivers fill up the oceans fully, but Indra ensures that Turavasu and Yadu are able to cross the oceans.

R 8 Richa 8/28/1 मनुवैंवस्वतः, विश्वे देवाः, गायत्री

For this Richa, the Rishi is Vaivasvat Manu. All Devtas together are addressed as the Vishwe Devta. The Chanda is Gayatri.

> ये त्रिंशति त्र्यंस्पुरो देवासों बर्हिरासंदन् ।
> विदन्नहं द्वितासनन् ॥8/28/1

Meaning of words/combination of words

ये त्रिंशति त्र्यंस्पुरो देवासों These thirty-three Devtas बर्हिरासंदन् who came to the Yajna from outside विदन्नहं they understood our desires द्वितासनन् and bestowed upon us, two kinds of wealth.

This Richa translates to: 'These thirty-three Devtas, who came to the Yajna from outside, they understood our desires and bestowed upon us, two kinds of wealth.'

This Richa's Rishi, Vaivasvat Manu, acknowledges that Devtas who came from the outer universe and were thirty-three in number, understood the desires or needs of men who are the descendants of Manu. They bestowed upon men, two kinds of wealth: Daivik and Earthly that is, divine and terrestrial.

In this and the next Suktas, Devtas are identified by their individual names.

R 9 Richa 8/30/2 मनुर्वैवस्वत:, विश्वे देवा:, पुरउष्णिक्

For this Richa, the Rishi is Vaivasvat Manu. The Devta is all Devtas co-addressed together. The Chanda is Purushnik.

> इतिं स्तुतासों असथा रिशादसो ये स्थ त्रयंश्च त्रिंशच्चं ।
> मनोंदेंवा यज्ञियासः ॥8/30/2

Meaning of words/combination of words

इतिं स्तुतासों So adored by Manu असथा रिशादसो destroyers of violent foes ये स्थ त्रयंश्च त्रिंशच्चं these thirty-three Devtas मनोंदेंवा worshipped by the wise यज्ञियासः may they be praised by our Yajnas.

This Richa translates to: 'So adored (by Manu), these thirty-three Devtas are destroyers of violent foes, they are worshipped by knowledgeable people, they deserve to be praised by our Yajnas.'

In this Richa, Manu reconfirms that Devtas are thirty-three in number. Some of the Devtas, who are referred to in Rigveda frequently may be mentioned here:

- Two Ashwini Kumars who travel on their bird-like spaceships, orbit the Earth on this one ship together.
- Mitra and Varuna are the masters of this universe. They reside in Heaven, that is, Dyulok.
- Agni is the master of all energy fields including man's bodily field.
- Aryaman
- Indradev, wielder of Vajra, chief of all Devtas.
- Rudras are eleven in number. They use water-medicine for cures, hold a sharp weapon. These are Prana, Apana, Vyana, Udana,

Samana, Nag, Koorma, Kukala, Devdutta, Dhananjaya, and one soul called 'Jivatma.
- Pushan, owner of wealth, knows all hidden and explicit treasures.
- Vishnu who measured all the three Lokas with his feet in one of his Avatars.
- Vayu, Devta of wind.

The thirty-three Devtas are considered as consisting of eight Vasus (Prithvi, Jal, Agni, Vayu, Akash, Chandrama, Surya, and Nakshatra), eleven Rudras consisting of Prana, Apana, Vyana, Udana, Samana, Nag, Koorma, Kukala, Devdutta, Dhananjaya, and one soul called 'Jivatma' or 'Rudra', and twelve Adityas. The Adityas also refer to the twelve months of the year (Samvatsar) or alternatively, twelve Devta-children of Aditi, who may also be associated with individual months. In the Mahabharat, the twelve Devta-children of Aditi are listed as Vivasvan, Aryaman, Twashta, Savitra, Bhaga, Dhata, Mitra, Varuna, Amsa, Pushan, Indra and Vishnu[6].

Summary and Key Points

Agriculture, in terms of its seeds, its implements, its art and practices, and the natural inputs required for the seed to grow into a full crop namely sunlight, water, and wind are all gifts from Devtas to mankind.

Agriculture is conceptualized by the Rishis as a Yajna. Associated with each Yajna, there is a Devta, a Rishi, a Mantra or Stotra. The process involves offering of Havi along with the praise in acknowledgement of the contribution of the Devta, while praying for blessings in the form of food grains, wealth, knowledge, and progeny. All these elements are present in agriculture. Every aspect of agriculture, every activity of agriculture in Rigveda is guided by Devtas. That is why, in acknowledgement, men are supposed to offer symbolically, the output

---

[6] Dalal, R. (2010). *Hinduism: An alphabetical guide*. Penguin Books India.

of agriculture, that is grains, to the Devtas. Some of the key points of this Chapter are given below.

- In the Rigvaidic Richas, Devtas associated with agriculture are Indra, the Ashwini Kumars, Mitra, Varun, and Pushan.
- The first seeds given by the Devtas are those of Yava (Jau).
- The agricultural practices are taught by Devtas to Manu.
- The first implement of agriculture namely, the plough was also given by Indra to Manu.
- Devtas are thirty-three in number consisting of three main groups namely, 12 Adityas, 11 Rudras, and 8 Vasus and 2 Ashwini Kumars.

Chapter 3 Kshetra and Kshetrapati

In understanding the place of agriculture in Rigveda, it is important to understand the concept of Kshetra and Kshetrapati. The word Kshetra refers to what is commonly known in modern times as 'Khet' or agricultural field. The word 'Khet' used in day-to-day Hindi is clearly a derivative of Kshetra which literally means a 'field'. This field is associated with a Devta who has been referred to as Kshetrapati that is the owner of the field. These concepts occur in Sukta 57 in Mandal 4 of Rigveda. This is one of the main Suktas in Rigveda devoted entirely to the activities of agriculture. It may be referred to as the 'Krishi-Sukta'. In Sukta 57, there are 8 Richas. The Rishi for this Sukta is Vamadev for all the Richas. For each Richa, there is an associated Devta. There are four Devtas namely, Kshetrapati (Richas 1 to 3), Shuna (Richa 4), Shunaseera (Richas 5 and 8) and Sita (Richas 6 and 7). There are three types of Chandas namely, Ushnik, Anushtup and Trishtup. In this Sukta, the first Richa refers to land or field and the owner or knower of land.

Krishi Sukta in Rigveda: Mandal 4, Sukta 57

R 10 Richa 4/57/1 वामदेवो गौतमः, क्षेत्रपतिः, अनुष्टुप्

For this Richa, the Rishi is Vamadev Gautam. The Devta is Kshetrapati. The Chanda is Anushtup.

> क्षेत्रस्य पतिना वयं हितेनेव जयामसि ।
> गामश्वं पोषयित्वा स नो मृळातीदृशे ॥ 4/57/1

Meaning of Words/Combination of words

क्षेत्रस्य पतिना Owner of land or field वयं हितेनेव for our welfare जयामसि being victorious or successful गामश्वं पोषयित्वा for the nourishment of cattle and horses नो us मृळातीदृशे being made rich and happy.

This Richa translates as follows: 'Together with our brother-like Kshetrapati, the owner of the area, we will be victorious over the area. He may provide nourishment for us and our cattle and horses. He may give us wealth and make us happy.'

The Devta in this Richa is Kshetrapati. Kshetrapati is the master or owner of the field. He is also supposed to be the 'knower' of the field. It may stand for Bhudev, Devta of land. As a Devta of the land, he would know all the relevant features of the land including sources of water in the proximity as well as the nature of the soil, etc. That knowledge would come in handy when the concerned land is used for agriculture. Kshetrapati may also stand for Ishwar, owner and knower of all fields. Such an interpretation is given in Srimad Bhagvad Gita in Chapter 13 where the words Kshetra and Kshetragya occur and Kshetra refers to the field of the human body.

Kshetrapati may also stand for the king of the people residing in the area, who is a representative of the Creator. He is described as 'brother-like' that is somebody who is pre-oriented towards our welfare, that is, human welfare as well as the welfare of all the beings of that area. He may therefore use all the knowledge about the agricultural field to guide the farmers in regard to their activities.

R 11 Richa 4/57/2 वामदेवो गौतमः, क्षेत्रपतिः, त्रिष्टुप्

For this Richa, the Rishi is Vamadev Gautam. The Devta is Kshetrapati. The Chanda is Anushtup.

> क्षेत्रस्य पते मधुमन्तमूर्मिं धेनुरिव पयो अस्मासु धुक्ष्व ।
> मधुश्चुतं घृतमिव सुपूतमृतस्य नः पतयो मृळयन्तु ॥ 4/57/2

Meaning of Words/Combination of words

क्षेत्रस्य पते Belonging to the owner of the field मधुमन्तमूर्मिं full of sweetness and liquid flows धेनुरिव पयो like the cow gives milk अस्मासु धुक्ष्व please give for us, output मधुश्चुतं dropping like honey घृतमिव like clarified butter सुपूतमृतस्य पतयो Devtas who follow truthful actions नः मृळयन्तु please make us happy.

Agriculture in Rigveda: Seeds of India's Civilizational Prosperity

Thus the Richa can be translated as follows: 'O Master of the field, just as cow gives us milk, bestow upon us, sweet free-flowing abundant water, dropping like honey, smooth as ghee (clarified butter), sweet and purified. May the Devtas, who follow truthful actions, make us happy.'

The purport is that since the Kshetrapati knows the area in and around the field fully, he can show us all the sources of water that may be accessed like rivers, ponds and wells. Water is recognized as the critical input for agriculture. The chosen field for cultivation as guided by the master of the field is such that available water is of the highest quality, free flowing, abundant in quantity, and full of sweetness and nourishment. This would lead to nourishing and tasteful output. The agricultural field is so good that everything that derives from it is full of sweetness. Such a healthy and wholesome input to the human body would produce happiness and truthful actions. Thus, the complete cycle of inputs and outputs eventually produces human actions and happiness. The last verse of the Richa makes reference to this eventual outcome: 'May the Devtas bless us with truthful actions, so that the outcome of our actions may make us happy.' Guided by the Devtas, our actions would be appropriate, suited for the purpose at hand, leading to optimal outcomes. By implication and in contrast, a society of humans fed on agricultural output that is based on artificial fertilizers and chemicals would be characterized by disease, falsehood, untruthful actions, conflict and unhappiness.

R 12 Richa 4/57/3 वामदेवो गौतमः, क्षेत्रपतिः, त्रिष्टुप्

For this Richa, the Rishi is Vamadev Gautam. The Devta is Kshetrapati. The Chanda is Anushtup.

मधुमतीरोषधीर्द्याव् आपो मधुमन्नो भवत्वन्तरिक्षम् ।
क्षेत्रस्य पतिर्मधुमान् अस्त्वरिष्यन्तो अन्वेनं चरेम ॥ 4/57/3

Meaning of words/combination of words

मधुमतीरोषधीर्द्याव् Herbs are full of honey like sweetness. Here, 'Aushadhi' means herbs or medicinal plants आपो मधुमन्नो water and food may be full of honey like sweetness भवत्वन्तरिक्षम् the skies may be kind to us अस्त्वरिष्यन्तो without being troubled by enemies अन्वेनं चरेम let us follow our leader, क्षेत्रस्य पति the King or the Kshetrapati.

Thus, the Richa translates as follows: 'May the herbs of the field be sweet for us, may the heavens, the waters, the sky be kind to us, may the Master of the field be gracious to us, let us, undeterred by foes, have recourse to him.'

The purport is that let vegetations and herbs or medicinal plants (such as Brihi and Priyangu) be full of sweetness, let the water taste sweet, let the entire area and its surroundings yield honey-like sweet output, let the Master of the field bestow upon us, honey like blessings. Let the skies be kind to us by bestowing upon us, ample rainfall. Let us follow the Kshetrapati, that is, the King or the Master of the area, who will protect us from the enemies and make us rich and happy.

R 13 Richa 4/57/4 वामदेवो गौतमः, शुनः, अनुष्टुप्

For this Richa, the Rishi is Vamadev Gautam. The Devta is Shuna. The Chanda is Anushtup.

> शुनं वाहाः शुनं नरः शुनं कृषतु लाङ्गलम् ।
> शुनं वरत्रा बध्न्यन्तां शुनमष्ट्रामुदिङ्गय ॥ 4/57/4

Meaning of words/combination of words

शुनं (Shunam) is translated as the auspicious one. Shunam is considered as making reference to 'that resulting in growth and prosperity', 'happily', 'auspiciously'. वाहाः (Vahah) refers to animals who pull the plough or a cart, such as bullocks. लाङ्गलम् (Langalam) is the plough. वरत्रा (Varatra) refers to the yoke. अष्ट्राम् (Ashtram) refers to a goad or chabuk, which is used as a spur or guide for livestock. There is thus a reference to some of the early farming implements.

Thus, this Richa translates as follows: 'Powerful and auspicious oxen pull the plough happily, let men happily engage in agricultural activities, let the plough be used for furroughing the field happily, let the oxen be yoked together happily, let (even) the goad be wielded happily.'

This Richa underlines the symbiotic relationship between men, animals, and implements engaged in the agricultural activities. In this Richa, a number of farming implements are introduced such as a plough, a yoke, and a goad. Oxen used for pulling the plough and men engaged in agricultural activities interact with each other and operate on the land with such smoothness and felicity, that even while labouring on the farmland, they are happy. In conventional Economics, production and consumption are considered dichotomous activities, one producing output and the other producing satisfaction. Here, what is described implies that production and consumption take place simultaneously and the engagement in productive activity itself results in happiness.

R 14 Richa 4/57/5 *वामदेवो गौतमः, शुनासीरौ, पुर उष्णिक्*

For this Richa, the Rishi is Vamadev Gautam. The Devta is Shunaseera. The Chanda is Anushtup.

> शुनांसीराविमां वाचं जुषेथां यद्दिवि चक्रथुः पयः ।
> तेनेमामुपं सिञ्चतम् ॥ 4/57/5

Meaning of words/combination of words

शुनांसीराविमां Shuna and Seera refer to two Devtas. According to Rishi Shaunak, these refer to Indra and Vayu. According to Nirukta, these refer to Indra and Aditya. वाचं voice or praise जुषेथां listen. Thus, it means, the two of you, please listen to this praise of yours. यद्दिवि चक्रथुः पयः this water that you have created in Heaven. Alternatively, Seera may refer to a river in Dyulok, that is the abode of the Devtas *[see, p.268 Hindi Rigveda, Rigveda translation in Hindi by Ram Govind Trivedi (1954)]*. Flowing Seera river lets wavy water fall on Earth तेनेमामुपं सिञ्चतम् with that same divine water, let the Earth be saturated.

Thus, the Richa means: 'Shuna and Seera, that is Indra and Aditya [the Rain and Sun Devtas], be pleased with our praise (for them) and sprinkle this divine wavy water, which you have created in Heaven, on Earth, saturating it.'

The purport is that Devtas of rain and sunlight may be pleased with our praise of theirs and bless the Earth with ample sunlight and rain so that our crops can grow in plenty since water and sunlight are the main nourishment for our crops. Thus, the key elements of nature which contribute to the agricultural output mainly water received from the rainfall and sunlight received from the Sun are praised in acknowledgement of their contribution to the human endeavour for survival and growth.

Alternatively, it may mean that Devtas of rain and water may ensure that water from the land of Devtas may be shared with us on Earth implying that the quality of water made available to us may be the same as that in Dyulok, the abode of the Devtas.

R 15 Richa 4/57/6 *वामदेवो गौतमः, सीता, अनुष्टुप्*

For this Richa, the Rishi is Vamadev Gautam. The Devta is Sita[7]. The Chanda is Anushtup.

अर्वाचीं सुभगे भव् सीते वन्दांमहे त्वा ।
यथां नः सुभगासंसि यथां नः सुफलांसंसि ॥ 4/57/6

Meaning of words/combination of words

सुभगे सीते Auspicious Earth or soil that gives great prosperity अर्वाचीं भव् please be kind to us यथां so that you सुभगासंसि give us or bless us with great fortune सुफलासंसि bless us with abundant fruits नः for us.

---

[7] In Kautilya's Arthashastra (Chapter 2, Sukta 24.1), the head of the department of Agriculture was given the title of 'Sitaadhyaksha' associating the word Sita with all agricultural matters.

Thus, the Richa may be translated as: 'O Sita, giver of great fortune, please be kind to us, we worship you. Bless us with great fortune, reward us with abundant fruits.'

In understanding this Richa, it may be recognized that Sita is referred to as the mark made on the soil by a furrough. She is the Devta of soil, fertility and fruition. She is the fertile layer of Earth. She is Earth itself. Thus, with the combination of water, sunlight, and fertility of Earth, with their blessings, we may be rewarded with an abundant crop.

R 16 Richa 4/57/7 वामदेवो गौतमः, सीता, अनुष्टुप्

For this Richa, the Rishi is Vamadev. The Devta is Sita. The Chanda is Anushtup.

> इन्द्रः सीतां नि गृह्णातु तां पूषानुं यच्छतु ।
> सा नः पयस्वती दुहामुत्तरामुत्तरां समाम् ॥ 4/57/7

Meaning of words/combination of words

इन्द्रः सीतां नि गृह्णातु May Indra hold the wood of the plough. Here, Sita is referred to as the wood, which the plough is made of and which is the fruit of the Earth. तां पूषानुं यच्छतु let Pushan Devta guide the movement of the plough सा नः पयस्वती let the Earth be full of water for us दुहामुत्तरामुत्तरां yielding crops again and again.

This Richa may be translated as follows: 'May Indra Devta accept (or hold) the wood that holds or is used to guide the furrough. May Pushan Devta regulate (or guide) the (movement of) that furrough. May the Earth be full of water, may she yield crops for us again and again.'

The purport is that the movement of the plough should be efficient so that the land is properly cultivated. Ploughing the land is thus visualized as an art that preserves the fertility of the land. Working with the plough should be so smooth as if it is being guided by the Devtas Indra and Pushan. With ample water, it may produce abundant crops for us, season after season.

R 17 Richa 4/57/8 वामदेवो गौतमः, शुनासीरौ, त्रिष्टुप्

For this Richa, the Rishi is Vamadev. The Devta is Shunaseera. The Chanda is Anushtup.

शुनं नः फाला वि कृषन्तु भूमिं शुनं कीनाशां अभि यन्तु वाहैः ।
शुनं पर्जन्यो मधुना पयोभिः शुनासीरा शुनमस्मासुं धत्तम् ॥ 4/57/8

Meaning of words/combination of words

शुनं Happily फाला वि कृषन्तु भूमिं plough furroughs the land कीनाशां अभि यन्तु वाहैः farmers guide the oxen पर्जन्यो मधुना पयोभिः Parjanya Devta give us sweet water शुनासीरा शुनमस्मासुं धत्तम् Indra and Vayu Devtas, please bless us with happiness.

Thus, the Richa may be translated as:'Let the plough furrough the Earth happily, farmers guide the strong oxen happily, let (Parjanya Devta) bless us with sweet rain, Indra (Devta of rain) and Vayu (Devta of fortune and Devta of wind), please confer upon us ample happiness (in this endeavor)'.

The purport of this Richa is that all the natural forces be aligned in such a balanced way and all the farmer's work be efficient in combination with the farm animals, that none is tired or exhausted. Working together produces comfort and happiness. Enjoying the work implies that happiness is the outcome of that effort. This Richa emphasises that no negative vibrations should be caused by the agricultural activities that may emanate either from the discomfort of the farmer or of the animals used in the farming activity or any stress on the tools used. Instead, there should be a generation of positive vibrations in which all cooperating life forms and instruments feel happy. The absence of negative vibrations and the presence of positive vibrations ensure a robust growth of the plants and its nourishing features. In this cooperative activity, salient forces of nature are also involved such as rain, sun and wind. With ample water available for the soil, all the sub-soil life forms also feel ample positive vibrations.

Agriculture in Rigveda: Seeds of India's Civilizational Prosperity

These Richas are meant to be recited as part of the Yajnas that are to be performed while the agricultural activities are undertaken. Their sound waves make all participants feel at ease, in equilibrium with nature and with the creation around them. The participants include men, animals, nature, Devtas and even the agricultural implements which are otherwise supposed to be inanimate objects. Their coming together in harmony leads to the sense of happiness that makes all the physical actions feel effortless.

Agriculture is discussed in Rigveda in other Mandals also by a number of Rishis. The Sukta discussed next refers mainly to harvesting activities.

In Mandal 10, Sukta 94, the process of planting seeds is described.

R 18 Richa 10/94/13 अर्बुदः काद्रवेयः सर्पः, ग्रावाणः, जगती

The Rishi is Arbud. The Devta is Kadravayah Sarpa. The Chanda is Jagati.

> तदिद्ध्यन्त्यद्रयो विमोचने यामंत्रञ्जस्पा इव घेदुंपुब्दिभिः ।
> वपंन्तो बीजमिव धान्याकृतं पृञ्चन्ति सोमं न मिंनन्ति
> बप्संतः ॥ 10/94/13

Meaning of words/combination of words

तदिद्ध्यन्त्यद्रयो विमोचने Respected stones, at the time of preparing for the Somaras यामंत्रञ्जस्पा इव घेदुंपुब्दिभिः produce sound like the noise made by rapidly moving chariots वपंन्तो बीजमिव धान्याकृतं पृञ्चन्ति these stones take care of the Soma like the oxen who help in the sowing of seeds of grain सोमं न मिंनन्ति बप्संतः they do not harm the seeds.

This Richa translates to: 'The stones proclaim it with their clamour at the issue of the Soma juice, like the quick-proceeding chariots on the road, like the cultivators whose oxen while being used for sowing the seeds do not hurt the seeds as while the Soma juice is being produced, the stones do not hurt the Soma plant or its parts.'

In the processing of seeds, implements as well as strength may be used to clean up the grains. But in this process, grains that serve as seeds are to be handled carefully so as not to harm them. Only then the seeds would germinate properly. This is an art that cultivators have learnt well. In this Richa, this is compared with the process of making the Soma juice where stones are used. They are used in a manner such that the Soma ingredients are not damaged.

In the next Richa, it is said that fertile agricultural fields are recognized as a form of wealth. In Richa of the tenth Mandal, this idea is expressed by Rishi Shabar who derives from the lineage of Kakshivaan.

R 19 Richa 10/33/6 शबरः काक्षीवतः, गावः, त्रिष्टुप्

The Rishi is Shabar who derives from the lineage of Kakshivaan. The Devta is Gau, that is, Cow. The Chanda is Trishtup.

> यस्य प्रस्वादसो गिरं उपमश्रवसः पितुः ।
> क्षेत्रं न रण्वमूचुषें ॥10/33/6

Meaning of words/combination of words

यस्य whose प्रस्वादसो गिरं words were sweet उपमश्रवसः पितुः your father's, O King, Upamshravas क्षेत्रं न रण्वमूचुषें like pleasant fields appropriate for being given as a gift.

This Richa translates to: 'O King, Upamshravas, the words of your father were sweet, like a pleasant field ready to be given as gift.'

Here, agricultural fields that are fertile and therefore pleasant are recognized as a form of desirable wealth. These fields are considered suitable for being given as a gift. Somebody in need would be extremely pleased to receive them. Similarly, spoken words should be sweet and therefore pleasant to hear to somebody who has been addressed.

In the tenth Mandal, Rishi Ailoosh asserts that agriculture is the appropriate way of earning income. He cautions not to give into the temptation of gambling, that is, games of dice. Instead, it would be far more desirable to pursue agriculture and thereby earn income by engaging in honest, happiness-producing activities that are guided by the Devtas and in this process, accumulate wealth. This would be a

Agriculture in Rigveda: Seeds of India's Civilizational Prosperity

legitimate and satisfying method of production and earning income which will keep a balance in one's life so that one is kept away from the vices of gambling.

R 20 Richa 10/34/13 कवष ऐलूषः, अक्षो मौजवान् वा, ऋषिः

For this Richa, the Rishi is Kavash from the lineage of Ailoosh. The Devta is Akshah or Maujwan. The Chanda is called Rishi.

अ॒क्षैर्मा दी॒व्यः कृ॒षिमित्कृष॑स्व वि॒त्ते र॑मस्व ब॒हु मन्य॑मानः ।
तत्र॒ गाव॑ः कितव॒ तत्र॑ जा॒या तन्मे॒ वि च॑ष्टे सवि॒तायम॒र्यः ॥10/34/13

Meaning of words/combination of words

अक्षैर्मा दीव्यः Never play with dice कृषिमित्कृषस्व instead pursue agriculture वित्ते रमस्व बहु मन्यमानः consider it to be plenty and derive happiness in the wealth that is produced from agriculture तत्र गावः there are the cows कितव O gambler तत्र जाया there is your wife तन्मे वि चष्टे सवितायमर्यः this is what Savita has declared to me.

This Richa translates to: 'Giving serious attention to my advice, do not ever play with dice. Instead pursue agriculture, take pleasure in the wealth (acquired from agriculture). O gambler, in agricultural fields, there are the cows and there is your wife. You have to look after them. This is what the Devta Savita had declared to me.'

Thus, gambling as a social evil was recognized in the Rigvaidic period. Savita Devta has instructed that gambling should not be pursued as a means of earning income. Instead, one should pursue agriculture and thereby produce sanctified income and wealth. Such wealth would be sustainable and welfare promoting. This would enable the farmer to lead a happy family life and maintain one's cattle. The farmer would also feel satisfied that in the agricultural field, he is able to see the cows as well as his wife who are not only cooperating with him but who are also his responsibilities. If he were to engage in gambling, he is sure to ignore his wife and family as well as his cattle.

Krishi Sukta in Atharvaveda: Kanda 3, Sukta 17

In Atharvaveda, in Kanda 3, Sukta 17, Mantras 1 to 9 are devoted to agriculture. Their Rishi is Vishwamitra. In their scope and reference to Devtas, these Mantras are very similar to the Krishi Sukta in Rigveda (Mandal 4, Sukta 57, Richas 1 to 9). These Atharvaveda Mantras complement the message from Rigveda. In other places also, in Atharvaveda, Mantras devoted to agriculture are given. We will make reference to some of them. The Atharvaveda Mantras given in this Volume are sequenced as M1, M2, and so on.

References to Atharvaveda Mantras indicate the Kanda (Chapter), Sukta and the sequence of the Mantra in the Sukta. For each Mantra, first the Rishi, followed by the Devta of the Mantra and finally the Chanda used in the Mantra are given. In these Mantras, the Rishi and the Devta are common. However, the Chandas differ as indicated below.

M 2 Atharvaveda Mantra 3/17/1 विश्वामित्रः, सीता, आर्षी गायत्री

For this Mantra, the Rishi is Vishwamitra. Devta is Sita. Metre is Arshigayatri.

> सीरा युञ्जन्ति कवयो युगा वि तन्वते पृथक् ।
> धीरा देवेषु सुमन्यौ ॥3/17/1

Meaning of words/combination of words

सीरा युञ्जन्ति Join together the plough ropes धीरा देवेषु कवयो wise men who are devoted to the Devtas युगा वि तन्वते पृथक् and separate the yokes that were put on the oxen and lay these on either side सुमन्यौ with a good or well-dispositioned mind, seeking happiness.

This Mantra translates to: 'Wise men who are devoted to the Devtas bind the plough-ropes firmly, putting on the yokes on the oxen on either side separately (properly), apply the plough (on the field) with a good mental disposition, seeking happiness.'

Agriculture in Rigveda: Seeds of India's Civilizational Prosperity

The purport is that engaging in the regular activity of agriculture, that is ploughing the field, itself generates happiness and a firm devotion to the Devtas. The Devta for this Mantra is Sita, that is, the Devta of fertility of the soil. Ploughing the field, engaging the oxen in this endeavour, is a spontaneous, organically integrated act in which men, Devtas, animals, and nature are inter-linked. The dedication to the Devta(s), makes this act of cultivation as a form of Yajna.

M 3 Atharvaveda Mantra 3/17/2 विश्वामित्रः, सीता, त्रिष्टुप्

For this Mantra, the Rishi is Vishwamitra. Devta is Sita and the Metre is Trishtup.

> युनक्त सीरा वि युगा तंनोत कृते योनौ वपतेह बीजम्।
> विराजः श्रुष्टिः सभंरा असन्नो नेदीय् इत् सृण्यः पक्कमा यंवन्॥ 3/17/2

Meaning of words/combination of words

युनक्त सीरा Join the ploughs युगा वि तनोत spread out the yokes कृते योनौ वपतेह बीजम् sow seeds here in the prepared field (womb) विराजः श्रुष्टिः सभंराः असन्नो for us, may the output of grains be full नेदीय इत्सृण्यः पक्कमा यवन् the sickles may bring closer to us, the mature grain.

This Mantra translates to: 'Harness the ploughs, place the yokes, sow the seeds in the prepared field. May the output be plentiful and may the ripe grain come close to the sickle.'

Here, the agricultural field is compared to a womb, that is womb of mother Earth. Plentiful nourishment in the form of ripe grain would emerge, but in this process, men would have played an elaborate role by preparing the field, applying the plough, harvesting the grain and then processing it. The term योनौ meaning womb implies a comparison of sowing with impregnation. The term यवन् may specifically mean barley or 'Jau' but may refer generically to all grains.

M 4 Atharvaveda Mantra 3/17/3 विश्वामित्रः, सीता, पथ्यापङ्क्तिः

For this Mantra, the Rishi is Vishwamitra. Devta is Sita. Metre is Pathyapankti.

लाङ्गलं पवीरवत्सुशीमं सोमसत्सरु ।
उदिदव्यतु गामविंप्रस्थावद्रथवाहनं पीबरीं च प्रफर्व्यऽम्॥3/17/3

Meaning of words/combination of words

लाङ्गलं The plough पवीरवत्सुशीमं सोमसत्सरु which is hard as 'Vajra' with a wooden handle, which is comfortable to apply गामविंप्रस्थावद्रथवाहनं cows, goats, horses or bulls of a fast-going vehicle पीबरीं च प्रफर्व्यऽम् healthy women उदिदव्यतु may all emerge (from the efforts of that plough).

This Mantra translates to: 'This plough, which is firm as a weapon, which has a wooden handle, which is easy to drive, may lead to healthy and strong women in the family and strong cows, goats, horses, and bulls.'

The purport is that it is the plough which is symbolically the cause of the grains that provide nourishment for our family members and our domesticated animals. This is the reward of successful agriculture. But one should recognize that our main tool namely, the plough itself should be well-made, hard and firm with a sharp edge and our vehicles should be fast, our animals should be strong, our women should be healthy so that engaging in agriculture remains an activity that gives reward and pleasure.

The reference to सोमसत्सरु implies as if the plough is being driven by the Devtas who drink the Somaras. This again equates the agricultural activity to performance of a Yajna. The reference to Devta becomes even clearer in the next Mantra.

Agriculture in Rigveda: Seeds of India's Civilizational Prosperity

M 5 Atharvaveda Mantra 3/17/4 विश्वामित्रः, सीता, अनुष्टुप्

For this Mantra, the Rishi is Vishwamitra. Devta is Sita. Metre is Anushtup.

> इन्द्रः सीताम् नि गृह्णातु ताम् पूषाभि रक्षतु ।
> सा नः पयस्वती दुहामुत्तारमुत्तारम् समाम् ॥3/17/4

Meaning of words/combination of words

इन्द्रः सीताम् नि गृह्णातु May Indra hold the handle (furrow) of the plough ताम् पूषाभि रक्षतु May Pushan protect it सा नः पयस्वती providing us with nourishment दुहामुत्तारमुत्तारम् समाम् may that handle of the plough be full of milk (juice) in equal measure in the years as they come in succession.

This Mantra translates to: 'May Indra supervise the application of the plough by guiding the furrow, may Devta Pushan protect it, may it be full of juice, giving us nourishment year after year evenly.'

Rishi Vishwamitra makes reference to and invokes two Devtas in the act of applying the plough on land so that it is done under divine guidance and protection. The involvement of Indra who is the Devta of rains ensures ample water for the crops to draw juices from and the involvement of Pushan ensures sunlight and protection from various unanticipated risks. In this manner, when agriculture is carried out, it will feed us and our future generations with nourishing food and prosperity. Further, the output may be reaped evenly over time, season after season, thereby avoiding volatility.

M 6 Atharvaveda Mantra 3/17/5 विश्वामित्रः, सीता, त्रिष्टुप्

For this Mantra, the Rishi is Vishwamitra. Devta is Sita. Metre is Anushtup.

> शुनं सुफाला वि तुदन्तु भूमिं शुनं कीनाशा अनु यन्तु वाहान् ।
> शुनासीरा हविषा तोशमाना सुपिप्पला ओषधीः कर्तस्मै ॥3/17/5

Meaning of words/combination of words

शुनं सुफाला वि तुदन्तु भूमिं May the beautiful furrow dig up the land happily शुनं कीनाशा अनु यन्तु वाहान् may the farmers happily come behind the oxen

शुनासीरा may the Devtas of wind and sunlight (Vayu and Pushan) हविषा तोशमाना be satisfied with our Yajnas सुपिप्पला ओषधी: कर्तस्मै make the plants bring forth ample output.

This Mantra translates to: 'May the furrow happily till the land, may the farmers happily follow the oxen, may Vayu and Sun make the plants bring forth, ample produce.'

The purport is that all aspects of the agricultural activities themselves yield happiness, be it tilling the land by applying the plough with the help of oxen or ensuring growth of plants, fed by water, wind and sunlight. Nursed in this manner, the output is sure to be abundant and nourishing. Shuna is the Devta of happiness and Seera is the Devta of energy. The word 'Kinasha' has been used for 'Kisan' or farmer. Reference may also be made to the interpretation of 'Shuna Seera' in the case of Rigveda Richas in the Krishi-Sukta, as discussed earlier in this Chapter.

M 7 Atharvaveda Mantra 3/17/6 विश्वामित्र:, सीता, अनुष्टुप्

For this Mantra, the Rishi is Vishwamitra. Devta is Sita. Metre is Anushtup.

> शुनं वाहा शुनं नर: शुनं कृषतु लाङ्गलं ।
> शुनं वरत्रा बध्यन्तां शुनमष्ट्रामुदिङ्गय ॥3/17/6

Meaning of words/combination of words

शुनं वाहा May the bulls be happy शुनं नर: may men be happy शुनं कृषतु लाङ्गलं may the plough used in agriculture be happy शुनं वरत्रा बध्यन्तां may the straps be tied happily शुनमष्ट्रामुदिङ्गय may the driving goad be happily applied.

This Mantra translates to: 'May the oxen be driven smoothly, may the farmers work comfortably, may the plough be furrowed effortlessly, may the straps be tied painlessly, may the driving goad be applied gently.'

All the entities involved in the agricultural act namely, bulls, men, implements such as the plough, tools such as the ropes and the goad, all work together in such harmonious coordination that all operations become efficient, smooth, yielding happiness while avoiding discomfort all along. Such coordination in the agricultural activities happens when men who are engaged in it are efficient and are guided by the Devtas.

M 8 Atharvaveda Mantra 3/17/7 विश्वामित्रः, सीता, विराट् पुर उष्णिक्

For this Mantra, the Rishi is Vishwamitra. Devta is Sita. Metre is Viratpurushnik.

> शुनसीरेह स्म मे जुषेथाम् ।
> यद्दिवि चक्रथुः पयस्तेनेमामुप सिञ्चतम् ॥3/17/7

Meaning of words/combination of words

शुनसीरेह Vayu and Sun स्म मे जुषेथाम् here, please accept my havan or offering through the Yajna यद्दिवि चक्रथुः पयस्तेनेमामुप सिञ्चतम् that water (milk) which you have made in the sky, please keep irrigating this land with that (water).

This Mantra translates to: 'O Devtas of wind and energy, please accept my offering (Yajna), and please keep irrigating this Earth with the milk, that is divine water, that you have made in Heaven.'

This Mantra makes reference to the formation of rain as the result of the joint effort of wind and sunlight. By raining down this pure, milk-like, nutritious water, please keep irrigating our land so that our agricultural activities can keep yielding nourishing output.

M 9 Atharvaveda Mantra 3/17/8 विश्वामित्रः, सीता, निचृत्

For this Mantra, the Rishi is Vishwamitra. Devta is Sita. Metre is Nichrat.

> सीते वन्दामहे त्वार्वाची सुभगे भव ।
> यथा नः सुमना असो यथा नः सुफला भुवः ॥3/17/8

Meaning of words/combination of words

सीते O Sita, Devta of soil fertility (or tilled field) वन्दामहे we worship you सुभगे O prosperity-bringing land त्वार्वाची please look at (pay attention to) us यथा नः सुमना भव so that you may be of a favourable mind for us असो यथा नः सुफला भुवः so that you may be giver of excellent fruits for us.

This Mantra translates to: 'O Sita, the Devta of fertility, deliverer of prosperity, we venerate you. Please be oriented towards us with a favourable disposition, so that you may bring forth excellent fruits for us.'

The purport is that the fertility of soil should be preserved, treating it as a divine gift, worthy of worshipping and praising. When the soil is well-treated and it is pleased with us, it will respond by delivering good fortune and prosperity for us. This may be contrasted with how, in current times, we have ill-treated soil with pollutants and excessive chemicals. The response of the soil is to transfer these chemicals back into the output that it yields resulting into such health hazards that reduce both the quality and extent of life. It is at our own peril that we displease and upset the Devta of soil fertility.

M 10 Atharvaveda Mantra 3/17/9 विश्वामित्रः, सीता, त्रिष्टुप्

For this Mantra, the Rishi is Vishwamitra. Devta is Sita. Metre is Trishtup.

घृतेन सीता मधुना समक्ता विश्वैर्देवैरनुमता मरुद्भिः ।
सा नः सीते पयसाभ्या ववृत्स्वोजस्वती घृतवत्पिन्वमाना ॥3/17/9

Meaning of words/combination of words

घृतेन सीता मधुना समक्ता Venerable land, well irrigated with purified milk and honey विश्वैर्देवैरनुमता मरुद्भिः approved by all Devtas and winds सा नः सीते पयसाभ्या please bring forth for us milk all-around ववृत्स्वोजस्वती घृतवत्पिन्वमाना that tilled land venerated by purified milk.

This Richa translates to: 'Irrigated by ghee (clarified butter) and honey, liked by all Devtas and wind Devtas, O milk-venerated soil, please deliver milk-nourished abundant output for us.'

The implication is that if we treat the soil with milk and honey, that is, treating it with clean and healthy water for irrigation, that same water will enter into the grains that will be produced from this soil aided by natural forces such as sunlight, winds, and rain. Inputs are translated into outputs by divine interventions and understanding, according to the pre-coding of the seeds, which may be considered as the gift from the Devtas. Respecting this cyclical interdependence is a Yajna or knowledge that the Mantra asserts that men should follow for their own welfare.

Kshetra as Human Body

The concept of human body being a Kshetra, that is a field, has been explicitly stated in Srimad Bhagvad Gita by Sri Krishna himself. Just as in Rigveda, Kshetra and Kshetrapati are enunciated, in Gita, Kshetra and Kshetragya are distinguished.

G 8 Srimad Bhagvad Gita: Chapter 13, Shloka 2

> इदं शरीरं कौन्तेय क्षेत्रमित्यभिधीयते ।
> एतद्यो वेत्ति तं प्राहुः क्षेत्रज्ञ इति तद्विदः ॥ 13-2

Meaning of words/combination of words

O Arjun, this body is termed as Kṣhetra (the field of activities), and the one who knows this body is called Kṣhetrajna (the knower of the field) by the sages who discern the truth about both. *[Translation by Swami Mukundananda, 2014]*

Putting these together, the circuit of interlinkages is completed. In agriculture, the output of the field consisting of food grains becomes an input into the other field that is human body. The output of this field is 'Bhava', that is feelings and emotions and eventually the recognition or acknowledgment that we are all parts of the supreme entity, which generates the sense of Bhakti or devotion and worship. This whole circuit needs to be recognized in its entirety. That is why the inputs into the agricultural field, the pure and nourishing water full of honey and ghee (clarified butter), the divine seeds, and the divine sunlight produce the food grains that nourish the human body. Within the human body also, Indra, Agni, Mitra, Varuna, the Ashwini Kumars and all other Devtas guide the working of the human limbs and senses to produce the outcomes in terms of the Bhavas. The purity and quality of the output from one field translates into the purity and quality of the other field. That is why it is important to be careful as to how the agricultural field is ploughed, seeded, cropped, and reaped. That is why Sri Krishna distinguishes between Sattvik, Rajasik, and Tamasik food.

The circuit of interdependence includes the animal world particularly cows and bees for they produce milk, ghee (clarified butter) and honey, taking their inputs from the output of the field, the grass, the flowers, the herbs, plants, and trees.

In Yajurveda also, Mantras ranging from 67 to 73 in Chapter 12 are devoted entirely to agriculture. The messages contained in these Mantras are similar to the ones that we have discussed in this Volume as drawn from Rigveda and Atharvaveda.

Summary and Key Points

In Rigveda, Sukta 57 of Mandal 4 consisting of 8 Mantras, is devoted entirely to agriculture. The entire agricultural process may be clearly understood in these Richas as Yajnas. Similarly, Sukta 17 in Kanda 3 of Atharvaveda, is devoted entirely to agriculture. These two Suktas respectively in Rigveda and Atharvaveda broadly cover the same subject matter including Devtas and agricultural processes. In Yajurveda also, Mantras ranging from 67 to 73 in Chapter 12 are devoted entirely to agriculture.

In understanding the place of agriculture in Rigveda, it is important to understand the concept of Kshetra and Kshetrapati. The word Kshetra refers to what is now known as 'Khet' or agricultural field. The word 'Khet' used in day-to-day Hindi in contemporary times is clearly a derivative of Kshetra. This field is associated with a Devta who has been referred to as Kshetrapati, that is, the owner and the knower of the field.

Rigveda's Sukta 4/57 along with various supplementary Suktas discussed in this Chapter have served as the foundation for India's civilizational prosperity by not only ensuring abundant and high-quality agricultural outputs, season after season, but by prescribing an approach to agriculture which is wholesome, sustainable, comprehensively organic, respectful of all lifeforms, and well-coordinated with nature which is guided by the Devtas having distinct responsibilities concerning different natural forces such as rainfall, wind, energy, sunlight, water and trees. The subject of trees and their role in not only providing medicinal support to mankind but also in the completion of the water cycle through rainfall, its retention under the soil with the help of the roots of the trees and other plants, its flow back to the oceans through the rivers is dealt in detail in Rigveda. Subsequently, in Chapter 7 we have discussed the acknowledgement by the Rishis of major medicinal plants and trees in the Aushadhi Sukta.

In Sukta 57 of Mandal 4 of Rigveda, three main Chandas that are used are Trishtup, Anushtup, and Purushnik. Anushtup has the property that it holds or supports other Rashmis or it adopts to their form. It acts like a Mother Rashmi or all-encompassing Rashmi. Trishtup has the property that it works as the centre for other Rashmis. It holds other Rashmis in three ways. The vibrations created by these Chandas are vital for agricultural growth since several natural forces are to be brought together such as rain, sunlight and wind. The reference to Purushnik is particularly important when the seeds are getting converted into seedlings and then plants require considerable energy in the form of sunlight. These observations are based on Naishthik Acharya Agnivrit (2017). All of these natural elements interact with the soil and this is the reason why the fertility of soil is worshiped as a Devta. Some key points of this Chapter are summarized below.

> ➤ The agricultural farm is to be understood as a 'field', that is, 'kshetra', associated with which there is an owner and knower, that is 'Kshetrapati' of the field.

> ➤ Kshetrapati may be taken to refer to 'Paramatma' also and Kshetra may be taken to refer to as the human body. The growth of the body which serves as the vehicle for the journey of the 'Atman' through the finite lifetime of an individual lifeform is

therefore comparable to the working of the agricultural field which goes through cycle after cycle of maturity and repetition.

- The participants in the agricultural endeavour include Devtas, water, sunlight, wind, soil, implements, seeds, and animals. All of these have to act in a coordinated way guided by the farmer or the owner of the field.

- Each separate activity on the farm is to be performed by the farmer like it is a Yajna in which acknowledgement of the presiding or guiding Devta and prayer to the Devta for the fulfilment of the endeavour ensures beneficial outcomes.

- The farmer has to organize activities on the farm such that each participant enjoys his or its role. This ensures that no negative vibrations are generated and in fact, when the relevant Richas are recited repeatedly in the prescribed manner, powerful positive vibrations are added to the effort of the farmer. This ensures that the outcome is more than the sum of the individual activities.

- In modern times, the positive role of vibrations has been recognized extensively and in many contemporary experiments, music is played to ensure that the plants, as they grow, remain pleased. Such experiments would prove to be even more beneficial if the chants are of the Richas contained in the Sukta 57 of Mandal 4 of Rigveda.

- The matured crop is most juicy, nourishing, and healthy for mankind that is, the potential consumers if the necessary inputs including the water that has been used is pure, clean and largely drawn from rivers or from the Earth which is fed by the rivers which is at the sub-soil level.

The farmer, his implements, elements of nature namely, winds, sunlight, rain, water sourced from ground, and cattle, are integrally and organically interlinked over the season of a crop. This benign relationship, guided by Devtas ensure for the mankind, ample, juicy, nourishing crops, on which men along with their families and their cattle and other farm animals, can sustain themselves and flourish. Fertility of the soil needs to be maintained and worshipped. This would ensure that all the sub-soil life forms which contribute to the fertility of the soil are also nourished. All the participants in the agricultural activity namely, the farmer, the forces of nature such as wind, sun and rain, the animals such as the cows and the oxen, the implements, and the life forms present in the sub-soil levels cooperate with each other, taking care of each other, and in this process, remain happy and away from discomfort so that no negative vibrations are generated and there are positive vibrations at all stages of the growth of the plants. The yield from the crops of agriculture carried out in this manner will be most nourishing and health-preserving for the population that depends on such agriculture.

Chapter 4 Earth and Sources of Water

India's ancient Rishis recognized the key role of water and its sources for agriculture. They identified rivers, riverbeds, streams, underground wells, and ponds as the main sources of water for the agricultural fields. They also acknowledged the importance of rainfall and in fact, the entire cycle of water from rivers falling into the ocean, evaporation of water, formation of clouds, followed by rainfall, charging of wells and underground reservoirs, and also flowing back to the ocean through the rivers, thereby completing the cycle.

The main Devtas who are associated with water and rainfall include Indra, Varuna, Parjanya, and the Ashwini Kumars. Earth that is, Prithvi itself is acknowledged as a Devta. In fact, the Rishis recognized our Earth as a water planet, a planet distinguished among a large number of stars and planets, by the profuse presence of water. It is also notable that Earth and Dyulok, the planet of Devtas, are frequently referred to together throughout the Rigveda, both being full of water.

Earth as Devta: A Water Planet

The Vaidic Rishis acknowledged the distinguishing feature of Earth who is a Devta along with a planet referred to as Dyulok, as being water planets. Thus, in Richa 1 of Sukta 70 of Mandal 6 of the Rigveda, Rishi Bharadwaj refers to Earth along with Dyulok.

R 21 Richa 6/70/1 बार्हस्पत्यो भरद्वाजः, द्यावापृथिवी, जगती

For this Richa, the Rishi is Bharadwaj from the lineage of Brihaspati. Devta is Earth. Chanda is Jagati.

घृतवती भुवनानामभिश्रियोर्वी पृथ्वी मंधुदुघे सुपेशंसा ।
द्यावांपृथिवी वरुणस्यु धर्मणा विष्कंभिते अ॒जरे॒ भूरिरेतसा ॥6/70/1

Meaning of words/combination of words

घृतवती full of water भुवनानामभिश्रियोर्वी giving shelter to all beings and being spacious पृथ्वी Earth मंधुदुघे सुपेशांसा yielding sweet, tasty food, that is, beautiful food अजरे un-decaying भूरिरेतसा having many life-seeds द्यावांपृथिवी divine Earth वरुणस्य धर्मणा विष्कंभिते subject to the rules of Varuna.

This Richa translates to: 'Beautiful and divine, Earth and Dyulok, the shelter of all created beings, you are full of water, spacious, yielding sweet food and fruits, un-decaying, bearing many kinds of life-seeds, regulated by the rules of Varuna Devta.'

Varuna Devta manages the presence and flow of water both in Dyulok and Bhulok, that is Earth. Divine Earth has a special place amongst the planets. It is full of water, full of life-bearing seeds, and it nurtures life. It is spacious enough to accommodate a variety of living beings, plants, and animals. It yields sweet and abundant food and fruits. Earth's place in the cosmic system and its motion are governed by the regulations set by Varuna Devta.

In this Mantra, the words Prithivi (Earth) and Dyava-Prithvi (Dyulok, heaven, Svarga and Earth) are both used. This is taken to mean that the characteristics defined here for Earth are common with Dyulok, that is, heaven. The word Prithivi in Sanskrit, which refers to Earth, is related to or derives from King Prithu. It may be interpreted as 'Divine Earth, daughter of Prithu'.

In the same Sukta (70 of Mandal 6), Rishi Bharadwaj refers to the qualities of water on Earth in Richa 4.

R 22 Richa 6/70/4 बार्हस्पत्यो भरद्वाज:, द्यावापृथिवी, जगती

For this Richa, the Rishi is Bharadwaj, descendant of Brihaspati. Devta is Earth. Chanda is Jagati.

घृतेन द्यावांपृथिवी अभीवृते घृतश्रियां घृतपृचां घृतावृधां ।
उर्वी पृथ्वी होंतृवूर्ये पुरोहिंते ते इद्विप्रां ईळते सुम्नमिष्टयें ॥४॥६/७०/४

Agriculture in Rigveda: Seeds of India's Civilizational Prosperity

Meaning of words/combination of words

द्यावापृथिवी heaven (Svarga) and Earth अभीवृते they are surrounded घृतेन by water घृतश्रियां they are characterized by the beauty of water घृतपृचां they have affectionate relation with water घृतावृधा they are augmenters of water उर्वी पृथ्वी vast and manifold होतृवूर्ये you, Earth are propitiated with Yajna पुरोहिते the pious इद्रिप्रां and the knowledgeable ते ईळते pray for you सुम्नमिष्टये for the sake of obtaining the desirable (happiness) with a harmonious or good mind.

This Richa translates to: 'Dyulok and Earth are surrounded by water. They are distinguished by the beauty of water, they hold water affectionately and they are the augmenters of water. Earth, vast and without limit, when Yajna is performed, you are the first to be propitiated. The pious and knowledgeable (men) pray to you for obtaining the desirable (happiness) with a good or harmonious mind.'

It is thus, the abundance of water, that characterises both Dyulok and Earth. They exhibit the beauty of water. Earth is known as the blue planet because of abundance of water. The Rishis hold water dear to them. They even cause water to increase in volume. Alternatively, the term 'augmenters' may be taken to mean 'where water is in motion or dynamic'. It is with water, that the Earth is able to lead to desirable outcomes for men, when with a pious mind and knowledge, they perform Yajnas.

Qualities of Earthly water are further eulogized in Richa 5 of Sukta 70.

R 23 Richa 6/70/5 बार्हस्पत्यो भरद्वाज:, द्यावापृथिवी, जगती

For this Richa, the Rishi is Bharadwaj. Devta is Earth. Chanda is Jagati.

> मधुं नो द्यावापृथिवी मिमिक्षतां मधुश्चुतां मधुदुघे मधुव्रते ।
> दधाने यज्ञं द्रविणं च देवता महि श्रवो वाजमस्मे सुवीर्यम् ॥6/70/5

Meaning of words/combination of words

मधुं नो द्यावापृथिवी मिमिक्षतां O Heaven and Earth, please make us meet (let us access) the sweet water मधुश्चुतां you are discharger of sweet water

मधुदुघे मधुंव्रते you make sweet water that is, rain, it is your nature to provide sweet rain दधाने यज्ञं द्रविणं च देवता you are bearer of Yajna, wealth, and divinity महि श्रवो वाजमस्मे सुवीर्यम् you grant for us, excellent seed for progeny, reputation and strength.

This Richa translates to: 'O Heaven and Earth, let us access sweet water, you are the dischargers of sweet water, it is in your nature to provide sweet rain, you are the bearer of Yajna, wealth, and divinity. Please grant us reputation, strength, and excellent seed for our progeny.'

In this Richa, the emphasis is on the abundance of sweet water on Earth as well as in Heaven. Earth is given to discharge sweet water through rain and rivers, making life and prosperity possible. Prosperity comes from producing food-grains through agriculture. Food-grains may then be used for performing Yajnas.

In Rigveda, the interdependence of the land of Devtas (Dyulok) and Earth, that is the land of mankind, is emphasised time and again. In both places, water is available in plenty. Earth being full of water, becomes the bearer of life. Rishi Bharadwaj emphasises the role of Dyulok and Bhulok as father and mother of Devtas, mankind and other forms of life. Some of these Richas are discussed below.

R 24 Richa 6/70/6 बार्हस्पत्यो भरद्वाज:, द्यावापृथिवी, जगती

For this Richa, the Rishi is Bharadwaj, descendent of Brihaspati. Devta is Earth. The Chanda is Jagati.

> ऊर्जं नो द्यौश्च पृथिवी च पिन्वतां पिता माता विश्वविदा सुदंससा ।
> संरराणे रोदसी विश्वशंभुवा सनिं वाजं रयिमस्मे समिन्वताम् ॥
> 6/70/6

Meaning of words/combination of words

द्यौश्च पृथिवी च पिता माता Dyulok and Earth are like our father and mother ऊर्जं नो पिन्वतां may they augment our strength विश्वविदा they are all knowing सुदंससा they are performers of good deeds संरराणे रोदसी समिन्वताम् (they are) mutually cooperating, doers of excellent actions

विश्वशम्भुवा leading to the welfare of all of us सुनिं वाजं रयिमस्मे bestowing upon us prosperity, reputation, and strength.

This Richa translates to: 'May Dyulok who is our father, and Earth who is our mother, who are all-knowing, and doers of good deeds, augment our strength. By mutually cooperating, they perform excellent actions leading to the welfare of all beings. May they grant us prosperity, strength, and reputation.'

In this Richa, Heaven and Earth, that is the abodes of the Devtas and men respectively are seen as father and mother, who by mutual coordination cause the welfare of all beings. For human beings, may they grant prosperity in the form of wealth, food, strength, and reputation. Beings on the Earth are born from the elements of the Earth and of the Dyulok. All the physical elements may derive from Earth, and all the informational elements, the subtle bodies, and the consciousness may derive from Dyulok.

In the process of creation of beings on the Earth, in the Rigvaidic enunciation, Devtas who came from the Dyulok and Rishis who resided on the Earth played a key role. Devtas are also supposed to bear the responsibility of regulating various dimensions of nature such as air, water, space, fire, and energy. These elements reside both in the external atmosphere and inside the bodies of humans as well as all other lifeforms. By mutual cooperation of these divine and earthly forces, creation became possible and is being sustained. Mankind is blessed enough to play a key role in the progress and sustenance of this continuing creation for which, through this Richa, the Rishis, on behalf of mankind, are thankful to the divine and earthly forces.

A notable reference to Earth and her properties comes in the elaborate Bhumi Sukta in Kanda 12 of Atharvaveda. This entire Sukta is devoted to Earth. One special Mantra explaining the property of Earth to 'spread out' and to be the 'first' for sustaining creation of lifeforms and mankind is in Mantra 55.

M 11 Atharvaveda Mantra 12/1/55 अथर्वा, भूमिः, त्रिष्टुप्

For this Mantra, the Rishi is Atharva. The Devta is Bhumi or Prithvi that is Earth or land. The Chanda is Trishtup.

> अ॒दो यद् देँवि॒ प्रथमाना पुरस्तादु॒ देवैरु॒क्ता व्यसर्पो महित्वम्।
> आ त्वां सुभूतमंविशत् तु॒दानीमकंल्पयथाः प्रदिशश्चतंस्रः ॥ 12/1/55

Meaning of words/combination of words

अ॒दो यद् देँवि॒ at that time, O Goddess, that is Devi प्रथमाना when for the first time पुरस्तादु॒ देवैरु॒क्ता Devtas named you as the broad one implying that Prithvi literally means the broad one or the all-encompassing one व्यसर्पो महित्वम् you then extended to greatness आ त्वां सुभूतमंविशत् then prosperity entered in you तु॒दानीमकंल्पयथाः प्रदिशश्चतंस्रः then you defined the four of your regions.

This translates to: 'At that time, O Goddess, when spreading out and becoming the first (prathamana), you were named Prithvi (meaning the expanded one) by the Devtas, you extended to greatness, then prosperity entered into you and you specified your four regions.'

Here, Rishi Atharva says that the literal meaning of Prithvi is the 'broad' or the 'big' one which accommodates all. For this property, Devtas named Earth as Prithvi meaning the one that holds it all together. At that time, Prithvi's greatness was recognized by the Devtas and it is said that Prithvi was blessed with extensive resources which would ensure prosperity for all who find their shelter or residence in you. In fact, Devtas made reference to four regions of the Earth which are all blessed with ample resources.

We now make reference to Rishi Vashishtha and Richas visualised by him as given in Mandal 7. Different sources of water are referred to in Sukta 2 of Mandal 7 by Rishi Vashishtha.

R 25 Richa 7/49/2 मैत्रावरुणिर्वसिष्ठः, आपः, त्रिष्टुप्

For this Richa, the Rishi is Vashishta who derives from Devtas Mitra and Varuna. Devta is Water. The Chanda is Trishtup.

> या आपों दिव्या उत वा स्त्रवन्ति ख़निर्त्रिमा उत वा याः स्वयंजाः ।
> समुद्रार्था याः शुचयः पावकास्ता आपों देवीरिह मामंवन्तु ॥ 7/49/2

Meaning of words/combination of words

या आपों दिव्या those waters that are from the sky (or divine) उत वा स्त्रवन्ति those that flow in rivers ख़निर्त्रिमा उत वा those that are obtained by digging from under the Earth याः स्वयंजाः those that spring out on their own समुद्रार्था those that flow into the ocean याः शुचयः पावकास्ता those that cause purity and cleanliness आपों देवीरिह मामंवन्तु may these divine waters protect me here on Earth.

This Richa translates to: 'May the waters that are in the sky, or those that flow (on the Earth), those (whose channels) have been dug, or those that have sprung up spontaneously, and those that seek the ocean (that is river-water), all pure and purifying, may those divine waters protect me here (on Earth).'

Waters on Earth may emanate from different sources and destinations. But they have a divine attribute since they are pure and purifying. Water plays a protective role for mankind. It serves to sustain life. The expression 'Waters that seek the oceans' refers to rivers. Water emanates from the skies, from the Earth and from the ocean. In fact, there is a clear cycle of interlinkage in these three sources of water. From the ocean water or the water that is on the surface of the Earth, by the warming up from the sun, water evaporates, rises up so as to form the clouds. Clouds then rain down and the extent of this rain is facilitated by trees which help in the formation of depressions. Forest areas usually get a high incidence of rainfall. Much of this water is absorbed by the Earth below and the trees so that the cycle is repeated. In the process of evaporation and collection as clouds, all the impurities of water remain on ground while the water that comes down in the form of rain is purified. This process is sometimes disturbed by excessive chemical pollution on Earth and in the air which leads to rainfall that may be contaminated by metals and impurities resulting into the phenomenon called 'acid rain'. However, the natural processes involve cleaning up of all impurities through the heat of the sun and the impact of the winds.

References to 'Koop' (Well) and 'Avat' (ditches created by digging) are available in many places in Rigveda. The water of these wells never diminished. The water from the well was drawn out with wheels created from stones (Ashmachakra), to which pots that could hold water were tied by using ropes (Barwa) (Rigveda 10/25/4).

After drawing the water from the well, it was poured into a wooden receptacle (Aahav). Wells were used not only for drawing water for people and animals, but also for irrigation of the fields. Well water would reach the fields by flowing through wide lanes prepared for this purpose so as to make the fields fertile. This method of drawing water from wells still prevails in many areas in India. This is described in Rigveda 8/69/12.

R 26 Richa 8/69/12 प्रियमेध आङ्गिरस:, वरुण:, अनुष्टुप्

For this Richa, the Rishi is Priyamedh of the family of Angira. Devta is Varuna. The Chanda is Anushtup.

> सुदेवो अंसि वरुण॒ यस्यं ते स॒प्त सिन्धंव: ।
> अ॒नुक्षरंन्ति का॒कुदं सूम्यँ सुषिरामिंव ॥8/69/12

Meaning of words/combination of words

सुदेवो अंसि वरुण॒ you are well-provided by the Devtas यस्यं ते स॒प्त सिन्धंव: from whom the seven rivers or streams flow out अ॒नुक्षरंन्ति का॒कुदं as if they are flowing through a tube सूम्यँ सुषिरामिंव which ensures a smooth flow.

This Richa translates to: 'You are well-provided by the Devtas, O Varuna. You through whose gullet, the seven rivers flow, as if through a tube that provides easy flow'.

In this Richa, there is a recognition of an artificial construct such as a tube which is made for facilitating the flow of water from one place to another without any obstruction or loss of water in the process of reaching its destination. There is a praise to Varuna, Devta of water, that he has been endowed with well-wishing Devtas. Varuna ensures that water flows through various channels to reach suitable destinations for the sustenance of mankind and life forms on Earth.

Rivers and River-beds

As a source of water, rivers have the most prominent place in Rigveda. Water flows in the Rigvaidic rivers ceaselessly, forcefully, and in abundance. Agriculture first developed in India on the two sides of the rivers, using the fertility and abundance of underground water on land in the proximity of the rivers. Rivers could be connected by canals or channels to the agricultural fields. Ponds and wells could be dug for accessing water and the water table is likely to be close to the surface, if the land is located in the proximity of a river. Thus, agriculture developed along the banks of the prominent rivers and the land between pairs of rivers called 'Doabas'. Civilization evolved along that same course using the surplus output that was made possible by the abundance and easy access to water.

In Rigveda, the most prominent river is Saraswati. The timing and route of Saraswati may be used to guide us about the timing and location of the Indic-Vedic civilization. Saraswati originated in the Himalayas and went westwards to the ocean near modern day Gujarat. It dried up around 2000BCE. It must have been in full flow of water around 3000BCE to any time further back in antiquity. People argue about the peak of the Vaidic civilization from 3000BCE to about 22000 BCE or further back. In recent times, many scholarly works have been published, tracing the origins and spread of the river Saraswati and the civilization that developed on its banks. [See, for example, Bakshi (2020), Oak (2021), and Bhaty (2021)].

In terms of the spread, Saraswati and its tributaries and distributaries on both the western and eastern sides, provided the large fertile riverbeds along which agriculture prospered in the Rigvaidic times. On the western side, Sindhu was the most prominent river, and on the eastern side, Ganga was the most prominent river. These rivers and their tributaries served a large land area with abundant water and fertile land giving rise to abundant output of grains, vegetables, herbs, and other plants, which supported growth and sustenance of a large population and economic activities. This also enabled the development of agglomerations of population in cities and towns, which undertook extensive industrial and technolgical activities as well as trade using boats and ships that plied through rivers and oceans. In fact, the Saraswati civilization and the Vaidic civilization may be considered as synonymous and synchronous.

References to Saraswati in Rigveda

Saraswati is described in all her glory in a number of Rigvaidic Richas. The references are so frequent, and the descriptions are so detailed, that the importance of Saraswati is self-established. It is also convincing that without being real, it could not have survived in common and shared memory of the Indian population at large. In Table 4, we have listed the references to Saraswati in Rigveda. Saraswati is mentioned in all the 10 Mandals except Mandal 4. The maximum references are in Mandal 10 followed by Mandals 7 and 6. Along with Saraswati, some Richas are devoted to Saraswan, the meaning of which is discussed later in this Volume.

Table 4: Reference to Saraswati in Rigveda

Sukta	Richas	Total no. of Richas	Sukta	Richas	Total no. of Richas	Notes
Mandal 1		11	**Mandal 7**		18	
3	10,11,12	3	2	8	1	
13	9,10	2	9	5	1	
89	3	1	35	11	1	
142	9, 10	2	36	6	1	
164	49,52	2	39	5	1	

Sukta	Richas	Total no. of Richas	Sukta	Richas	Total no. of Richas	Notes
188	8	1	40	3	1	
Mandal 2		7	95	1 to 6	6	Richa 3 devoted to Saraswan
1	11	1	96	1 to 6	6	Richas 4 to 6 devoted to Saraswan
3	8	1	Mandal 8		4	
30	8	1	21	17,18	2	
32	8	1	38	10	1	
41	16,17,18	3	54	4	1	
Mandal 3		3	Mandal 9		3	
4	8	1	5	8	1	
23	4	1	67	32	1	
54	13	1	81	4	1	
Mandal 5		4	Mandal 10		31	
5	8	1	17	7,8,9	3	
42	12	1	30	12	1	
43	11	1	64	9	1	
46	2	1	65	1	1	
Mandal 6		17	65	13	1	
49	7	1	66	5	1	Devoted to Saraswan
50	12	1	75	1 to 9	9	Nadi Sukta Richa 5 mentions Saraswati
52	6	1	110	8	1	
61	1 to 14	14	125	1 to 8	8	Devoted to Vagambharni
--			131	5	1	
--			141	5	1	
--			184	2	3	
--			Total		98	

Source: Rigveda and compilation by Kalyanaraman
These references include those to Saraswan also. Further, the Manta 10/125 pertains to Saraswati although it is referred to as Vagambharni.

Saraswati as Mother and Devi

The most cited Richa eulogizing Saraswati is in Mandal 2, Sukta 41. Three Richas that are devoted to Saraswati in this Mandal are Richas 16, 17, and 18.

R 27 Richa 2/41/16 गृत्समद (आङ्गिरसः शौनहोत्रः पश्चाद्) भार्गवः शौनकः, सरस्वती, अनुष्टुप्

For this Richa, the Rishi is Gritsamad. The Devta is Saraswati. The Chanda is Anushtup.

> अम्बितमे नदीतमे देवितमे सरस्वति
> अप्रशस्ता इव स्मसि प्रशस्तिमम्ब नस्कृधि ॥2/41/16

Meaning of words/combination of words

सरस्वति O Saraswati अम्बितमे (you are) the best of mothers नदीतमे the best of rivers देवितमे the best of goddesses (Devis) अप्रशस्ता without your blessings, we are without any repute इव स्मसि प्रशस्तिमम्ब नस्कृधि please give us distinction (by lending to us your name).

This Richa translates to: 'O Saraswati, you are the best of mothers, the best of rivers, the best of Devis. We are, as if of no repute, without you. Grant us, mother, distinction by lending to us, your name'.

The purport is that Saraswati, the river, is also recognized as a Devi and a mother, therefore the Vedamata, the one who blesses and nurtures the community of men who live in the vicinity of her two banks. Not only that Saraswati is the most reputed river, but she is also the benevolent among the goddesses, and the most benevolent among the mothers. In fact, the Yajna-performers acknowledge that their distinction, that is their identity and name, come from being in the area under the sway of river Saraswati, fully dependent on the river for the succour and prosperity that it provides. These men, the Yajna-performers, implore Saraswati to lend her name to them so that they may be known by her name. It is only appropriate therefore, to call that civilization which developed on her banks and nearby areas, as the Saraswati Civilization.

In fact, the reputation of men who settled on the banks of Saraswati should derive from all three aspects of Saraswati. The first one is as a mother. In her mother's role, Saraswati is the cause of great prosperity and men living around and dependent on Sararswati should therefore be known for their prosperity and abundance of food. The second aspect is that of the great river. For this reason, men who settled on the banks of Saraswati, and cultures that evolved and developed around Saraswati, should then appropriately be known as the Saraswati Civilization. The third aspect is that of a goddess, that is, goddess of intellect and speech. People who worship Saraswati should then be known for their intellectual achievements and oral traditions.

Thus, for the Indians, our identity, our name, fame, repute, distinction, achievements and renown may all derive from the mother of mothers, Devi of the Devis, and river of rivers, namely, Saraswati.

R 28 Richa 2/41/17 गृत्समद (आङ्गिरसः शौनहोत्रः पश्चाद्) भार्गवः शौनकः, सरस्वती, अनुष्टुप्

For this Richa, the Rishi is Gritsamad. The Devta is Saraswati. The Chanda is Anushtup.

> त्वे विश्वां सरस्वति श्रितायूँषि देव्याम् ।
> शुनहोंत्रेषु मत्स्व प्रजां देवि दिदिड्ढि नः ॥2/41/17

Meaning of words/combination of words

सरस्वति O Saraswati त्वे विश्वां देव्याम् in you, who is divine श्रितायूँषि all existence is collected शुनहोंत्रेषु मत्स्व please be pleased by the pious Yajnas of the Shunhotras देवि दिदिड्ढि नः प्रजां O goddess, please give us progeny.

This Richa translates to: 'O Saraswati, in and around you, who is divine, all existence, that is all who have life, are collected. Please rejoice amongst the Shunhotras (who perform Yajnas for you). Grant us, O Devi, progeny for us.'

The Saraswati river is responsible for all that lives and thrives around the river since the surrounding land has become fertile. By undertaking economic activities, particularly agriculture, the next generations can be born and sustained by the blessings of the Devi.

R 29 Richa 2/41/18 गृत्समद (आङ्गिरसः शौनहोत्रः पश्चाद्) भार्गवः शौनकः, सरस्वती, बृहती

For this Richa, the Rishi is Gritsamad. The Devta is Saraswati. The Chanda is Brihati.

> इमा ब्रह्म सरस्वति जुषस्व वाजिनीवति ।
> या ते मन्मं गृत्समदा ऋतावरि प्रिया देवेषु जुह्वति ॥2/41/18

Meaning of words/combination of words

सरस्वति O Saraswati वाजिनीवति abundant in food and water ऋतावरि pursuing the path of truth गृत्समदा we the modest (without pride) worshippers या ते मन्मं प्रिया देवेषु जुह्वति offer in your praise that which pleases you and is precious for the Devtas इमा ब्रह्म जुषस्व please listen to those praises.

This Richa translates to: 'O Saraswati, abounding in food and water, please listen to these praises offered by us who are without pride, may the praises be pleasing to you and precious for the Devtas.'

The implication is that since water is abundant in Saraswti, food is also abundant. Men are entirely dependent on river Saraswati. The worshippers remain modest in acknowledging their dependence on Saraswati. They perform Yajnas, singing your praises. Men request river Saraswati to listen to these praises which the Devtas also value.

R 30 Richa 7/2/8 ऋजिश्वा भारद्वाजः, विश्वे देवाः, त्रिष्टुप्

For this Richa, the Rishi is Bharadwaj. All Devtas are the Devta for this Richa. The Chanda is Trishtup.

> आ भारती भारतीभिः सजोषा इळा देवैर्मनुष्येभिरग्निः ।
> सरस्वती सारस्वतेभिरुवर्क्तिस्त्रो देवीर्बर्हिरेदं सदन्तु ॥7/2/8

Meaning of words/combination of words

आ भारती भारतीभिः Devi Bharati is associated with the Bharatis सजोषा इळां देवैर्मनुष्येभिरग्निः Devi Ila is associated with the Devtas and men सरस्वती सारस्वतेभिर्वाक्तिस्रो Devi Saraswati and Devta Agni are associated with the Saraswats, that is, those who derive from Saraswati देवीर्बर्हिरेदं सदन्तु may all the three Devis be seated together on this sacred Kusha.

This Richa translates to: 'May Devi Bharati, associated with the Bharatis, Devi Ila with the Devtas and men and Agni and Saraswati with the Saraswats, may the three goddesses be seated before us upon this sacred grass.'

The meaning is that the followers of Devi Bharati call themselves Bharatis. Devotees of Devi Ila are men and the Devtas. Believers in Agni and Saraswati refer to themselves as the Saraswats. Thus, the reference is to all men and Devtas who reside on Earth and some of whom prefer to call themselves as deriving from or dependent on Bharati and Saraswati. All the three Devis may be present together so that they can be praised together. Once so praised, they would ensure the welfare of all mankind and of all Devtas.

R 31 Richa 7/2/9 ऋजिश्वा भारद्वाजः, विश्वे देवाः, त्रिष्टुप्

For this Richa, the Rishi is Bharadwaj. All Devtas are the Devta for this Richa. The Chanda is Trishtup.

> इळा सरस्वती मही तिस्रो देवीर्मयोभुवः ।
> बर्हिः सीदन्त्वस्रिधः ॥7/2/9

Meaning of words/combination of words

इळा सरस्वती मही Ila, Saraswati, and Mahi तिस्रो देवीर्मयोभुवः the three Devis who do not age, who are givers of delight बर्हिः सीदन्त्वस्रिधः may they be seated on the sacred Kusha.

This Richa translates to: 'May the three undecaying goddesses, givers of delight, Ila, Saraswati, and Mahi, sit together upon the sacred Kusha'.

This means that Ila, Saraswati, and Mahi remain ever young and with their blessings, their followers and worshippers which include both Devtas and men, are able to experience great delight.

R 32 Richa 6/49/7 ऋजिश्वा भारद्वाज:, विश्वे देवा:, त्रिष्टुप्

For this Richa, the Rishi is Bharadwaj. All Devtas are the Devta for this Richa. The Chanda is Trishtup.

> पावीरवी कन्यां चित्रायुः सरंस्वती वीरपत्नी धियं धात् ।
> ग्राभिरच्छिंद्रं शरणं सजोषां दुराधर्षं गृणते शर्म यंसत् ॥6/49/7

Meaning of words/combination of words

पावीरवी purifying कन्यां amiable, beautiful चित्रायुः graceful, giving excellent nourishment सरंस्वती Saraswati वीरपत्नी taking care of the brave धियं धात् bear our actions based on our intellect ग्राभिरच्छिंद्रं शरणं सजोषां दुराधर्षं living amicably with wives of Devtas, (bestow upon us) a habitation without defects where cold and winds do not bother us गृणते praising you शर्म यंसत् give us happiness.

This Richa translates to: 'May the purifying, amiable, graceful Saraswati, the one who takes care of the brave, accept our praise. May she, together with the wives of the Devtas or tributaries flowing together, being well pleased, bestow upon us, a habitation which is impenetrable to wind and rain and free from defects and unhappiness'.

This Richa means that Saraswati is praised here as graceful, amiable, and beautiful. She has come down from the mountains to the plains. She has received water from many tributaries that is, other rivers who are also considered Devis or goddesses. On these plains, men wishing to settle down, pray for houses that are protected from wind and rain, that are free from defects, so that one is sheltered and happy. On the plains thus, human habitations spread out on the banks of Saraswati and its tributaries, nourished and made prosperous through agriculture and economic activities.

R 33 Richa 6/52/6 ऋजिक्षा भारद्वाज:, विश्वे देवा:, त्रिष्टुप्

For this Richa, the Rishi is Bharadwaj. All Devtas are the Devta for this Richa. The Chanda is Trishtup.

> दिष्टमवृसागंमिष्टु: सरंस्वती सिन्धुंभि: पिन्वंमाना ।
> पर्जन्यों नु ओषंधीभिर्मयोभुरग्नि: सुशंस: सुहव: पितेवं ॥6/52/6

Meaning of words/combination of words

दिष्टमवृसागंमिष्टु: Indra with his protective means may come to us सरंस्वती सिन्धुंभि: पिन्वंमाना may Saraswati dwelling with her tributary rivers protect us पर्जन्यों नु ओषंधीभिर्मयोभुरग्नि: Parjanya (the cloud Devta) with plants that he nourishes, give us happiness and Agni सुशंस: well praised सुहव: and earnestly invoked पितेवं be (protective) like a father.

This Richa translates to: 'May Indra come to us with all his protective means. May Saraswati dwelling with her tributary rivers, protect us. May Parjanya, with the plants (that he nourishes), give us happiness, and may Agni, well-praised and well-invoked by us, be (protective like) a father to us'.

In this Richa, all the Devtas critical for agriculture and growth of plants and vegetation are praised together: Indra, Devta of rainfall, Saraswati carrying ground water along with her tributaries making vast lands on their banks and intermediate lands fertile, Parjanya, spreading rain for nourishing plants and vegetation, and Agni, representing sunlight. Together these Devtas may ensure for men, who are praising and worshipping them earnestly, protection and happiness. As summarized in Table 4, among all the references to Saraswati in Rigveda, Sukta 61 of Mandal 6 is special since all the Richas of this Sukta are devoted to Saraswati. That is why it is often referred to as the Saraswati Sukta.

The Saraswati Sukta: Mandal 6 Sukta 61

The 61st Sukta of the sixth Mandal in Rigveda is devoted entirely to Saraswati. This Sukta may be referred to as the Saraswati Sukta. In this Sukta, there are fourteen Richas.

In this Sukta, for all the Richas, the Rishi is Bharadwaj and the Devta is Saraswati. The Chandas differ according to the Richas.

R 34 Richa 6/61/1 बार्हस्पत्यो भरद्वाज:, सरस्वती, निचृत् जगती

For this Richa, the Rishi is Bharadwaj. Devta is Saraswati. The Chanda is Nichrat Jagati.

> इयमददाद्रभसमृणच्युतं दिवोदासं वध्र्यश्वाय दाशुषे ।
> या शश्वन्तमाचखादावसं पणिं ता ते दात्राणि तविषा सरस्वति ॥6/61/1

Meaning of words/combination of words

इयमददाद्रभसमृणच्युतं (Saraswati) gave (the son) endowed with speed and capable of acquitting debt दिवोदासं by the name of Divodas वध्र्यश्वाय for Vadhryashwa, दाशुषे known for giving oblations सरस्वति O (Devi) Saraswati या who शश्वन्तमाचखादावसं destroyed the niggard or miser always causing misery पणिं by the name of Pani ता ते दात्राणि तविषा these are your great bounties.

This Richa translates to: 'Saraswati gave to the donor of the oblations, Vadhryashwa, a son named Divodas who was endowed with speed, and who acquitted the debt, thereby destroying the miser who was given to always cause misery. Such are the great bounties of Saraswati.'

In this Richa, one of the great deeds performed by Devi Saraswati is described. With her blessings, Divodas was born to Vadhryashwa who was troubled by a miser money lender named Pani. Divodas could travel rapidly on a boat from his place to the place where Pani lived, travelling with speed on the river Saraswati. He acquitted the debt of his father. This Richa indicates that rapid travelling was possible by boat on Saraswati. It also indicates that in the commercial universe of the Saraswati civilization, money lending was prevalent and that charging high interest rates could also have been in vogue, but it was to be discouraged.

Agriculture in Rigveda: Seeds of India's Civilizational Prosperity

In this Richa, Saraswati is visualized as the giver of sons, giver of riches, giver of speed, and destroyer of misery and deprivation. Those who praise Saraswati, are thus blessed with progeny, riches, and swiftness.

R 35 Richa 6/61/2 बार्हस्पत्यो भरद्वाजः, सरस्वती, जगती

For this Richa, the Rishi is Bharadwaj. Devta is Saraswati. The Chanda is Jagati.

> इयं शुष्मेभिर्बिसखा इवारुजत्सानुं गिरीणां तविषेभिरूर्मिभिः ।
> पारावतघ्नीमवंसे सुवृक्तिभिः सरस्वतीमा विवासेम धीतिभिः ॥6/61/2

Meaning of words/combination of words

इयं this (Saraswati) शुष्मेभिर्बिसखा इवारुजत्सानुं falls on precipices (or big Himalayan rocks) like a digger of the lotus fibres गिरीणां breaks the upper parts of the mountains तविषेभिरूर्मिभिः your impetuous and mighty waves पारावतघ्नीमवंसे सरस्वती this Saraswati is the under-miner (the one who erodes) of both her banks मा विवासेम धीतिभिः we adore you for our protection with steadfastness सुवृक्तिभिः with good praises.

This Richa translates to: 'With impetuous and powerful waves, she (Saraswati) breaks down the rocks of the mountains (with ease), like a digger of the lotus fibres. Saraswati erodes both of her banks easily. We adore Saraswati for our protection, with good praises and with steadfastness.'

The Rishi recognizes the impact of the mighty Saraswati in the upper parts of the mountains. She easily breaks up the rocks in the upper reaches of the mountains. Rocks are broken with speed and spontaneity, as if these are lotus fibres. Saraswati is so mighty that she keeps destroying both her banks, often overrunning them. Clearly, the water flow in Saraswati is powerful, torrent-like, abundant, and full of strong flows. As she comes down from the higher reaches of the mountains, she carries with her, large boulders and rocks, which get broken down further as she descends. This process would keep bringing rich minerals of the rocks of the Himalaya's upper reaches to the areas in the plains thereby enriching the soil with mineral and fertility.

R 36 Richa 6/61/3 बार्हस्पत्यो भरद्वाज:, सरस्वती, निचृत् जगती

For this Richa, the Rishi is Bharadwaj. Devta is Saraswati. The Chanda is Nichrat Jagati.

> सरस्वति देवनिदो नि बर्हय प्रजां विश्वस्य बृसंयस्य मायिन: ।
> उत क्षितिभ्योऽवनीरविन्दो विषमेभ्यो अस्रवो वाजिनीवति ॥6/61/3

Meaning of words/combination of words

सरस्वति O Saraswati नि बर्हय प्रजां destroy (get rid of) these people देवनिदो who are the revilers of the Devtas विश्वस्य बृसंयस्य मायिनं: also destroy all the offspring of the villainous Vrisaya उत क्षितिभ्योऽवनीरविन्दो for the welfare of mankind विषमेभ्यो अस्रवो you have released large parts of lands and showered water on these men वाजिनीवति O giver of food and nourishment.

This Richa translates to: 'O Saraswati, destroy the revilers of the Devtas, as also all the offspring of the villainous Vrisaya. O giver of food, you have acquired for men, large lands and showered water upon them.'

Saraswati, in the course of her downward flow from the mountains, released large tracts of lands and irrigated these with her strong flow of water for the welfare of mankind, so that the community of men can be nourished and sustained by cultivation of food. With such strength as gained by the benevolence of Saraswati, these men are then able to drive away from these areas, people who did not believe in the Devtas or who refuted their existence. This includes the descendants of Vrisaya, a prominent non-believer of Devtas and Yajnas.

Agriculture in Rigveda: Seeds of India's Civilizational Prosperity

R 37 Richa 6/61/4 बार्हस्पत्यो भरद्वाज:, सरस्वती, निचृत् गायत्री

For this Richa, the Rishi is Bharadwaj. Devta is Saraswati. The Chanda is Nichrat Gayatri.

> प्र णो देवी सरस्वती वाजेभिर्वाजिनीवती ।
> धीनामवित्र्यवतु ॥6/61/4

Meaning of words/combination of words

देवी सरस्वती O Devi Saraswati वाजेभिर्वाजिनीवती You are the bearer of food and the giver of food धीनामवित्र्यवतु प्र णो protector of our intellect, protect us.

This Richa translates to: 'Devi Saraswati, accepting sacrifice of food in our Yajna, be the giver of food. Being the protector of our intellects, please protect us.'

The purport is that Devi Saraswati is the great giver of food. She gives us food which is many times what we offer to her in our Yajnas. She is also the Devi of intellect and learning. May she protect us, both with respect to our minds and our bodies. In this Richa, the reference is both to Saraswati as the River Devta who provides food by irrigating through her waters, the adjacent lands, and as the Devta of the intellect and speech, who protects men by giving them the power to think and express themselves.

R 38 Richa 6/61/5 बार्हस्पत्यो भरद्वाज:, सरस्वती, विराट् गायत्री

For this Richa, the Rishi is Bharadwaj. Devta is Saraswati. The Chanda is Virat Gayatri.

> यस्त्वां देवि सरस्वत्युपब्रूते धने हिते ।
> इन्द्रं न वृत्रतूर्ये ॥6/61/5

Meaning of words/combination of words

देवि सरस्वत्युपब्रूते O Devi Saraswati, those who call for you धनें हिते engaged in a war for the sake of wealth यस्त्वां इन्द्रं न वृत्रतूर्ये protect them in a manner similar to Indra who was praised when overcoming Vritra in a war.

This Richa translates to: 'Devi Saraswati, protect them, who call for you when engaged in war for the sake of wealth, and those who glorify you like Indra who was engaged in war with Vritra.'

Saraswati is the Devi of both strength and intellect. Those who worship her are victorious in all conflicts. They are blessed with prosperity, strength and wealth.

R 39 Richa 6/61/6 बार्हस्पत्यो भरद्वाज:, सरस्वती, विराट गायत्री

For this Richa, the Rishi is Bharadwaj. Devta is Saraswati. The Chanda is Virat Gayatri.

> देवि सरस्वत्यवा वाजेषु वाजिनि ।
> रदां पूषेवं नः सनिम् ॥6/61/6

Meaning of words/combination of words

त्वं देवि सरस्वत्यवा वाजिनि O divine and powerful Devi Saraswati वाजेषु please protect us in battles रदां पूषेवं नः सनिम् and like Pusha Devta, give us wealth.

This Richa translates to: 'Divine Saraswati, abounding in strength, protect us in battles, and, like Pushan Devta, give us wealth.'

Saraswati is powerful and generous. Men performing Yajna and praising her appeal to both of these attributes for protection and obtaining strength and wealth.

Agriculture in Rigveda: Seeds of India's Civilizational Prosperity

R 40 Richa 6/61/7 बार्हस्पत्यो भरद्वाजः, सरस्वती, गायत्री

For this Richa, the Rishi is Bharadwaj. Devta is Saraswati. The Chanda is Gayatri.

> उत स्या नः सरस्वती घोरा हिरण्यवर्तनिः ।
> वृत्रघ्नी वंष्टि सुष्टुतिम् ॥6/61/7

Meaning of words/combination of words

उत स्या सरस्वती घोरा हिरण्यवर्तनिः and this fierce Saraswati who rides on a golden chariot with wheels वृत्रघ्नी destroyer of Vritra नः वंष्टि सुष्टुतिम् is desirous of hearing our pleasing praises for her.

This Richa translates to: 'May the fierce Saraswati, riding on a golden chariot, the destroyer of enemies, be pleased by our earnest praises.'

Saraswati as a river, is acknowledged to be fierce due to the force of the flow of its water. That water glitters like gold when sunshine falls on the flowing river. This is why Rishi Bharadwaj compares the majestic flow of the river with that of the galloping of a golden chariot. She is the destroyer of all obstacles that come her way. We recognize her role in protecting and nourishing us, and she is pleased with our praises for her.

R 41 Richa 6/61/8 बार्हस्पत्यो भरद्वाजः, सरस्वती, गायत्री

For this Richa, the Rishi is Bharadwaj. Devta is Saraswati. The Chanda is Gayatri.

> यस्यां अनन्तो अहुतस्त्वेषश्चरिष्णुरर्णवः ।
> अमश्चरति रोरुवत् ॥6/61/8

Meaning of words/combination of words

यस्यां whose अनन्तो limitless अहुतस्त्वेषश्चरिष्णुरर्णवः constantly flowing unstoppable (water) अमश्चरति flow of water रोरुवत् roars while travelling. [In this Richa, we may note the origin of the English word 'Roar'].

This Richa translates to: 'Whose mighty, limitless, undeviating, splendid, progressive, water-flow proceeds roaringly.'

Saraswati was a river whose strength is recognized in this Richa indicating the limitless flow of water that hurtles down, making great noise without deviating from its course, flowing persistently. Clearly, Saraswati was the largest and the most impressive river in her heyday.

R 42 Richa 6/61/9 बार्हस्पत्यो भरद्वाजः, सरस्वती, निचृत् गायत्री

For this Richa, the Rishi is Bharadwaj. Devta is Saraswati. The Chanda is Nichrat Gayatri.

> सा नो॒ विश्वा॒ अति॒ द्विष॑: स्वसृ॒र॑न्या ऋता॒वरी ।
> अत॒न्नहे॑व॒ सूर्य॑: ॥6/61/9

Meaning of words/combination of words

सा नो॒ विश्वा॒ अति॒ द्विष॑: This Saraswati overcomes all our enemies स्वसृ॒र॑न्या takes us beyond the sister rivers ऋता॒वरी that truth-abiding Saraswati अत॒न्नहे॑व॒ सूर्य॑: like the Sun spreads light during the day.

This Richa translates to: 'She overcomes all our adversaries and brings to us, her other water-laden sisters as the ever-rolling Sun spreads light during the day.'

The purport is that through Saraswati, men are able to access the waters of all her tributaries. Such abundance of water is comparable to the spread of light by the Sun, which brightens up the space universally. With this abundance of water augmented by sunlight, rich, nourishing and abundant food becomes accessible, providing strength to men who perform Yajnas. These men are then able to defeat all the adversaries who are the non-believers in Yajnas.

Agriculture in Rigveda: Seeds of India's Civilizational Prosperity

R 43 Richa 6/61/10 बाईस्पत्यो भरद्वाज:, सरस्वती, विराट गायत्री

For this Richa, the Rishi is Bharadwaj. Devta is Saraswati. The Chanda is Virat Gayatri.

> उत नः प्रिया प्रियासुं सप्तस्वंसा सुजुंष्टा ।
> सरस्वती स्तोम्यां भूत् ॥6/61/10

Meaning of words/combination of words

उत नः प्रिया प्रियासुं she is beloved among the beloveds सप्तस्वंसा सुजुंष्टा she is the most likable among the seven sister rivers सरस्वती स्तोम्यां भूत् this Saraswati has become praiseworthy.

This Richa translates to: 'Saraswati, who has seven sisters and who is the dearest amongst these sisters who are all dear to us, she is the most praiseworthy for us'.

This Richa places Saraswati in the context of other prominent rivers of those days such as Sindhu, Ganga, Yamuna, Shutudri, Purushni, Asiknya, Marudvridha, Vitasta, Sushoma, and Arjikiya. For the inhabitants of those times, Saraswati is the most beloved for the prosperity that she has led to, mainly through the agricultural activities.

R 44 Richa 6/61/11 बाईस्पत्यो भरद्वाज:, सरस्वती, निचृत् गायत्री

For this Richa, the Rishi is Bharadwaj. Devta is Saraswati. The Chanda is Nichrat Gayatri.

> आपप्रुषी पार्थिवान्युरु रजों अन्तरिक्षम् ।
> सरस्वती निदस्पांतु ॥6/61/11

Meaning of words/combination of words

आपप्रुषी पार्थिवान्युरु रजों अन्तरिक्षम् Giver of earthly wealth and filler of the entire space with radiance सरस्वती O Saraswati निदस्पांतु protect us from those who blame us.

This Richa translates to: 'May Saraswati, who fills us up with earthly wealth and the vast space with her radiance, defend us from the revilers.'

The purport is that as river Saraswati, she gives us earthly wealth, and as Devi Saraswati, she fills the entire universe with radiance. May she protect us from the people who do not understand her greatness or who blame us for performing Yajnas in her praise or in the praise of Devtas.

R 45 Richa 6/61/12 बाईस्पत्यो भरद्वाजः, सरस्वती, निचृत् गायत्री

For this Richa, the Rishi is Bharadwaj. Devta is Saraswati. The Chanda is Nichrat Gayatri.

त्रिषृधस्थां सप्तधांतुः पञ्चं जाता वर्धयंती ।
वाजेंवाज़े हव्यां भूत् ॥6/61/12

Meaning of words/combination of words

त्रिषृधस्थां resident of three places सप्तधांतुः associated with seven powers or bearer of seven metals पञ्चं जाता वर्धयंती increasing welfare of five classes of men वाजेंवाज़े हव्यां भूत् she is praiseworthy in every battle, in every action.

This Richa translates to: 'Residing in the three worlds, comprising seven elements, increasing the welfare of the five races or five peoples, she may be worshipped in every battle and in every action.'

In this Richa, there is reference to three worlds that is planets or spaces in the universe namely, Earth, Dyulok (heaven, that is residence of the Devtas), and the intermediate space. Saraswati flows in all of these places. Saraswati is also associated with seven fundamental elements or metals. She is also known to be the protector of five tribes or five peoples who resided in that part of India where Saraswati flowed. These five peoples are mentioned in the Rigveda in the context of the Dasrajna Yuddha (7/18) as Puru, Yadu, Turvasa, Anu, and Druhyu. It is best not to call these as races or tribes since these were five descendants from the same common parentage. In fact, these were all sons or descendants of Yayati.

R 46 Richa 6/61/13 बार्हस्पत्यो भरद्वाजः, सरस्वती, निचृत् जगती

For this Richa, the Rishi is Bharadwaj. Devta is Saraswati. The Chanda is Nichrat Jagati.

> प्र या महिम्ना महिनासु चेकिते द्युम्नेभिरन्या अपसामपस्तमा ।
> रथं इव बृहती विभ्वने कृतोपस्तुत्यां चिकितुषा सरस्वती ॥6/61/13

Meaning of words/combination of words

सरस्वती Saraswati प्र या महिम्ना who is eminent in greatness महिनासु and glories चेकिते द्युम्नेभिरन्या अपसामपस्तमा most impetuous among all streams रथं इव बृहती विभ्वने created vast in capacity like a chariot कृतोपस्तुत्यां she is to be glorified चिकितुषा by discerning worshippers.

This Richa translates to: 'Saraswati, who is distinguished amongst all the rivers as eminent in her greatness, in her glories, she is the most impetuous among all streams. She, who has been created vast in capacity as a chariot, she is to be glorified by the discerning worshippers.'

This Richa emphasizes that among all the rivers flowing on Earth or in Dyulok or in any other planet in the universe, Saraswati is the most eminent in her greatness, in her glories, in her vastness, in her speed, and in the impetuous flow of her water. Those who understand her contribution and powers, always glorify her.

R 47 Richa 6/61/14 बार्हस्पत्यो भरद्वाजः, सरस्वती, पंक्ति

For this Richa, the Rishi is Bharadwaj. Devta is Saraswati. The Chanda is Pankti.

> सरस्वत्यभि नो नेषि वस्यो मापं स्फरीः पयसा मा नु आ धक् ।
> जुषस्व नः सख्या वेश्या च मा त्वत्क्षेत्राण्यरणानि गन्म ॥6/61/14

Meaning of words/combination of words

सरस्वत्यभि नो नेषि वस्यो O Saraswati, take us to desirable wealth मापं स्फरीः पयसा do not overwhelm us with your abundance of water मा नु आ धक् do not drive us away from you जुषस्व नः सख्या वेश्या be pleased by our friendly services and access to our habitations च मा त्वत्क्षेत्राण्यरंणानि गन्म do not let us go to fields that may be distant from you or unacceptable to you.

This Richa translates to 'O Saraswati, guide us to the desirable wealth. Do not harm us by your excess force of water. Be pleased by our friendly (services) and proximity of our habitations and let us not go to fields located away from you.'

In this Richa, men are praising Saraswati. Being in the proximity of Saraswati has led them on to the path of prosperity. They are praying that excess flow of water, that is floods or unpredictable changes in the course of the river, may not harm or disturb them so that they may remain in close proximity, carrying on their agricultural activities on the most fertile land. Men who reside in the vicinity of Saraswati do not wish to settle in other lands or on the banks of other rivers because they have found that being in the cradle of river Saraswati enables them to remain most prosperous and devoted to the Devtas.

Thus, the Saraswati Sukta in Mandal 6 has fourteen Richas. However, in Mandals preceding and following Mandal 6 (except Mandal 4), there are a number of other Richas that are devoted to praising Saraswati. Some of these are given below.

R 48 Richa 1/3/10 *मधुच्छन्दा वैश्वामित्र:, सरस्वती, गायत्री*

For this Richa, the Rishi is Madhuchanda from lineage of Vishwamitra. Devta is Saraswati. The Chanda is Gayatri.

> पावका न: सरस्वती वाजेभिर्वाजिनीवती।
> यज्ञं वष्टु धियावसु: ॥ 1/3/10

Meaning of words/combination of words

पावका न: सरस्वती Saraswati purifies us वाजेभिर्वाजिनीवती she gives us food, therefore she is known as the food giver यज्ञं वष्टु धियावसु: from the wealth generated by our intellect-driven actions, may our Yajnas succeed.

Agriculture in Rigveda: Seeds of India's Civilizational Prosperity

This Richa translates to: 'Saraswati purifies us and by giving us food, she is our food-bestower. From the intellect-driven actions, wealth is generated, may that make our Yajnas succeed.'

In this Richa, Rishi Madhuchanda, a later age Rishi focuses on the Saraswati both as the giver of food in her role as a river and her role as the Devi of intellect. In fact, when actions are driven by the power of intellect, they become momentous just as the might of the flow of the Saraswati waters.

R 49 Richa 1/3/11 मधुच्छन्दा वैश्वामित्रः, सरस्वती, गायत्री

For this Richa, the Rishi is Madhuchanda from lineage of Vishwamitra. Devta is Saraswati. The Chanda is Gayatri.

> चोद॒यित्री सू॒नृतानां॑ चेत॒न्ती सुम॒ती॒नाम्।
> य॒ज्ञं द॑धे सरस्वती॥ 1/3/11

Meaning of words/combination of words

चोद॒यित्री सू॒नृतानां॑ inspirer of truthful actions चेत॒न्ती सुम॒ती॒नाम् augmenter of excellent intellects य॒ज्ञं द॑धे सरस्वती Saraswati, the Devi of intellect sustains the Yajnas fully.

This Richa translates to: 'Saraswati inspires us to perform truthful actions. She augments in us, excellent intellects. She fully sustains our Yajnas'.

Saraswati, as the Devi of intellect, gives us the power to distinguish between truthful and false actions. She builds in us this power of intellect and enables us to perform the Yajnas.

R 50 Richa 1/3/12 मधुच्छन्दा वैश्वामित्रः, सरस्वती, गायत्री

For this Richa, the Rishi is Madhuchanda from lineage of Vishwamitra. Devta is Saraswati. The Chanda is Gayatri.

> म॒हो अर्णः॑ सरस्व॒ती प्र चेतयति के॒तुना॑।
> धियो॒ विश्वा॒ वि रा॑जति॥ 1/3/12

Meaning of words/combination of words

म॒हो अर्ण॒: सर॒स्वती॒ प्र चे॑तयति के॒तुना॑ from intellect born knowledge, Saraswati enables us to understand this great ocean of universe धियो॒ विश्वा॒ वि रा॑जति she enlightens us with all kinds of understandings.

This Richa translates to: 'Saraswati makes us understand from intellect-born knowledge, the grand universe. She enlightens us by providing all kinds of understandings.'

In this Richa also, the Rishi emphasizes the role that Saraswati plays as the Devi of intellect. She makes us understand, through the intellectual power of discernment, the mysteries of the great universe of actions. These understandings reside in speech and in the meaning of the spoken words. Saraswati resides in our speech and those blessed by her, break the sway of ignorance like her mighty waters break the surrounding rocks.

Like the Saraswati Sukta in Mandal 6, there is another prominent Sukta in Mandal 10 which makes reference to a number of other rivers apart from Saraswati. Clearly, this Sukta pertains to times when Saraswati had started drying up and other rivers had gained prominence.

The Nadi Sukta: Mandal 10 Sukta 75
recognizing the prominence of river Sindhu

R 51 Richa 10/75/1 सि॒न्धु॒क्षित् प्रैयमेध॒:, नद्य॒:, जगती

For this Richa, the Rishi is Sindhukshit, the son of Priyamedha. The Devtas are the Rivers. The Metre is Jagati.

> प्र सु व॑ आपो महि॒मान॑मुत्त॒मं का॒रुर्वो॑चाति॒ सद॑ने वि॒वस्व॑तः ।
> प्र स॒प्तस॑प्त त्रे॒धा हि च॒क्रमु॒: प्र सृ॒त्वरी॑णाम॒ति सिन्धु॒रोज॑सा ॥10/75/1

Meaning of words/combination of words

प्र सु व॑ आपो O waters महि॒मान॑मुत्त॒मं your greatness का॒रुर्वो॑चाति is praised well सद॑ने वि॒वस्व॑तः in the house of the performer of the Yajna प्र स॒प्तस॑प्त they flow by sevens त्रेधा हि चक्रमुः through the three worlds (Earth, Heaven, and Space) प्र सृत्वरीणामति सिन्धुरोजंसा Sindhu surpasses all in strength.

This Richa translates to: 'O waters, in the dwelling of the performer of the Yajna, the worshipper praises your excellent glory. These waters flow in multiples of seven through the three worlds, but the Sindhu surpasses all the other streams in strength'.

This refer to times when Saraswati had started drying up. Sindhu had become the most powerful river. The Rishi who visualized this Richa was named after the river Sindhu as Sindhukshit. He compares the might of Sindhu with all the waters that flow on the Earth, in Heaven and in the Space in groups of seven rivers each. Among all these rivers, Sindhu is the most powerful. The Indian civilization had moved both west and east of the erstwhile capture area of Saraswati and had prospered.

R 52 Richa 10/75/2 सिन्धुक्षित् प्रैयमेधः, नद्यः, जगती

For this Richa, the Rishi is Sindhukshit, the son of Priyamedha. The Devtas are the Rivers. The Metre is Jagati.

**प्र तेंऽरदृद्धरुणो यातंवे पुथः सिन्धो यद्वाजाँ अभ्यद्रंवस्त्वम् ।
भूम्या अधिं प्रवतां यासि सानुना यदेषामग्रं जगंतामिरज्यसिं ॥10/75/2**

Meaning of words/combination of words

सिन्धो O river Sindhu यातंवे पुथः अभ्यद्रंवस्त्वम् at the time when you started flowing towards these fertile lands प्र तेंऽरदृद्धरुणो यद्वाजाँ Varuna Devta made a path for you by digging the Earth भूम्या अधिं प्रवतां यासि you travel over an excellent path on the ground सानुना यदेषामग्रं जगंतामिरज्यसिं that is why you become the basis for the beings over there.

This Richa translates to: 'O Sindhu, when you started flowing towards these fertile lands, Varuna Devta tore open a path for you. You travel over an excellent path on the ground. By providing food to all, you reign in the sight of all beings'.

In this Richa, the majestic position of river Sindhu is recognized as its path has been made by divine intervention. It goes through fertile lands and makes them yield ample crops. In the eyes of those who behold its majesty, the river reigns among all rivers.

R 53 Richa 10/75/3 सिन्धुक्षित् प्रैयमेध:, नद्य:, जगती

For this Richa, the Rishi is Sindhukshit, the son of Priyamedha. The Devtas are the Rivers. The Metre is Jagati.

दिवि स्वनो यंतते भूम्योपर्यन्नन्तं शुष्मुमुदियर्ति भानुनां ।
अभ्रादिव प्र स्तनयन्ति वृष्ट्य: सिन्धुर्यदेति वृषभो न रोरुवत्
॥३॥ 10/75/3

Meaning of words/combination of words

दिवि स्वनो यंतते भूम्योपर्यन्नन्तं her sound on Earth encompasses even the Heavens शुष्मुमुदियर्ति भानुनां she travels with tremendous force with shining waves अभ्रादिव प्र स्तनयन्ति वृष्ट्य: like rains fall thundering from the cloud सिन्धुर्यदेति वृषभो न रोरुवत् Sindhu advances, roaring like a bull.

This Richa translates to: 'Her sound on Earth covers the Heavens, she travels with tremendous force with shining waves like rains fall from thundering clouds. Thus, Sindhu advances, roaring like a bull'.

Like Saraswati of the yester years, river Sindhu also proceeds with great speed and noise. Her waters shine in the Sun. Her waters sound like the roar of a charging bull. *[We may note again, the Sanskrit origin of the word 'roar']*

R 54 Richa 10/75/4 सिन्धुक्षित् प्रैयमेध:, नद्य:, जगती

For this Richa, the Rishi is Sindhukshit, the son of Priyamedha. The Devtas are the Rivers. The Metre is Jagati.

अभि त्वां सिन्धो शिशुमिन्न मातरो वाश्रा अर्षन्ति पयसेव धेनव: ।
राजेव युध्वां नयसि त्वमिस्चिचौ यदांसामग्रं प्रवतामिनंक्षसि ॥10/75/4

Meaning of words/combination of words

Agriculture in Rigveda: Seeds of India's Civilizational Prosperity

अ॒भि त्वा॑ सि॒न्धो Towards you Sindhu शिशु॒मिन्न मा॒तरो॑ like mothers go towards their children प॒यंसेव॑ धे॒नवः and cows ready to give milk go towards their calves with affection वा॒श्रा अ॒र्षन्ति॑ like these other rivers come towards you राजे॑व॒ यु॒ध्वां नय॑सि and like a king goes towards battle त्वमिसि॒चौ you take these rivers serving you यदा॑सा॒मग्रं॑ प्र॒व॒ता॒मिन॒क्षसि when you lead these streams moving ahead.

This Richa translates to: 'Like mothers go for their sons, cows ready to give milk rush towards their calves, the other rivers rush towards you, O Sindhu, and you with your both banks take these streams with you like a king going for battle takes along those who serve him. You lead these streams that are marching along'.

In this Richa, reference is made to the centrality of river Sindhu among rivers that either join Sindhu on the way or are moving towards the same direction that is, westwards. Sindhu and her tributaries have become central to the Indian civilisation at this time towards the end of Saraswati civilization.

R 55 Richa 10/75/5 सि॒न्धु॒क्षित् प्रैयमेध॒ः, नद्यः॑, जगती

For this Richa, the Rishi is Sindhukshit, the son of Priyamedha. The Devtas are the Rivers. The Metre is Jagati.

इ॒मं मे॑ ग॒ङ्गे य॑मुने सरस्वति॒ शुतु॑द्रि स्तोमं॑ सचता॒ परु॒ष्ण्या ।
असि॒क्न्या म॒रुद्वृधे॑ वि॒तस्त॒याऽऽर्जी॑कीये शृणु॒ह्या सु॒षोम॑या ॥ 10/75/5

Meaning of words/combination of words

ग॒ङ्गे यमुने सरस्वति॒ O Ganga, Yamuna, Saraswati शुतु॑द्रि Shutudri परु॒ष्ण्या Parushni असि॒क्न्या Asikni म॒रुद्वृधे॑ Marudvridha वि॒तस्त॒याऽऽर्जी॑कीये Vitasta and Arjikiya सु॒षोम॑या and Sushoma इ॒मं मे॑ स्तोमं॑ सचता॒ शृणु॒ह्या (All of you) please accept this, my praise.

This Richa translates to: 'Please accept this my praise, O Ganga, Yamuna, Saraswati, Shutudri, Parushni, Marudvridha with Asikni, and Vitasta, listen also Arjikiya with Sushoma'.

In this Richa, ten major rivers of the time are acknowledged other than Sindhu. Saraswati is also referred to. Now it is well past its peak days. The coverage of these rivers extends to vast areas of India. Ganga is gaining in prominence by this time.

R 56 Richa 10/75/6 सिन्धुक्षित् प्रैयमेधः, नद्यः, जगती

For this Richa, the Rishi is Sindhukshit, the son of Priyamedha. The Devtas are the Rivers. The Metre is Jagati.

> तृष्टामया प्रथमं यातवे सजूः सुसर्त्वा रसया श्वेत्या त्या ।
> त्वं सिन्धो कुभया गोमतीं क्रुमुं मेहत्वा सरथं याभिरीयसे ॥10/75/6

Meaning of words/combination of words

सिन्धो O Sindhu त्वं क्रुमुं गोमतीं यातवे you, for meeting the fast-moving Gomati प्रथमं तृष्टामया सजूः you first united with Trishtatma and moved on सुसर्त्वा रसया श्वेत्या कुभया मेहत्वा त्या then joined with Susartu, the Rasa, the Shweti, the Kubha, and the Mehatnu सरथं याभिरीयसे then proceeded as if riding together on a chariot.

This Richa translates to: 'O Sindhu, in order to meet the fast-moving Gomati, you first united with the Trishtatma, thereafter you joined with the Susartu, the Rasa, the Shweti, the Kubha, and the Mehatnu, and then proceeded together as if on a chariot'.

In this Richa, those rivers are named which join Sindhu along the way namely, Trishtatma, Susartu, Rasa, Shweti, Kubha, and Mehatnu, that is six rivers. Together with Sindhu, these seven rivers proceed rapidly towards the fast-moving great river Gomati near modern day Gujarat.

R 57 Richa 10/75/7 सिन्धुक्षित् प्रैयमेधः, नद्यः, जगती

For this Richa, the Rishi is Sindhukshit, the son of Priyamedha. The Devtas are the Rivers. The Metre is Jagati.

> ऋजीत्येनी रुशन्ती महित्वा परि ज्रयांसि भरते रजांसि ।
> अदब्धा सिन्धुरुपसामपस्तमाऽश्वा न चित्रा वपुषीव दर्शता ॥10/75/7

Agriculture in Rigveda: Seeds of India's Civilizational Prosperity

Meaning of words/combination of words

ऋजीत्येनी रुशंती Straight flowing, white coloured, bright shining महित्वा in its might परि व्रयांसि भरते रजांसि bears along the rapid waters अदब्धा सिन्धुरुपसांमुपस्तमाऽश्वा the unobstructed Sindhu is the river among rivers, she is speckled like a mare न चित्रा वपुषीव दर्शता and beautiful like a pretty and healthy woman.

This Richa translates to: 'Straight-flowing, white-coloured, and bright-shining (Sindhu) bears along in its might, the rapid waters, flowing unobstructed. It is the river among rivers, speckled like a mare. She looks beautiful like a pretty and healthy woman'.

In this Richa, all the attributes of the river Sindhu are captured. She flows straight, her waters are white and bright, and her flow is uninterrupted. She appears like a running mare, and she is beautiful as if a fair coloured bright and healthy maiden. She is described as the river among rivers just as the Rishis had earlier described Saraswati as the river among rivers in her own heyday.

R 58 Richa 10/75/8 सिन्धुक्षित् प्रैयमेधः, नद्यः, जगती

For this Richa, the Rishi is Sindhukshit, the son of Priyamedha. The Devtas are the Rivers. The Metre is Jagati.

स्वश्वा सिन्धुः सुरथां सुवासां हिरण्ययीं सुकृता वाजिनीवती ।
ऊर्णावती युवतिः सीलमांवत्युताधि वस्ते सुभगां मधुवृधम् ॥10/75/8

Meaning of words/combination of words

सिन्धुः That Sindhu is characterized by स्वश्वा grand horses सुरथां great chariots सुवासां excellent clothes हिरण्ययीं beautiful gold ornaments सुकृता she is doer of pious acts वाजिनीवती rich in food ऊर्णावती rich in wool युवतिः she is ever young सीलमांवत्युताधिं abounding in Silam plants वस्ते सुभगां मधुवृधम् and the auspicious river abounds in honey-growing flowers.

This Richa translates to: 'This Sindhu is rich in grand horses, great chariots, excellent clothes and beautiful gold ornaments. She is the doer of pious acts. She is rich in food and wool. She is ever young and full of Silam plants. The auspicious river abounds in honey-growing flowers'.

This Richa asserts that the entire area under the sway of river Sindhu is extremely prosperous. The surrounding land is full of grand horses (a horse is also known as 'Sindhu'), great chariots. It is rich in clothes, wool, food, and gold ornaments. Holy rites are performed all around. There is youthfulness and freshness all around with abundant vegetation and flowers.

R 59 Richa 10/75/9 सिन्धुक्षित् प्रैयमेध:, नद्य:, जगती

For this Richa, the Rishi is Sindhukshit, the son of Priyamedha. The Devtas are the Rivers. The Metre is Jagati.

**सुखं रथं युयुजे सिन्धुरश्विनं तेन् वाजं सनिषदुस्मित्राजौ ।
मृहान्ह्यस्य महिमा पंनुस्यतेऽदंब्धस्यु स्वयंशसो विरुप्शिनं: ॥10/75/9**

Meaning of words/combination of words

सिन्धुरश्विनं सुखं रथं Sindhu harnesses her comfortable chariot with good horses युयुजे तेन् वाजं सनिषदुस्मित्राजौ by that chariot she may give us abundant food मृहान्ह्यस्य महिमा पंनुस्यतेऽदंब्धस्यु in this battle and in the Yajnas, great praises are sung for Sindhu स्वयंशसो विरुप्शिनं: Sindhu's chariot is invincible, reputed, and great.

This Richa translates to: 'Sindhu harnesses her comfortable well-horsed chariot. With that chariot, may she bring food for us. Great praises are sung in battle and in Yajnas for Sindhu. Her chariots are inviolable, great, and renowned'.

In this Richa, the reference to the chariot may be considered as that of the speed of the flow of water of river Sindhu. Sindhu flows straight and fast, and unobstructed. It brings abundant food and prosperity to residents on both sides of the river. They sing praises of the mighty Sindhu in their battles and in their Yajnas. Sindhu's name is the cause of their name and renown. These people have become great with their association with Sindhu.

In Rigveda, Mandal 10, Sukta 75, in all, eighteen rivers have been named. Ten of these are Ganga, Yamuna, Saraswati, Shatudri, Parushni, Asikni, Marudvridha, Vitasta, Arjikiya, and Sushoma. In addition, along with Sindhu, six other rivers are mentioned as Trishtatma, Susartu, Rasa, Shweti, Kubha, and Mehatnu. Further, finally Sindhu meets the river Gomati.

Of these, the Parushni is identified with Iravati, and the Arjikiya with Vipasha. In Mahabharata also, a number of rivers are mentioned in Book 3 entitled 'Vanparva' in the context of a discussion on Tirthas (holy places) in India. Some of the rivers mentioned are Saraswati, Drishadwati, Shalukni, Panchananda, Ekahansa, Vaitarini, Kausiki, Ganga, Renuka, Nanda, Kirtika, Visala, Kampana, Plaksha, Apaga, Narmada, Payaswini, Brahamasara, Payoshni, Venna, Bhimarathi, Yamuna, Bhagirathi, Jala, and Upajala. Apart from Tirthas relating to rivers, Mahabharata also gives the names of a number of lakes, ponds, and wells which are recognized as Tirthas in ancient India. All of these refer to water bodies. The ancient Indian landscape was dotted with many of these water bodies which also often served as sources of irrigation apart from their spiritual values which raised them to the status of Tirthas.

Apart from this main Sukta which describes the main rivers providing abundant water across the vast landmass of India, there are some other Richas in Rigveda where the number of prominent rivers in India is mentioned. For example, in Richa 10 of Sukta 43, seven rivers are mentioned. Here, the word 'Sindhu' is used generically for indicating a river.

R 60 Richa 10/43/3 कृष्ण आङ्गिरसः, इन्द्रः, जगती

For this Richa in Sukta 43 of Mandal 10, the Rishi is Krishna from the lineage of Angiras. The Devta is Indra. The Metre is Jagati.

> विषूवृदिन्द्रो अमंतेरुत क्षुधः स इद्रायो मघवा वस्वं ईशते ।
> तस्येदिमे प्रवणे सप्त सिन्धंवो वयो वर्धन्ति वृषभस्यं शुष्मिणः ॥10/43/3

Meaning of words/combination of words

विषूवृदिन्द्रो अमंतेरुत क्षुधः May Indra be all around us to protect us from hunger and ill thoughts स इद्रायो मघवा वस्वं ईशते that same Indra is the lord of all wealth and prosperity तस्येदिमे प्रवणे सप्त सिन्धंवो वयो वर्धन्ति वृषभस्यं शुष्मिणः of that same Indra, who is strong and who absorbs everything and causes the rain. These famous seven rivers augment all the food grains in this land.

This Richa translates to: 'May Indra, remaining present around us, protect us from hunger and ill-thoughts. Indra is the owner of all wealth and prosperity. He is strong, absorbing everything, and causing rain. The prominent seven rivers augment the food grains in this land'.

This Richa refers to the role of Indra Devta as being responsible for abundant food, wealth and prosperity for the citizens who reside in this land, implying India, where it is by the rain caused by Indra that water always remains abundant. As the Devta of rain, Indra also absorbs all the shocks and calamities which may befall the residents of the area served by these rivers. There is a complementarity between these residents and Indra since they perform Yajnas in praise of Indra.

Mention of 90/ 99 rivers

In Mandal 1, there are references to the number of rivers in India of those days as 90 and 99 in two different places. The latter reference may also be for the number of medicines linked to river water. The implication is that in ancient times, like the modern times, India was dotted with a number of rivers, which were spread throughout its land mass.

Agriculture in Rigveda: Seeds of India's Civilizational Prosperity

Consequently, agriculture as an economic activity had reason to spread throughout its geography and accordingly, the population would also have spread out. Population may still have been denser in the river-basin areas of major rivers such as Saraswati, Sindhu, and Ganga. Perhaps, there were three phases: first being the era when population resided mostly around Saraswati; then, in the second phase, when Saraswati had started drying up, the peak of the culture and economic activities shifted to Sindhu; and lastly, it may have shifted towards Ganga or the Ganga-Jamuna Doaab, which is continuing in modern times. But in general, agricultural activities would have spread throughout along the vast river network of India. These two Richas are given below.

R 61 Richa 1/121/13 कक्षीवान् दैर्घतमस औशिजः, इन्द्रो विश्वे देवा वा, त्रिष्टुप्

For this Richa, the Rishi is Kakshivan. Devta is Indra along with all Devtas. The Chanda is Trishtup.

त्वं सूरो हरितो रामयो नॄन् भरंच्चक्रमेतंशो नायमिंद्र ।
प्रास्यं पारं नंवृतिं नाव्यांनामपिं कर्तमंवर्तयोऽयंज्यून् ॥1/121/13

Meaning of words/combination of words

त्वं हरितो रामयो नॄन् you express rays that soak up liquids causing men's welfare भरंच्चक्रमेतंशो नायमिंद्र सूरो O Indra, bright as the Sun, the wheels of your chariot keep running नंवृतिं नाव्यांनामपिं capable of being crossed by boats, these ninety rivers प्रास्यं पारं कर्तमंवर्तयोऽयंज्यून् throwing on the other banks, those who do not perform Yajnas, you have done a great service to men.

This Richa translates to: 'O Indra, bright as the Sun, the wheels of your chariot keep running, expressing rays that soak up liquids. You have done a great favour to mankind by driving those people out who do not perform Yajnas, beyond the shores of the ninety rivers that can only be crossed by boats'.

In this Richa, ninety rivers are mentioned. A distinction is made between population that lives inside the area covered by these ninety rivers and population that has been driven out beyond the shores of these rivers. These are people who do not acknowledge the presence of the Devtas by performing Yajnas.

The second Richa in this context is also in Mandal 1 but the relevant Sukta is the last Sukta of this Mandal which is Sukta 191.

R 62 Richa 1/191/13 अगस्त्यो मैत्रावरुणिः, अप् त्रिण सूर्यः, महाबृहती

For Richa 13, the Rishi is Agastya who is the descendent of Mitra and Varuna. Devta is Apatrina Surya. The Chanda is Mahabrihati.

> नुवानां नंवतीनां विषस्य रोपुंषीणाम् ।
> सर्वासामग्रभं नामाऽऽरे अंस्य योजंनं हरिष्ठा मधुं त्वा मधुला चंकार ॥
> 1/191/13

Meaning of words/combination of words

विषस्य रोपुंषीणाम् destroyers of poison are नुवानां नंवतीनां ninety-nine rivers or (water-based) medicines सर्वासामग्रभं नामाऽऽरे I take all their names अंस्य योजंनं हरिष्ठा may Sun, driven by the golden horses, take this (poison) far away मधुं त्वा मधुला चंकार the medicine called *Madhula* turns this poison into ambrosia.

This Richa translates to: 'I recite the name of ninety-nine rivers or medicinal antidotes to poisons. Although far off, the Sun, drawn by his horses will overtake the poison, the science of antidotes will turn this (that is, the poison) with the medicine called *Madhula,* into ambrosia'.

In this Richa, devoted to the treatment of poisons, the number ninety-nine is mentioned. Some translators have taken this to mean rivers [*e.g. Wilson in English and Ram Govind Trivedi in Hindi*], some to medicinal herbs that work as antidotes to different kinds of poison. One particular medicinal herb by the name of *Madhula* is so powerful that it may turn even poison into nectar.

Mandal 7 Suktas 95 and 96: Saraswati, Saraswan, and Nationhood

Rishi Vashishta makes reference to both Saraswati and Saraswan in Richa 3 of Sukta 95 and Richas 4 to 6 of Sukta 96 respectively. Saraswan may refer to a great water body or water reservoir. Thus, Saraswan may stand for large water bodies such as clouds, oceans, and glaciers. Saraswati originates from the Himalayan glaciers, now being identified as the Saraswati glaciers. Saraswati finally merges into the great ocean in India's south-west. Saraswati is fed with water along its course through profuse rain clouds. Thus, the pairing of Saraswati and Saraswan seems spontaneous and natural.

In fact, human body (possibly, most animal bodies) consists of a very large segment of water. As such, the human body can also be referred to as Saraswan. From this Saraswan, intelligent speech flows out in the form of Saraswati. Thus, Saraswan-Saraswati combination, which is otherwise found or referred to in nature, is also endogenized in the human body where water organises itself in such an intelligent way as to utilize information to express thoughts, feelings and emotions.

Mandal 7 Sukta 95

R 63 Richa 7/95/1 मैत्रावरुणिर्वसिष्ठ:, सरस्वती, त्रिष्टुप्

For this Richa, the Rishi is Vashishtha. The Devta is Saraswati. The Metre is Trishtup.

> प्र क्षोदसा धायसा सस्र एषा सरस्वती धरुणमायसी पू: ।
> प्रबाबधाना रथ्येव याति विश्वा अपो महिना सिन्धुरन्या: ॥7/95/1

Meaning of words/combination of words

एषा सरस्वती this Saraswati प्र क्षोदसा धायसा flows rapidly with all sustaining water सस्र धरुणमायसी पू: like a city made of iron प्रबाबधाना in its might रथ्येव as a charioteer याति विश्वां clears all अपो महिना sweeping away सिन्धुरन्या: all other waters.

This Richa may be translated as: 'This Saraswati, firm as a city made of iron, flows rapidly with all sustaining water, sweeping away in its might, all other waters, as a charioteer (clears the road ahead)'.

Rishi Vashistha highlights the might of Saraswati by making a comparison with a city made of iron. There is thus a reference to iron in Rigveda by the Sanskrit word 'Aayasi', that means made of iron. The flow of its water is so powerful as if a complete city of iron is afloat. Along its course, it meets various other rivers but sweeps them all, that is, carries them all along with its own waters. Yet the waters of Saraswati are all sustaining, great life giver, great nourisher of the population that inhabit its areas on and beyond its banks and in its vicinity.

R 64 Richa 7/95/2 मैत्रावरुणिर्वसिष्ठ:, सरस्वती, त्रिष्टुप्

For this Richa, the Rishi is Vashishtha. The Devta is Saraswati. The Metre is Trishtup.

> एकांचेतत्सरंस्वती नदीनां शुचिर्यती गिरिभ्य आ संमुद्रात् ।
> रायश्चेतंन्ती भुवंनस्य भूरेंघृतं पयों दुदुहे नाहुंषाय ॥7/95/2

Meaning of words/combination of words

एकांचेतत्सरंस्वती Saraswati, unique and the chief नदीनां among the rivers शुचिर्यती the purest गिरिभ्य starting from the mountains आ संमुद्रात् going to the ocean रायश्चेतंन्ती भुवंनस्य distributing riches amongst many places भूरेंघृतं पयों दुदुहे milked for him, butter and ghee (clarified butter) नाहुंषाय on the request of Nahush.

This Richa translates to: 'Saraswati, chief and purest of rivers, flowing from the mountains to the ocean, understood the request of Nahush, and while distributing riches among the many existing places, milked for him, butter and ghee' (clarified butter).

Rishi Vashistha, in his praise of Saraswati, asserts and acknowledges that Saraswati is the purest and the mightiest of all rivers. It originates from the mountains and flows all the way towards the ocean. Along its course, it gives rise to streams of butter and ghee (clarified butter) where these may indirectly derive from Saraswati waters since she nourishes the cattle who reside on her banks and from whose milk, butter and ghee (clarified butter) are produced. This implies that for the nourishment of men and cattle through agriculture and animal husbandry, Saraswati waters played a key role.

The story of Nahusha gives an important message. After Indra successfully killed Vritra, he went into a deep state of remorse and vacated his position in Svarga. Devtas being left without a leader, looked for somebody who could replace him. They identified, amongst men, Nahusha as being brave as well as handsome enough to take Indra's position. Nahusha was doubtful to take up this position but Devtas assured him that all of them would help him perform the duties of the King of Devtas. At first, Nahusha recognized his position and knew that he was able to rule only with the help of other Devtas. But soon, he mistook his position and considered that it was his own strength, power, and beauty that enabled him to rule over the Devtas. In this self-indulgence, he lost his humility and became filled with unreasonable desires. He became enamored with Indra's wife. Learning of this, Indra's wife Sachi became very angry. Sachi went in search of Indra and narrated to him, her trouble. Indra told her a plan and accordingly, she went back to Nahusha and asked him to come to her in grand style being carried by the seven Rishis. In his haste, Nahusha kicked Agastya who was one of the Rishis carrying him. Agastya became angry and cursed him to become a 'Sarpa'. He was restored back to his earlier state as a king amongst men only after thousands of years. In the meanwhile, Indra came back to heaven. The downfall that occurs due to self-indulgence and self-deception is the lesson to be derived from the Nahusha story. In the Greek legends, there is a similar story of Narcissus who also got lost in self-indulgence. Sometimes, this is called the 'Narcissus Effect'. Going back to the original Nahusha story, it can also be referred to as the 'Nahusha Effect'.

R 65 Richa 7/95/3 मैत्रावरुणिर्वसिष्ठः, सरस्वान्, त्रिष्टुप्

For this Richa, the Rishi is Vashishtha. The Devta is Saraswan and the Metre is Trishtup.

> स वांवृधे नर्यो योषंणासु वृषा शिशुंर्वृषभो यज्ञियांसु ।
> स वांजिनं म्घवंद्भ्यो दधातिं वि सांतयें तन्वं मामृजीत ॥7/95/3

Meaning of words/combination of words

स वांवृधे He (Saraswan) grows नर्यो for the benefit of men शिशुंर्वृषभो like a young bull योषंणासु वृषा यज्ञियांसु among his adorable wives (like the rains are wives of the clouds) devoted to the Yajnas स वांजिनं म्घवंद्भ्यो दधातिं for the worshipper, he provides a vigorous son वि सांतयें तन्वं मामृजीत and purifies the body, making it ready for work or for receiving the bounties.

This Richa translates to: 'The showerer (clouds), Saraswan, the friend of man, grows for the benefit of men, like a young bull. He grows among his many adorable wives (like the rains carried by the cloud) and bestows upon the worshippers, an energetic son. He purifies their bodies such that these are ready for work or for receiving bounties'.

This Richa is addressed to Saraswan, who is seen as a major water body like the clouds and /or the ocean. Saraswan is praised for the benefit it showers upon the Earth for men. Like a cloud, it continually expands among his wives that are like the rains. From the rains, he nourishes a vigorous son for the worshippers and prepares their bodies to do work, that is, blesses them with strong bodies so that they do work vigorously and enjoy the bounties or outcomes emanating from the blessings of the rains in the form of plentiful food.

Agriculture in Rigveda: Seeds of India's Civilizational Prosperity

R 66 Richa 7/95/4 मैत्रावरुणिर्वसिष्ठः, सरस्वती, त्रिष्टुप्

For this Richa, the Rishi is Vashishtha. The Devta is Saraswati and the Metre is Trishtup.

> उत स्या नः सरस्वती जुषाणोपं श्रवत्सुभगां यज्ञे अस्मिन् ।
> मितज्ञुभिर्नमस्यैरियाना राया युजा चिदुत्तरा सखिभ्यः ॥7/95/4

Meaning of words/combination of words

सरस्वती जुषाणोपं may the gracious Saraswati, rendered happy श्रवत्सुभगां may she, the auspicious one, hear यज्ञे अस्मिन् in this Yajna उत स्या नः our praises
मितज्ञुभिर्नमस्यैरियाना worshippers approach her on bended knees राया युजा she is very able and wealthy चिदुत्तरा सखिभ्यः most liberal to her friends causing their continuous progress.

This Richa translates to: 'May the auspicious and gracious Saraswati, (when) made happy, hear our praises in this Yajna. She is approached (by us) with bended knees and reverence, she is very able and endowed with riches, she is most liberal to her friends, causing their continuous progress'.

When Saraswati is approached with reverence, with bended knees, and Yajnas are performed in her praise, and men approach her with friendliness, she makes sure that they continually progress and prosper as she can gift them liberally with riches.

R 67 Richa 7/95/5 मैत्रावरुणिर्वसिष्ठः, सरस्वती, त्रिष्टुप्

For this Richa, the Rishi is Vashishtha. The Devta is Saraswati and the Metre is Trishtup.

> इमा जुह्वाना युष्मदा नमोभिः प्रति स्तोमं सरस्वति जुषस्व ।
> तव शर्मन्प्रियतमे दधाना उप स्थेयाम शरणं न वृक्षम् ॥7/95/5

Meaning of words/combination of words

इमा जुह्वाना these food grains, we offer to you in the Yajna युष्मदा नमोभिः प्रति with reverence and praise, to obtain even more affluence सरस्वति O Saraswati स्तोमं जुषस्व please listen to our praise तव शर्मन्प्रियतमे दधाना may we be retained in your dearest contentment उप स्थेयाम शरणं न वृक्षम् we recline upon you as a sheltering tree.

This Richa translates to: 'We offer to you, with reverence, these food grains in Yajna, O Saraswati, so that we may receive from you, more affluence. Please listen to our praises, may we be retained in your dearest contentment, may we keep relying on you, as if reclining on a sheltering tree'.

The purport is that men who offer food grains in Yajnas organized in the praise of Saraswati receive even more food and affluence. Men can keep relying on Saraswati for the blessing of affluence, so long as she is content with them. She is like a tree under which Yajna performing men can always take shelter.

R 68 Richa 7/95/6 मैत्रावरुणिर्वसिष्ठः, सरस्वती, त्रिष्टुप्

For this Richa, the Rishi is Vashishtha. The Devta is Saraswati and the Metre is Trishtup.

अयमुं ते सरस्वति वसिष्ठो द्वारावृतस्यं सुभगे व्यांवः ।
वर्धं शुभ्रे स्तुवते रासि वाजान्यूयं पांत स्वस्तिभिः सदां नः ॥7/95/6

Meaning of words/combination of words

सरस्वति सुभगे O auspicious Saraswati अयमुं ते वसिष्ठो द्वारावृतस्यं व्यांवः for you, Rishi Vashishtha has set open, the two doors of the Yajna वर्धं शुभ्रे स्तुवते O white-complexioned Saraswati, be magnified by our praises रासि वाजान्यूयं bring food for us who glorify you पांत स्वस्तिभिः सदां नः with your welfare-augmenting blessings, always cherish us.

This Richa translates to: 'O auspicious Saraswati, for you, Vashishtha has set open the two doors (the east and the west) of the Yajna. O white-complexioned Devi, be magnified by our praise and bestow food on us who glorify you and with your welfare-augmenting blessings, cherish us'.

The colour of Saraswati's waters is white. She is the Devta of Yajna for Vashishtha and his disciples. Their welfare should be ensured by the Devi through the gift of food and all other resources through which their welfare can be augmented.

Like Richa 3 of Sukta 95 of Mandal 7, Richas 4 to 6 of Sukta 96 of Mandal 7, whose Rishi is also Vashishtha, are also devoted to Saraswan as Devta. Saraswan metaphorically stands for large water bodies like an ocean, or clouds, or glaciers. By extension, Sarawan also stands for a reservoir of wisdom. Maharashi Dayanand, in his translation of these Rigvaidic Richas interprets Saraswan in this manner, as the Devta of wisdom.

Mandal 7 Sukta 96

The Devta of the first three verses is Saraswati, and that of the rest, is Saraswat. The Rishi is Vashishtha. The Metre of the first verse is Brihati, of the second, Satobrihati, of the third, Prastarapankti. For the remaining, the Chanda is Gayatri.

R 69 Richa 7/96/1 मैत्रावरुणिर्वसिष्ठ:, सरस्वती, बृहती

For this Richa, the Rishi is Vashishtha. The Devta is Saraswati and the Metre is Brihati.

> बृहदुं गायिषे॒ वचो॑ऽसु॒र्या॑ न॒दीनां᳭ ।
> सरंस्वती॒मिन्म॑ह॒या सुवृ॒क्तिभि॒: स्तोमै॑र्वसिष्ठ रोदंसी ॥7/96/1

Meaning of words/combination of words

बृहदुं गायिषे॒ वचो॑ऽसु॒र्या॑ न॒दीनाम् you sing a powerful praise for Saraswati who is the mightiest amongst rivers सरंस्वती॒मिन्म॑ह॒या सुवृ॒क्तिभि॒: स्तोमै॑र्वसिष्ठ रोदंसी O Vashishtha, praise Saraswati with selected praises, who resides both in Heaven and on Earth.

This Richa translates to: 'O Vashishtha, sing a powerful praise for Saraswati, who is the mightiest amongst rivers. Worship her with well-selected praises, for Saraswati resides both in Heaven and on Earth'.

Saraswati flows in Dyulok, which is the land of light and the place from where Devtas came, as well as on Earth. She is divine in both places. She is the mightiest in both places.

R 70 Richa 7/96/2 मैत्रावरुणिर्वसिष्ठ:, सरस्वती, सतोबृहती

For this Richa, the Rishi is Vashishtha. The Devta is Saraswati and the Metre is Satobrihati.

> उभे यत्ते महिना शुंभ्रे अन्धंसी अधिक्षियन्ति पूरव: ।
> सा नों बोध्यवित्री मरुत्संखा चोद राधों मघोनाम् ॥7/96/2

Meaning of words/combination of words

उभे यत्ते महिना शुंभ्रे O fair-coloured (Saraswati) with your greatness, men obtain both kinds of food, divine and earthly अन्धंसी अधिक्षियन्ति पूरव: that protectress river protects the citizens सा नों बोध्यवित्री she understands us मरुत्संखा she is the friend of Maruts चोद राधों मघोनाम् she bestows riches on those who are affluent in offering their praise (to you).

This Richa translates to: 'O fair-coloured Saraswati, with your greatness, men obtain both divine and earthly food. You are the protectress of the citizens, you understand us, you are the friend of the Maruts, you bestow riches upon those who are profuse in their praises of you'.

Saraswati's waters are white coloured. With her blessings, men access divine foods that is divine thoughts and expressions and earthly food for the nourishment of the body. Citizens, that is people who live in cities on your banks, are protected by you. You provide the natural barriers for these people to protect them. You understand their needs. With your friendship with the Maruts, we (who reside on your banks) have access to ample rain. You bestow riches upon those who acknowledge and express profusely, their praise for you.

R 71 Richa 7/96/3, मैत्रावरुणिर्विसिष्टः, सरस्वती, प्रस्तारपंक्ति:

For this Richa, the Rishi is Vashishtha. The Devta is Saraswati and the Metre is Prastarpankti.

> भद्रमिद्भद्रा कृणवृत्सरस्वृत्यकंवारी चेतति वाजिनींवती ।
> गृणाना जमदग्निवत्स्तुंवाना चं वसिष्ठवत् ॥7/96/3

Meaning of words/combination of words

भद्रमिद्भद्रा कृणवृत्सरस्वृत्यकंवारी May the auspicious Saraswati bestow promising fortune चेतति वाजिनींवती may she, who moves faultlessly, may who is the food-giving Devi, think of us गृणाना जमदग्निवत्स्तुंवाना चं वसिष्ठवत् you have been praised by Jamadagni, you are now glorified by Vashishtha.

This Richa translates to: 'May the auspicious Saraswati bestow promising fortune upon us. May she, the one who moves free of barriers, the Devi who is bestower of food, think of us (of our needs). You were glorified by Jamadagni, you are now glorified by Vashishtha'.

In this Richa, several qualities of Saraswati are acknowledged. She is herself auspicious. The food she provides is also auspicious. She, that is, her waters, move fast without obstructions. She blesses us with nourishment. This, she has been doing for long. She was praised in the past by Rishi Jamadagni. She is now praised by Rishi Vashishtha. This Richa indicates the long period over which Saraswati flowed in India, and throughout this period, she was praised by Rishis of different generations.

R 72 Richa 7/96/4 मैत्रावरुणिर्विसिष्टः, सरस्वती, गायत्री

For this Richa, the Rishi is Vashishtha. The Devta is Saraswati and the Metre is Gayatri.

> जनीयन्तो न्वग्रवः पुत्रीयन्तः सुदानवः ।
> सरस्वन्तं हवामहे ॥7/96/4

Meaning of words/combination of words

ज़नीयन्तो Desirous of wives पुत्रीयन्तः desirous of progeny सुदानंवः liberal in donations न्वग्रंवः us, approaching him, सरंस्वन्तं हवामहे worship Saraswan.

This Richa translates to: 'Desirous of wives and progeny, liberal in giving donations, we, approaching him, worship Saraswan'.

The purport is that Saraswan, the Devta of oceans and clouds, is the Devta who can give us the blessing of wives and progeny. Let us approach Saraswan and seek his blessings. Saraswan is supposed to have many wives in the form of clouds and progeny in the form of rains. He is thus the ideal Devta for asking for wives and progeny.

R 73 Richa 7/96/5 मैत्रावरुणिर्वसिष्ठः, सरस्वती, गायत्री

For this Richa, the Rishi is Vashishtha. The Devta is Saraswati and the Metre is Gayatri.

> ये तें सरस्व ऊर्मयो मधुंमन्तो घृतश्चुतः ।
> तेभिर्नोऽविता भंव ॥7/96/5

Meaning of words/combination of words

ये तें सरस्व ऊर्मयो with these waves of yours मधुंमन्तो घृतश्चुतः that are sweet and full of ghee (clarified butter) तेभिर्नोऽविता भंव with those, be our protector, O Saraswan.

This Richa translates to: 'With these waves of yours that are sweet and full of ghee (clarified butter), O Saraswan, be our protector'.

Saraswan means not only ocean full of water but also ocean of wisdom. The waves of Saraswan are the thoughts. These thoughts spread out happiness (sweetness) and affection, being full of ghee (clarified butter). With these wise thoughts, O Devta of wisdom, please protect us.

Agriculture in Rigveda: Seeds of India's Civilizational Prosperity

R 74 Richa 7/96/6 मैत्रावरुणिर्वसिष्ठ:, सरस्वती, गायत्री

For this Richa, the Rishi is Vashishtha. The Devta is Saraswati and the Metre is Gayatri.

> पीपिवांसं सरस्वतः स्तनं यो विश्वदर्शतः ।
> भक्षीमहि प्रजामिषम् ॥7/96/6

Meaning of words/combination of words

पीपिवांसं we drink from सरस्वतः स्तनं the breasts of Saraswan यो विश्वदर्शतः who sees the entire universe भक्षीमहि प्रजामिषम् from him, we obtain food and progeny.

This Richa translates to: 'May we drink from the sumptuous breasts of Saraswan, who sees the entire universe, so that we may obtain progeny and food'.

Saraswan is the Devta who refers to ocean, clouds, and wisdom. From the sumptuous breasts of wisdom, we draw wise thoughts and understand the universe. We are then able to propagate our progeny and satisfy our worldly needs.

In the context of the role of water in agriculture and as a basis of human prosperity, it is relevant to discuss the Rastri Sukta given in Mandal 10.

Mandal 10 Sukta 125: The Mysterious Rastri Sukta

The Rastri Sukta, which is the 125th Sukta of the tenth Mandal is a very special Sukta. It is one of the few Suktas in Rigveda which is in first person, a soliloquy. The Rishi is 'वागाम्भृणी', which refers to 'Vak' that is, speech and 'Ambhas' that is bearer of water or mother and 'rni', that is, holder of debt or obligation. The Devta of the Sukta is Atma or self. It is a mysterious Sukta where the Rishi addresses her own self. This Sukta refers to Saraswati in her roles as the Devta of speech, as a river, and as an entity that provides the concept of nationhood. Saraswati is however not explicitly mentioned in this Sukta. This Sukta is about water, water borne trade, agriculture, industry, prosperity and nationhood.

Kalyanaraman (2013)[8] has written elaborately about this Sukta. He refers to 'Rastri' occurring in the third Richa of this Sukta as the feminine form of Rastram, meaning 'nation'. Kalyanaraman observes that this Sukta signifies the navigable Saraswati river, which moves and creates the wealth of a nation, namely, the historic India. The word 'Vagambharni' is a metaphor which consists of three parts. 'Vak' वाच *f.* (fr. √ वच) that is, speech, knowledge or language (also of animals), and sounds, 'Ambhas' अम्भस deriving from अभ्र or अम्ब, which refers to water. The last syllable 'Rni' ऋण is a personification and feminine form of that debt which is owed, or which involves an obligation or duty. Thus, Kalyanaraman summarizes the expression 'Vagambharni' as a metaphor that signifies a knowledge/speech divinity who is a fortress of water and to whom debt is owed. The proclamation of Rishika Vagambharni in this Sukta is that debt is owed by all citizens of a nation because the wealth of a nation is created by that knowledge system and that fortress of water where the cargo of wealth moved on the navigable waterway for exchange, trade, and value creation. These meanings become clearer as we discuss the individual Richas of this powerful Sukta.

Manu, in Manu Samhita (ix.294) defines a nation as having seven limbs or constituent parts (of a kingdom) consisting of the king and his minister, his capital, his realm, his treasury, his army, and his allies. Thus, a kingdom is said to have seven limbs (anga). *[source: https://www.sacred-texts.com/hin/manu/manu09.htm]*

R 75 Richa 10/125/1 वागाम्भृणी, आत्मा, त्रिष्टुप्

For this Richa, the Rishi is Vagambharni. The Devta is her own self. The Metre is Trishtup.

> अहं रुद्रेभिर्वसुभिश्चराम्यहमादित्यैरुत विश्वदेवैः ।
> अहं मित्रावरुणोभा बिंभर्म्यहमिन्द्राग्नी अहमश्विनोभा ॥10/125/1

---

[8] http://bharatkalyan97.blogspot.com/2013/06/sarasvati-is-vagambhrini.html

Meaning of words/combination of words

अहं रुद्रेभिर्वसुभिश्चराम्यहमादित्यैरुत I proceed with Rudras, Vasus and Adityas विश्वदेवैः and all the Devtas अहं मित्रावरुणोभा बिभर्म्यहमिन्द्राग्नी अहमश्विनोभा I support both Mitra and Varuna, Agni and Indra, as well as the two Ashwins.

This Richa translates to: 'I proceed with the Rudras, the Vasus, the Adityas, and all Devtas. I hold aloft, Mitra and Varuna, Agni and Indra, and the two Ashwins'.

In this Richa, there is a basic emphasis on 'movement' or 'flow', the basic feature of Saraswati that is viewed as a divine river. In her movement, all the Devtas participate including the Rudras, Vasus, and Adityas. By her qualities and role, Saraswati holds up the reputation of Devtas such as Mitra, Varun, Agni, Indra, and the Ashwins. Saraswati is in the forefront of all Devtas, providing the flow and force for all their divine activities.

R 76 Richa 10/125/2 वागाम्भृणी, आत्मा, त्रिष्टुप्

For this Richa, the Rishi is Vagambharni. The Devta is her own self. The Metre is Jagati.

> अहं सोममाहनसं बिभर्म्यहं त्वष्टारमुत पूषणं भगम् ।
> अहं दधामि द्रविणं हविष्मते सुप्राव्ये३ यजमानाय सुन्वते ॥10/125/2

Meaning of words/combination of words

अहं 'I', सोममाहनसं foe-destroying Soma, support बिभर्म्यहं and I (also) support त्वष्टारमुत Twashta, पूषणं Pushan and भगम् Bhaga अहं दधामि द्रविणं I give wealth to the हविष्मते सुप्राव्ये३ यजमानाय सुन्वते performer of the Yajna, deserving of careful protection, who provides good offerings for the Devtas.

This Richa translates to: 'I sustain the foe-destroying Soma, as also Twashta, Pushan and Bhaga. I give wealth to the institutor of the Yajna, deserving of careful protection, who pours the Soma juice and provides good offerings'.

Saraswati is the one who supports or sustains all the Devtas. The list includes Soma, Twashta, Pushan and Bhaga. She also rewards with wealth, the performer of the Yajnas and with abundant offerings for the Devtas. Thus, Saraswati supports both Devtas and men.

The expression 'सोममाहनस' combines two words: सोम Soma and आहनस Ahanas, which means 'destroyer of the enemy'. Kalyanaraman argues that it means 'destroyer of the enemy' as well as 'ahangar' that is blacksmith. This is derived from 'asani' that is thunderbolt. We may recall Satyajit Ray's award-winning film, 'Ashuni Sanket' meaning the sign of the thunder. Kalyanaraman further asserts that in addition रुद्रतभवसतभःसोमत्वष्टा पूषणं भगम् are invoked. Such an invocation is an adoration of the creators and promoters of artisans who create wealth. For example, त्वष्टा is the Devta for metals or weapons-makers which also implies a carpenter and makers of carriages.

R 77 Richa 10/125/3 वागाम्भृणी, आत्मा, त्रिष्टुप्

For this Richa, the Rishi is Vagambharni. The Devta is her own self. The Metre is Trishtup.

> अ॒हं रा॒ष्ट्री सं॒ग॒म॒नी॒ वसू॑नां चिकि॒तुषीं प्रथ॒मा य॒ज्ञिया॑नाम् ।
> तां मां दे॒वा व्य॑दधुः पुरु॒त्रा भूरि॑स्थात्रां भूर्या॒वे॒शयं॑न्तीम् ॥10/125/3

Meaning of words/combination of words

अहं राष्ट्री I am the nation (or sovereign of the nation) संगमनी mover of wealth वसूनां of the Earth चिकितुषीं प्रथमा यज्ञियानाम् first to be acknowledged amongst those for whom Yajnas are performed तां मां देवा व्यदधुः Devtas have established me पुरुत्रा भूरिस्थात्रां in many homes and places भूर्याविशयंन्तीम् entering and abiding in numerous forms.

This Richa translates to: 'I am the sovereign owner of the nation, the bearer of treasures, cognizant (of the Supreme Being), the chief of the objects of worship. As such, the Devtas have established me in many places, abiding in manifold conditions, entering into numerous forms'.

Kalyanaraman argues that the metaphor of a navigable waterway is seen in the proclamation 'अहवसना सुंगमंनी:राष्ट्री', which means 'I am the gatherer and mover of the wealth of a nation'. The verb 'गमन' indicates 'to move or to go with'. He argues that the metaphor is that cargo of wealth based on metalworks moves on the navigable waterway and that wealth is signified as indicated by the plural 'gatherer and mover' of wealth. The term 'Vasana' indicates Devtas meaning the 'good or bright ones'.

This is where Saraswati proclaims her sovereignty over the nationhood by asserting that I am the nation 'अहं राष्ट्री'. 'Rashtri' refers to sovereignty which is the basis of the construction and identification of a nation. As referred to earlier, Manu-Smriti defines a 'Rastram', that is nation as consisting of seven main elements or foundations. The relevant descriptions as contained in Manu, Chapter VII, Suktas 155, 156, and 157, are given below. These are also quoted by Kalyanaraman in defining a nation.

"155. On the conduct of the middlemost (prince), on the doings of him who seeks conquest, on the behaviour of the neutral (king), and (on that) of the foe (let him) sedulously (mediate).

156. These (four) constituents (prakriti, form), briefly (speaking), the foundation of the circle (of neighbours) besides, eight others are enumerated (in the Institutes of Polity) and (thus) the (total) is declared to be twelve.

157. The minister, the kingdom, the fortress, the treasury, and the army are five other (constituent elements of the circle) for, these are mentioned in connection with each (of the first twelve. Thus, the whole circle consists), briefly (speaking, of) seventy-two (constituent parts)." [Source https://www.sacred-texts.com/hin/manu/manu07.htm]

R 78 Richa 10/125/4 वागाम्भृणी, आत्मा, त्रिष्टुप्

For this Richa, the Rishi is Vagambharni. The Devta is her own self. The Metre is Trishtup.

> मया॒ सो अन्नमत्ति॒ यो विपश्य॑ति॒ यः प्राणि॑ति॒ य ईं॑ शृणोत्यु॒क्तम् ।
> अ॒म॒न्त॒वो मां त उप॑ क्षियन्ति श्रु॒धि श्रु॑त श्रद्धि॒वं ते॑ वदामि ॥10/125/4

Meaning of words/combination of words

मया॒ through me सो अन्नमत्ति॒ he who eats food यो विपश्य॑ति who sees यः प्राणि॑ति who breathes य ईं॑ शृणोत्यु॒क्तम् and who hears what is spoken, he does so through me अ॒म॒न्त॒वो मां those who are ignorant of me त उप॑ क्षियन्ति they perish श्रु॒धि श्रु॑त listen to me, you who has hearing श्रद्धि॒वं ते॑ वदामि I tell you what is worth believing in.

This Richa translates to: 'He who eats food, (eats) through me, he, who sees, who breathes, and who hears what is spoken, does so, through me, he who is ignorant of me, or does not recognize me, perishes. You, who has hearing, listen to me, I tell you what is worth hearing'.

All faculties of hearing, seeing, breathing, and sustaining oneself by eating derive from the blessings of Saraswati. She is the one who provides the nourishment, which enables all the knowledge-senses and sense-organs to work. Those who do not recognize this, bring themselves to harm.

R 79 Richa 10/125/5 वागाम्भृणी, आत्मा, त्रिष्टुप्

For this Richa, the Rishi is Vagambharni. The Devta is her own self. The Metre is Trishtup.

> अ॒हमे॒व स्व॒यमि॒दं वदा॑मि॒ जुष्टं॑ दे॒वेभि॑रु॒त मानु॑षेभिः ।
> यं का॒मये॒ तंत॑मु॒ग्रं कृ॑णोमि॒ तं ब्र॒ह्माणं॒ तमृषिं॒ तं सु॒मेधा॑म् ॥10/125/5

Meaning of words/combination of words

अहमेव स्वयमिदं वंदामि This knowledge, I myself declare जुष्टं देवेभिरुत मानुषेभिः that is listened with Shraddha (reverence) by Devtas and men यं कामये whoever I wish तंतमुग्रं कृणोमि I render formidable तं making him (or her) ब्रह्माणं a Brahma तमृषिं a Rishi तं सुमेधाम् or a Sage.

This Richa translates to: 'I myself declare this, which is listened to by Devtas as well as men with respect. Whomsoever I wish, I render him (or her) formidable, making him (or her), a Brahma, a Rishi, or a Sage'.

This Richa speaks of the power above Brahma, Devta, or Rishi. Devi Saraswati reveals this knowledge that she has the power to raise the status of any person to that of the Brahman (or to that of the knower of the Brahman), or a Rishi or a Sage. In a physical sense, Ashrams and Gurukuls of many sages were located on the banks of Saraswati. With her blessing, they became great Rishis, wise men, and knowers of the Brahman.

R 80 Richa 10/125/6 वागाम्भृणी, आत्मा, त्रिष्टुप्

For this Richa, the Rishi is Vagambharni. The Devta is her own self. The Metre is Trishtup.

> अहं रुद्राय् धनुरा तंनोमि ब्रह्मद्विषे शरंवे हन्तवा उं ।
> अहं जनाय समदं कृणोम्यहं द्यावांपृथिवी आ विवेश ॥10/125/6

Meaning of words/combination of words

अहं रुद्राय् धनुरा तंनोमि I stretch the bow of Rudra ब्रह्मद्विषे शरंवे हन्तवा उं अहं for destroying the enemy of the Brahman जनाय समदं कृणोम्यहं I wage war with the enemies of my people, and द्यावांपृथिवी आ विवेश I occupy the whole space of Heaven and Earth.

This Richa translates to: 'For slaying the enemy of the Brahman, I bend the bow of Rudra, I wage war with men hostile (to my people), I pervade the whole of Heaven and Earth'.

This Richa highlights the underlying power of Saraswati that is, Vagambharni (वागाम्भृणी). It is that power, which energizes the Devtas and men. With that power, Rudra, with his bow, destroys the enemies (that is, non-believers) of the Brahman, and those hostile to the believers of Brahman who subsist according to the knowledge and principles of the Vedas.

R 81 Richa 10/125/7 वागाम्भृणी, आत्मा, त्रिष्टुप्

For this Richa, the Rishi is Vagambharni. The Devta is her own self. The Metre is Trishtup.

अ॒हं सु॑वे पि॒तरंमस्य मूर्धन्मम॒ योनि॑रप्स्व१॒न्तः संमुद्रे ।
ततो॒ वि ति॑ष्ठे भुव॒नानु॒ विश्वो॒तामूं द्यां व॒र्ष्मणोप॑ स्पृशामि ॥10/125/7

Meaning of words/combination of words

अ॒हं सु॑वे पि॒तरं॑मस्य मूर्धन्मम् I bring forth, this Heaven located at the head of this Earth योनि॑रप्स्व१॒न्तः संमुद्रे my birthplace is in the midst of ocean waters ततो॒ वि ति॑ष्ठे from that place, I spread out भुव॒नानु॒ विश्वो॒तामूं through all beings द्यां व॒र्ष्मणोप॑ स्पृशामि by my raised presence, I touch the Heaven.

This Richa translates to: 'I bring forth, this heaven located upon the head of this Earth. My birthplace is in the midst of the ocean waters. From this place, I spread through all beings, and raise my presence to touch the heaven'.

The purport is that all existence is due to contribution of water, which pervades all beings from Earth/ to heaven. The Rishika and Devta, Vagambharni extends from the centre of the oceans to the skies and heavens, that is, the entire interstellar space, making all beings possible.

R 82 Richa 10/125/8 वागाम्भृणी, आत्मा, त्रिष्टुप्

For this Richa, the Rishi is Vagambharni. The Devta is her own self. The Metre is Trishtup.

अ॒हमे॒व वातं॑ इव॒ प्र वाम्यारभमाणा॒ भुव॒नानि॒ विश्वा॑ ।
प॒रो दि॒वा प॒र एना॑ पृथि॒व्यैताव॑ती महि॒ना सं ब॑भूव ॥10/125/8

Meaning of words/combination of words

अहमेव विश्वां भुवंनानि वांम्यांरभंमाणा I alone, while creating all the worlds वातं
इवु प्र I spread out like wind to give form to all the created worlds पुरो द्विवा
पुर एना पृंथिव्यैतावंती I am beyond the Heaven and beyond the Earth महिना
सं बंभूव so vast I am, in greatness.

This Richa translates to: 'I alone, while creating all worlds, spread out like the wind, giving form to all these created worlds. I am beyond the Heaven and beyond the Earth, so vast I am, in greatness'.

Rishika Vagambharni or Devi Saraswati is the energy of the creator, that is Brahmaji. She is responsible for the creation of all the worlds, all the forms that exist. She spreads out and encompasses the entire universe. She is vaster than all the worlds that are all contained within her.

Historicity of River Saraswati

In recent years, there has been a debate as to whether river Saraswati existed in reality or whether it is only a myth. This debate is now more or less settled in favour of the reality and historicity of river Saraswati. A number of technical researchers, historians, and people drawn from various other disciplines have written at length, on the historicity and existence of Saraswati. Some of the important contributions are Valdiya (2002, 2016), Bakshi (2019), Kalyanaraman (2020), Nilesh Oak (2021)[9], Michel Danino (2010). Gupta et. al. (2004, 2011) has summarized some of the technical details. Their contention is based on numerous studies which have been conducted mostly in the last two to three decades by different experts and agencies for tracing the course(s) of the paleochannels highlighting the path of river Saraswati. These paleochannels are identified based on satellite/sensor and digital image processing technologies. These paleochannels and the extensive data pertaining to these, compiled from alternative investigative techniques confirm the existence of Saraswati without any remaining doubt.

---

[9]https://www.youtube.com/watch?v=zsY4Biuzras; https://www.youtube.com/watch?v=SUHbEmk9oqo; https://www.nature.com/articles/s41598-019-53489-4?fbclid=IwAR2wbUWzzICAW5LXIEe30Oo3UuI8HTPzAnpyHgSeQF0W-TPp21ybhkfr8Ak

Saraswati flowed parallel to the Indus as an independent river system originating from the Himalayas to the ocean, flowing westwards.

The historicity of Saraswati river is confirmed by collating information on the following features or characteristics.

1. Course of river Saraswati
2. Major epochs in the flow of Saraswati
3. Age of Saraswati
4. Rigvaidic references to Saraswati
5. Recent efforts for revival of river Saraswati

1. Course of Saraswati

The course of Saraswati has been worked out by scholars based on satellite imagery which shows a powerful, continuous, and wide drainage system in India's north-west region. Saraswati flowed more or less parallel to the river Indus and shifted its course within a much narrower zone of less than 40 km. The major (western most) channel of river Saraswati remained more or less constant and unchanged and is considered to be the actual Rigvaidic Saraswati river. These channels have features that match with those of the Vaidic Saraswati described in detail in Rigveda. River Saraswati had its major course through present day river Ghaggar and further passing through parts of Jaisalmer and adjoining region in Pakistan and finally discharging into the Rann of Kachchh. A major paleochannel of the river passes through Jaisalmer district while a considerable part of the river drained further, inside Pakistan.

Gupta et. al. (2004) observes: "The present study shows that river Saraswati never took a course to join river Luni. Luni has been from time to time joined by other streams/rivers (of much lower significance than Saraswati, e.g. Drishadvati) which drained along the Aravalli hills."

Figure 2: Course of river Saraswati

Simplified palaeochannel map showing the course of the river Saraswati, which is represented by Channel 1.

Source (Gupta et al, 2011)

The courses mapped in Figure 2 from Gupta et. al. (2011) are listed in order of their location from east to west.

The main Saraswati course: 4–10 km wide, extends from the river Ghaggar via Banawali–Anupgarh–north-west of Beriyanwala–Ganeriwala–west of Nawakot and Islamgarh–Tanot–Laungwalatar–west of Ghotaru–east of Pairewarotar–running parallel to the Indus River–north-east of Khipro– Munabao–east of Islamkot and meets the Rann of Kachchh.

The second major course extends from the river Ghaggar via Banawali–Anupgarh–north-west of Beriyanwala–Rukanpur–Nawakot–west of Islamgarh–Tanot–Laungwalatar–Ghotaru, running parallel to the Nara river and passing via Dhanana–west of Myajlar–Munabao–east of Islamkot and meeting the Rann of Kachch, with a 4–6 km wide channel.

This seems to act as a spillway for the excess waters of the Saraswati to pass through.

A third course originates from the main channel near Bijnot and passes through Bahla–Ratund–Mohangarh–Lanela–Dawa–Devran–Giral–Kanod–Gadra road–east of Munabao–east of Islamkot and meets the main channel east of Munabao, finally discharging into the Rann of Kachch. This channel (only a few hundred metres wide) joins the Kanod, Meetha and Khara Rann as well

The fourth course passes through Hisar–Sewani–Rajgarh–east of Churu–Fatehpur–Kalasar–Didwana–Kuchera–Falodi–Bhopalgarh–east of Taranau–Merta– Pipar–north of Luni–Kalyanpur–Pachpadra, and meets the Rann of Kachch, though a channel via Sirwa or directly through the present course of Luni through Sindari–Gudha and north-west of Sanchor.

The fifth course passes through Loharu–Nawalgarh–Sikar–Maulasi–Degana–Merta– Pipar–north of Luni–Kalyanpur–Pachpadra and meets the Rann of Kachchh through a channel via Sirwa or directly through the present course of Luni through Sindari–Gudha and north-west of Sanchor.

[Source: A. K. Gupta (2011) (downloaded on 15 September 2015) - Satellite imagery revealing an extinct river, Thar Desert, Indo-Pak region 5203]

2. Major Epochs

The river Saraswati, originating in the Himalayas, was a mighty perennial river of the Vaidic period. In the Rigveda, as discussed in this Chapter, it is described as 'Ambitame–Naditame–Devitame' – the 'greatest of Mothers, greatest of Goddesses and greatest of the Rivers'. Discovery of a large number of sites from the pre-Harappan and Harappan civilization along the banks of the Saraswati also indicate the grand size and might of this river. The first two courses (nos. 1 and 2) of paleochannels, originating from the river Ghaggar near Anupgarh in the Ganganagar district of Rajasthan state of India, and passing through the Jaisalmer district and eastern Pakistan (along the international border), have a channel width of about 10 km and, in a few places, about 4 km (compared to the maximum observed width of the Indus flood plains of the order of about 20 km). This matches the expected width of the Saraswati paleochannels if the Saraswati river was a mighty river. Channel 1 is more prominent and forms a well-developed river course joining the Rann of Kachchh as an independent river with no major shift along this course. Also, there is no other major paleo-drainage present in the area. Hence, Gupta et. al. (2011) consider it to be the main course of the extinct Saraswati river. The other paleo-river courses delineated along the Aravalli Hills (nos. 4 and 5) are much thinner, only a few hundred metres wide. These do not signify the grand size of the river Saraswati in the Rigveda and, hence, are considered to be courses of other smaller rivers or streams. Studies indicate some interesting facts. First, river Saraswati flowed as an independent river system parallel to the Indus river and did not change its course significantly and continuously, as suggested by many earlier works (Ghose et al. 1979, Bakliwal and Grover 1988). Second, with reference to Figure 2, the Beriyanwala (in India) route is found to be the main Saraswati channel joining the Rann of Kachchh. The earlier Marot route (in Pakistan) was believed to be the actual Saraswati route. On satellite imagery (Figure 2), prominent dry channels (white tones) can be seen clearly in conjunction with the existing (dark coloured) drainage course of the river Ghaggar westward from the Marot (towards the river Indus). This indicates that these channels must have finally joined with the river Indus and, hence, they cannot represent the course of the river Saraswati. Third, river Saraswati did not flow through the river Nara, as postulated by earlier works (Yashpal et al. 1980). Fourth, the present mapped course of river Saraswati is about 22 km east of the river Nara. After Banawali, downstream of Ghaggar, about 29% (295 km) of the buried course of the river Saraswati falls in the territory of India, while the remaining 71% (644 km) in Pakistan. A number of conclusions can be drawn based on the studies conducted and their discussions. These are given below.

- Clear signs of paleochannels on the satellite imagery in the form of a strong and continuous drainage pattern, approximately 10 kms wide in the Indo-Pak region, and its parallelism with the Indus river, indicate beyond doubt, the existence of a mighty paleo-river in this region.

- The occurrence of archaeological sites of pre-Harappan, Harappan and post-Harappan age along the paleochannels of the river, and the description of such a river in the ancient Indian (Vaidic/post-Vaidic) literature, indicate that the course is that of the river Saraswati. It also indicates the existence of a mighty paleo drainage system of Vaidic Saraswati river in this region. Such archaeological evidence based on human settlements located along the course of Saraswati have mounted in recent years (Figure 3).

- The presence of thin paleo-drainage courses and absence of Harappan sites along the Aravalli Hills, indicates that the river Saraswati never drained along the Aravalli Hills and hence did not shift its course from east to west, as believed by previous researchers.

- Tectonic movements in the Siwalik Hills region, due to uplift of the Himalayas and changes in climatic conditions, were the main cause of the drying of the river Saraswati and drainage desiccation in the region.

- Investigations carried out by the GWD, Rajasthan, indicate that Saraswati paleochannels are the store house of good quality potable water.

Figure 3: Distribution of Harappan settlements

Bhāratam Janam Meluhha settlements on Sarasvati-Sindhu Rivers from ca. 8th m. -2nd m. BCE

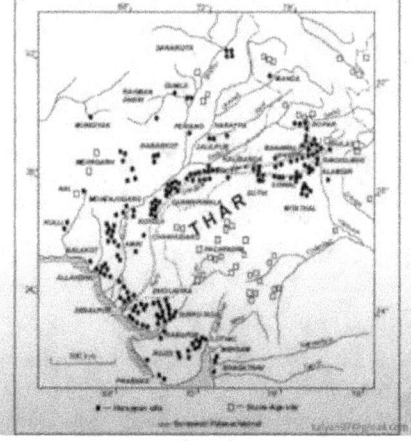

The broadly linear pattern of the distribution of the Harappan settlements (older than 5500 yr B.P. to about 3300 yr B.P.) coincides with the now waterless, sand-choked, extraordinarily wide channel of the Ghaggar-Hakra-Nara [From Valdiya, 2002]. Among the settlements is Ganweriwala, (Fig.6.2) the second biggest metropolis of the time. About 5 m below the Hakra bed the 100m thick sand body in the Fort Abbas reach point to its deposition by a large perennial river (Mughal, 1995). The U-Pb zircon dating demonstrates that the channel was active until about 4500 years B.P. (Clift et al., 2012). Samples of sediments close to the archaeological sites show similarities with the sediments of both the Beas and the Satluj rivers in the west and the Yamuna River in the east (Clift et al., 2012). Giosan et al., (2012) concede that the Yamuna may have contributed sediments to the Hakra before the Mature Harappan time, for they recovered 5300-year old sandy flood deposit at Fort Abbas. In other words, there are tell-tale evidence of the Himalayan rivers Satluj and the Yamuna flowing through the channel of the Ghaggar-Hakra until the Harappan times (Valdiya, 2016). http://jalshakti-dowr.gov.in/sites/default/files/Palaeochannel/ExpertCommittee_15thOct2016_0.pdf (p.75)

Source: a recent Kalyanaraman presentation on Samudramanthan
[link https://youtu.be/XqujleC4siM]

In a recent presentation, Professor B.B. Lal (2008)[10] has highlighted using crop layouts or patterns, the continuity of Indian civilization from the Saraswati times to the modern era. Figures 4 and 5 highlight this continuity. The layout of the land in earlier and present times in a criss-cross manner are clearly comparable.

---

[10] The Saraswati: The mother of Indian civilization. Inaugural address delivered on 24 October 2008 by Prof. BB Lal in the Conference on Vedic River Sarasvati and Hindu Civilization held at India International Centre, New Delhi

Figure 4 and 5: Continuity of Civilization

Source: Extracted from a Lecture given at the National Council of Educational Research and Training (NCERT), New Delhi by B. B. Lal - 'Why Perpetuate Myths?: A Fresh Look at Ancient Indian History' (http://www.geocities.ws/ifihhome/articles/bbl002.html) Around Kalibangan village. Picture on the left (Figure 4) belongs to earlier times showing the system of ploughing the field, which had the criss-cross pattern of furrows. The picture on the right (Figure 5) belongs to the present time field with mustard plants in the widely-distanced furrows and those of chickpea in the others.

3. Age of Saraswati: results from archaeological studies

A large number of archaeological sites have been discovered in the area covered by the Saraswati river basin. More than 1200 of the 1600 settlements including many prosperous towns of Harappan culture (5000–3500 before present) (Mughal, 1980 and 1992, Misra, 1995) and Ashramas of many Rishis (hermitages) existed along banks of Saraswati river (Valdiya, 2002). A large number of sites of Harappan culture have been found in the Saraswati river basin along the paleochannels mapped using satellite remote sensing and other methods (Kalyanaraman,1999). Out of the archaeological sites discovered by the Archaeological Survey of India in the Saraswati river basin, 54 sites of early-Harappan and Harappan period falling in western Rajasthan have been plotted on to the paleo channel map prepared from satellite data to observe if any correlation exists between the two types of data *(Source: Gazetteer of archaeological sites in Possehl, 2002).*

Figure 6: River Saraswati and habitation clusters

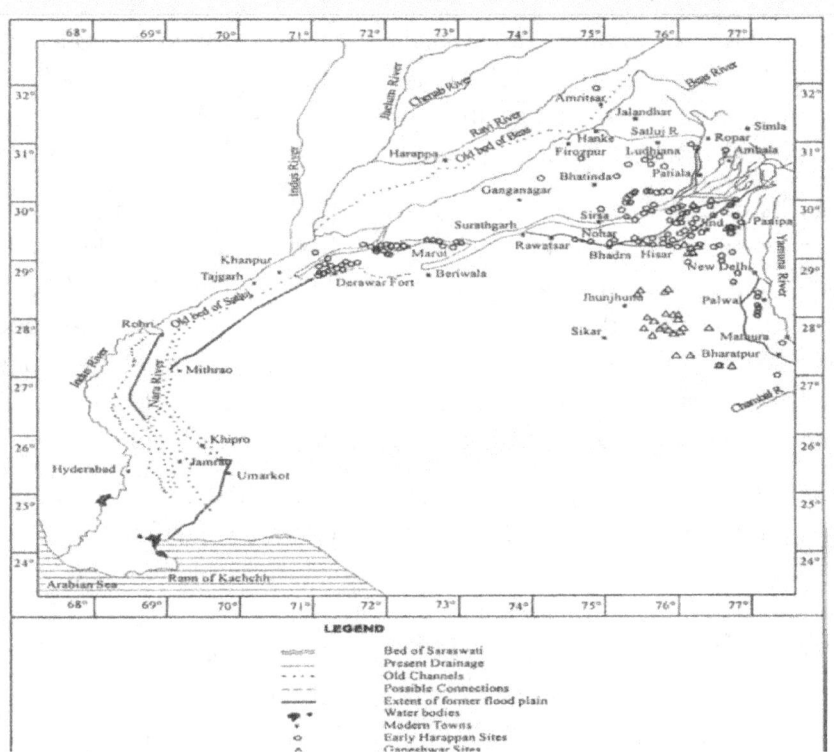

Source: Gupta et al. (2001).

It is observed that most of the archaeological sites of Harappan period discovered in Ganganagar and Hanumangarh districts fall along the Ghaggar river, indicating Ghaggar to be the paleo Saraswati course (Gupta et al., 2001) (Figure 6). More archaeological data of Harappan/pre-Harappan period is however needed from other districts in central part of Thar desert such as Jhunjhunun, Nagaur, Jodhpur, Pali, Barmer, Degana, Ajmer, etc., to confirm the existence of Saraswati paleo channels in these areas. A similar point has been made by Kalyanaraman in a recent presentation (Figure 3).

Age and Quality of Water

Water has been found in tube wells and dug wells along the course of the paleo-channels. This water has been dated using a variety of methods including carbon-dating. Together, these evidences confirm not only the existence of Saraswati but also its age.

Results of drilling analysis of lithology as well as ground water quality and age data obtained from drilling of 14 borewells on the identified paleo channels in Jaisalmer district has confirmed the presence of paleo channels on ground. Results show that the water quality is quite good for most of the drilled wells (Table 5). The quality of ground water along the paleo channels is much better for most of the drilled tube wells, as compared to tube/ dug wells located away from paleo channels.

Table 5: Ground water ages of samples collected along the paleo channels in Jaisalmer and Ganganagar districts, Rajasthan*

ID No.	Location	Well type	^{3}H (TR ± 0.5)	δ^{13}C	14 C ± 1σ (pMC)	Age (BP) (a), UC	Model Age, a (Pearson)
Jaisalmer samples							
D1	Dharmikua	DW	2.1	-9.6	79.5 (2.2)	1900	m
T1	Kishengarh	TW	0.3	-5.7	47.3 (1.4)	6190	m
D3	Kuriaberi	DW	0.5	-8.3	58.8 (1.6)	4390	1340
D4	Nathurakua	DW	0.3	7.9	69.3 (1.8)	3000	m
T2	Ghantiyali	TW	0.5	-4.0	31.2 (1.2)	9630	550
D5	Ghantiyali	DW	0.6	-	54.9 (1.5)	4960	-
D7	Gajesing ka tar	DW	2.1	-7.7	64.9 (1.9)	3570	m
T3	Ranau	TW	0.6	-7.4	48.8 (1.5)	5930	1930
T4	Sadewala	TW	0.4	-7.7	6.6 (0.7)	22450	18800
T5	Loungewala	TW	0.4	-5.6	10.4 (0.9)	18700	12400
T7	Ghotaru	TW	0.4	-7.3	20.7 (1.0)	13000	8910
D12	Ghotaru	DW	1.1	-	62.7 (1.7)	3860	-
T8	Asutar	TW	0.4	-7.5	36.1 (1.3)	8420	4540
D14	Langtala	HP	0.3	-6.2	68.6 (2.0)	3120	m
D15	Langtala	DW	1.0	-	64.8 (1.7)	3590	-
D17	Dostmoh. Kua	DW	1.0	-7.6	49.7 (1.5)	5780	2000
D18	Mituwala	DW	0.6	-11.0	57.9 (1.7)	4520	3800

DW: Dugwell; TW: Tubewell; DCB: Dug cum Bore well; TR: Tritium ratio; pMC: Per cent Modern carbon, UC: Uncorrected; m: Modern

*(Source: Ground Water Department (GWD), Govt. of Rajasthan, Jodhpur. Data analyzed by the BARC, Mumbai, for the GWD)

Source: Gupta et al (2004)

The prominence and the width of the paleo channels on the satellite data are supported by the data from archaeological findings, age and quality of ground water, sediment type, etc., as given in Table 5. The oldest age of water in this table relates to 22450 BP (before present with reference to 2004 when Gupta et. al. was published) pertaining to T4 Sadewala.

A recent Government of India publication[11] has given in full detail, research-based authentic data regarding the historicity of river Saraswati. More discussion on the historicity of river Saraswati, based on this publication, is provided in Appendix 5.

4. Revival of Saraswati

Attempts are being made to revive the Saraswati river. It has now been confirmed that the Saraswati revival project does not require environmental clearance. This clearance was based on documents submitted by the Haryana government in the context of the Saraswati revival project. Around 2300 BCE, the Saraswati river disappeared due to tectonic disturbances, impacting its tributaries (Bhaty, July 2021). At present, those advocating its revival, claim that the river is alive and flowing underground.

Works proposed for reviving Saraswati include the construction of Adi Badri Dam on Somb river, its piped link to the origin of the Saraswati river and the proposed Saraswati reservoir.

According to the state's pre-feasibility report for this project, the Saraswati river system in the Vaidic period included rivers like Ghaggar, Markanda, Chautang, Sutlej and Yamuna. The report referenced studies which have indicated that the Yamuna, as well as Sutlej, were tributaries of Saraswati river but around 3,700 BC, due to tectonic disturbances in the area, Saraswati's Yamuna tributary was diverted to its present course and Sutlej was deflected to the west later while the Saraswati river had started to disappear. The report claimed that the Saraswati originated at Adi Badri, a site of archaeological and religious significance, located

---

[11]http://cgwb.gov.in/Ground-Water/Final%20print%20version_Palaeochannel%20Expert%20Committee_15thOct2016.pdf

around 40 kilometres away from Yamunanagar town of Haryana, at the foothills of the Shivalik mountains, near the Somb river.

The revival project is being considered as a 'heritage project' with additional benefits like groundwater recharge, flood control, fish farming and recreation, and tourism. The concerned Committee also observed that the current project does not involve any components of irrigation or hydropower generation and that it involves infrastructure development and as such, it did not require environmental clearance.

As per latest developments, governments of Haryana and Himachal Pradesh have come together to construct a dam at Adi Badri, the starting point of river Saraswati, to ensure that through a canal, water starts flowing on a permanent basis in the identified channels of river Saraswati[12].

Revival of river Saraswati is crucial for the welfare and growth of modern India since it has been said in Rigveda that the people who lived around Saraswati and whose descendants are the modern Indians are dependent on Saraswati and their welfare and name derives from and (Rigveda 7/96/2). The period over which Saraswati has remained underground is also the period over which the Indian civilization suffered. We should now revive Saraswati to revive India's fortunes. We may also rename Harappan civilization as Saraswati civilization since Harappa was only one of the towns along the Saraswati river and it was also not the oldest one.

The expert committee (2016) setup by government of India to review available evidence on the historicity of Saraswati has made the following recommendations (See Appendix 5).

"The rivers carrying life-supporting-sustaining water and the cultural creations located on their banks must be regarded as prized heritages of

---

[12]https://indianexpress.com/article/india/haryana-himachal-mou-saraswati-river-revival-7732551/

tremendous importance. The archaeological heritage along the paleochannels of once great ancient river known as river Saraswati needs to be protected, preserved and properly safeguarded from modern developments. The most important among this heritage, such as Kalibangan, Banawali, Bhirrana, Baror, Binjor, to name a few, may be developed as centres of academic activities and research, facilitating people from all walks of life to visit all along the paleochannel of ancient river Saraswati from Adibadri to Dholavira.

Those spots where subsurface water has made spontaneous appearance, can then be developed the way the Sabarmati River Front in Ahmadabad has been developed — with gardens, orchards (or sylvan patches) public conveniences and museums. The museums would trace the history and archaeology of the region, house archaeological artefacts from nearby excavated sites, historical documents, virtual walk through and have galleries of photographs and maps portraying the history of the river, of the people and their culture of the place. Souvenir shops at these places will display replicas of most important artefacts, ornaments, jewellery, ceramics, handicrafts, to spread the information of long bustling activity on these rivers.

It may be emphasized that the paleochannels should not be dredged to remove the sediments that fill them or widened to make very smooth facile passage for very slowly moving underground water, as is being done in some places in the name of revival of a legendary river. Apart from causing great loss of the scarce water due to evaporation in the hot, dry land, the exposure of under-surface flowing water would lead to the kind of pollution that has converted the Yamuna and the Ganga into veritable gutters."

Summary and Key Points

India's ancient Rishis recognized the key role of water and its sources for agriculture. They identified rivers, riverbeds, streams, underground wells, and ponds as the main sources of water for the agricultural fields. They also acknowledged the importance of rainfall and in fact, the entire cycle of water from rivers falling into the ocean, evaporation of water, the formation of clouds, followed by rainfall, charging of the wells and underground reservoirs, and flowing back to the ocean through the rivers, thereby completing the cycle. Some of the main points highlighted in this Chapter are summarized below.

- Water is critical for agriculture as well as human body. In both cases, it serves as the main input or resource for sustenance. It is the quality and cleanliness of water used in agriculture or endogenized in human body that serves as critical determinant of human welfare and wellbeing.
- India is a land of a vast network of river systems. It is often characterized as the land of seven main rivers which have been served by a large number of tributaries and distributaries.
- Historically, Indian civilization developed and prospered based on agriculture and habitations that grew at first, on the banks of river Saraswati and afterwards, on the banks of river Sindhu and then river Ganga.
- The historicity of river Saraswati is not in doubt anymore based on satellite imagery regarding paleochannels and archaeological and other supporting data.
- Different sources of water including rain and clouds, glaciers and oceans, and rivers are all visualized as Devtas in Rigveda who are benevolent for mankind. Thus, Devtas like Saraswati and Saraswan, Indra, Varuna, and Parjanya are praised by different Rishis so that mankind can ensure that these sources are kept clean as entities of worship.
- With prosperous agriculture, industry and trade also developed in India along the courses of India's prominent rivers. In fact, these rivers were also used for water borne travel and trade. This interconnected community of farmers, traders, and industrialists gave rise to the concept of 'nationhood' which the Rigvaidic Rishis consider as emanating from river Saraswati.

It is important to recognize the cyclical nature of the flow of water from the ocean, to land through clouds and rainfall and the flowing back of these waters to the ocean through the rivers. All life forms are dependent on the maintenance of this interrelationship between mankind and nature.

Chapter 5 Rainfall and Rain-Devtas

In the context of agriculture, rainfall has always had an important role to play in India from the time of our ancient Rishis to modern days. In Rigveda, there are a number of Richas devoted to the Devtas who have control over rainfall. The main Devta having control over rainfall is Indra. Parjanya, who manages clouds, is another important Devta for controlling rainfall. Maruts or winds are also recognized as Devtas since they have a crucial role to play. One Sukta that is entirely devoted to the subject of rainfall with Parjanya as the Devta is Sukta 83 in Mandal 5. This Sukta has ten Richas that are all devoted to rains.

Parjanya Sukta: Mandal 5 Sukta 83

R 83 Richa 5/83/1 भौमोऽत्रिः, पर्जन्यः, त्रिष्टुप्

For this Richa, the Rishi is Bhauma in the lineage of Rishi Atri. The Devta is Parjanya. The Chanda is Trishtup (in Maharshi Dayananda translated Rigveda, Chanda for this Richa is given as Nichrat Trishtup).

> अच्छां वद तवसं गीर्भिराभिः स्तुहि पर्जन्यं नमसा विवास ।
> कनिक्रदद् वृषभो जीरदानू दधात्योषधीषु गर्भम् ॥5/83/1

Meaning of words/combination of words

तवसं पर्जन्यं For that Parjanya गीर्भिराभिः we, with our voice स्तुहि अच्छां वद (Men you) praise well नमसा विवास bowing down वृषभो who like a strong (bull) कनिक्रदद् जीरदानू the cloud that quickly gives the gift of shower रेतों दधात्योषधीषु गर्भम् by impregnating the plants with rain, saturating them with water and providing nourishment.

This Richa translates as follows: 'We address the mighty Parjanya who is the master of the clouds. We praise him with these Stotras, worshipping him with reverence. He, who is the thunderer, the showerer, and the beautiful, who impregnates the plants with rain'.

Devta Parjanya is the Devta of the rainclouds. He is powerful and he is the one who causes thunders and bestows upon us, showers. The water from these showers nourishes our crops.

R 84 Richa 5/83/2 भौमोऽत्रि:, पर्जन्य:, जगती

For this Richa, the Rishi is Bhauma in the lineage of Rishi Atri. The Devta is Parjanaya. The Chanda is Jagati. (in Maharshi Dayananda translated Rigveda, Chanda for this Richa is given as Swarat Trishtup)

> वि वृक्षान् हन्त्युत हन्ति रक्षसो विश्वं बिभायु भुवनं महावधात् ।
> उतानागा ईषते स्तनयन्हन्तिं यत् पर्जन्यः स्तनयन्हन्तिं दुष्कृतः ॥5/83/2

Meaning of words/combination of words

वृक्षान् the trees हन्त्युत (he) strikes down हन्ति रक्षसो destroys the Rakshasas विश्वं बिभायु terrifies the whole world भुवनं महावधात् his mighty weapon दुष्कृतं the wicked स्तनयन्हन्तिं kills while thundering or making great noise स्तनयन्हन्तिं maker of rain उतानागा ईषते and intends to protect the innocent.

This Richa translates to: 'He strikes down the trees, he destroys the Rakshasas, he terrifies the whole world with his mighty weapon. Even the innocent men run away from the sender of the rain, when Parjanya, thundering, slays the wicked'.

This Richa implies that the great rain Devta distinguishes between the wicked and the innocent. He protects the innocent and does not spare the wicked.

R 85 Richa 5/83/3 भौमोऽत्रि:, पर्जन्य:, जगती

For this Richa, the Rishi is Bhauma in the lineage of Rishi Atri. The Devta is Parjanaya. The Chanda is Jagati. (in Maharshi Dayananda translated Rigveda, Chanda for this Richa is given as Bhurik Trishtup)

> रथीव कशयाश्वाँ अभिक्षिपन्नाविर्दूतान् कृणुते वर्ष्याँ अह ।
> दूरात् सिंहस्यं स्तनथा उदीरते यत् पर्जन्यः कृणुते वर्ष्यं१ नभः ॥5/83/3

Agriculture in Rigveda: Seeds of India's Civilizational Prosperity

Meaning of words/combination of words

रथीव् like a charioteer, कशयाश्वाँ using a whip, drives the horses अभिक्षिपन्नाविर्दूतान् कृणुते वृष्ट्य्ाँ rapidly falling streams of water makes them visible दूरात् from a distance स्तनथा roars सिंहस्यं of a lion उदीरते are heard यत् when पर्जन्यः कृणुते वर्ष्यं नभः Parjanya makes rain in the sky.

This Richa translates to: 'Like a charioteer, urging his horses with his whip brings into view, the messenger of war, so Parjanya (driving the clouds in front of him), makes clouds, who are the messenger of rain, explicit. The clouds, roaring like a lion, proclaims from afar that Parjanya covers all the skies with rains'.

The purport is that the coming of impending rain is pre-announced with thunder and lightning when the skies become overcast. Let men find shelter or be ready for using the rainwater.

R 86 Richa 5/83/4 भौमोऽत्रिः, पर्जन्यः, जगती

For this Richa, the Rishi is Bhauma in the lineage of Rishi Atri. The Devta is Parjanya. The Chanda is Jagati. (in Maharshi Dayananda translated Rigveda, Chanda for this Richa is given as Nichrat Trishtup)

> प्र वाता वान्ति पतयन्ति विद्युत उदोषधीर्जिहंते पिन्वंते स्वः ।
> इरा विश्वस्मै भुवनाय जायते यत् पर्जन्यः पृथिवीं रेतसावति
> ॥४॥5/83/4

Meaning of words/combination of words

वाता Winds वान्ति blow विद्युत lightning पतयन्ति flash or fall उदोषधीर्जिहंते औषधीः जिहते plants start drinking water or spring up पिन्वंते स्वः skies or firmament starts gathering strength इरा पृथिवीं this Earth विश्वस्मै भुवनाय for the welfare of the world यत् पर्जन्यः when Parjanya (cloud); रेतसावति full of semen goes towards.

This Richa translates to: 'The winds blow strong, the lightnings flash, the plants spring up, the firmament dissolves. The Earth becomes fit for all creatures when clouds fertilise the soil with showers'.

The implication is that clouds full of the capacity to fertilize the Earth make the skies look as if they are gathering strength. At that time, winds blow and lightnings flash. Then plants draw nourishment from water for the welfare of the world. The Earth has been made ready for life in different forms including plants and biological life.

R 87 Richa 5/83/5 भौमोऽत्रि:, पर्जन्य:, त्रिष्टुप्

For this Richa, the Rishi is Bhauma in the lineage of Rishi Atri. The Devta is Parjanya. The Chanda is Trishtup.

> यस्यं व्रते पृथिवी नन्नमीति यस्यं व्रते शफवज्जभुरीति ।
> यस्यं व्रत ओषधीर्विश्वरूपा: स न: पर्जन्य महि शर्म यच्छ ॥5/83/5

Meaning of words/combination of words

यस्यं Whose व्रते action or sacrifice पृथिवी Earth नन्नमीति becomes fertile यस्यं whose व्रते action or sacrifice शफवज्जभुरीति all beings become nourishes यस्यं व्रत whose action ओषधीर्विश्वरूपा: plants take various forms स so that न: for us पर्जन्य cloud महि शर्म यच्छ gives abundant happiness.

This Richa translates to 'May you, Parjanya, through whose function the Earth is bowed down, through whose function hoofed cattle (or all beings) thrive, through whose function plants assume all kinds of forms, grant us great felicity (or happiness)'.

This Richa is an acknowledgement of the role that clouds play by carrying water and providing nourishment to plants and animals. This rainwater when combined with the soil and its fertility leads to an extensive variety of plants which serve both mankind and the vast animal world around men, weaving nature, men, and animals, in a tight link of interdependence, which is critical for human sustenance and happiness.

Agriculture in Rigveda: Seeds of India's Civilizational Prosperity

R 88 Richa 5/83/6 भौमोऽत्रिः, पर्जन्यः, त्रिष्टुप्

For this Richa, the Rishi is Bhauma in the lineage of Rishi Atri. The Devta is Parjanya. The Chanda is Trishtup.

> दिवो नों वृष्टिं मरुतो ररीध्वं प्र पिन्वत वृष्णो अश्वस्य धाराः ।
> अर्वाङ्‌एतेनं स्तनयित्‍नुनेह्यपो निषिञ्चन्नसुरः पिता नः ॥५/८३/६

Meaning of words/combination of words

मरुतो O Devtas of winds नों for us दिवो वृष्टिं ररीध्वं give rain from the skies प्र वृष्णो अश्वस्य धाराः streams from water carrying clouds पिन्वत nourish अर्वाङ्‌एतेनं come towards नः us स्तनयित्‍नुनेह्यपो with these thundering clouds निषिञ्चन्नसुरः send rain पिता our guardian.

This Richa translates to 'Send down for us, O Maruts, divine rain from Heaven. May drops of rainy charger (horse) descend. May Parjanya come down, sprinkling water by this thundering cloud. You are the sender of rain, you are our protector'.

This Richa describes that the clouds are formed from the evaporation of water from the seas and on the Earth. This water gets cleaned in rising up by the intervention of sunlight. It is blown up and down, as it rides on the clouds that are compared with horses who travel with speed by the help of winds so that it may be purified. Then this divine and purified water is sprinkled back on the Earth, leading to creation and sustenance of life.

R 89 Richa 5/87/7 भौमोऽत्रिः, पर्जन्यः, त्रिष्टुप्

For this Richa, the Rishi is Bhauma in the lineage of Rishi Atri. The Devta is Parjanya. The Chanda is Trishtup. (in Maharshi Dayananda translated Rigveda, Chanda for this Richa is given as Virat Trishtup)

> अभि क्रन्द स्तनय गर्भमा धां उद्न्वता परि दीया रथेन ।
> दृतिं सु कर्ष विषितं न्यञ्‌चं समा भवन्तूद्वतो निपादाः ॥५/८३/७

Meaning of words/combination of words

अभि क्रन्द Cry, that is, make noise स्तनय thunder and गर्भमा धा implant seeds in the trees उदन्वता in the form of water परि दीया go all around रथेन in a chariot like the cloud दृतिं pitcher full of water सु कर्षं न्यञ्चं empty down in the best way विषितं सुमा equalize भवन्तूद्व्रतों निपादाः up and down.

This Richa may be translated as 'Cry aloud over the Earth, thunder, impregnate the plants, traverse the sky with your water laden chariot, draw upon the tight-fastened, down-turned water bag, and may the high and low places be made level'.

The purport is that clouds express themselves by raining down, thereby completing a cycle of water from the oceans, Earth, and rivers, rising up to the sky in the form of vapour. In that process, all the dirt and infirmities are removed. Clean and high-quality water is then returned to the Earth in the form of rains which fall on mountains, valleys and plains. From there, they flow back to the rivers or are absorbed in the soil under the Earth. The extent to which it is retained under the Earth depends on the trees and plants and their roots. That water which flows through the river is also absorbed partly in the land on the two banks of the river. But a good part of the rainwater is returned to the seas and the cycle is restarted. The Richa asserts that again and again, water is distributed across different parts of the Earth according to their needs. This entire process is itself conceived as a Yajna. Clouds are metaphorically compared to horses or chariots, majestic and prone to speedy movement, so that they can cover a lot of ground and distribute their benefit in the form of water equally across the fields. Rain that falls on high ground then flows down to the lower grounds, thereby giving both plains and hills, equal benefit.

Agriculture in Rigveda: Seeds of India's Civilizational Prosperity

R 90 Richa 5/83/8 भौमोऽत्रिः, पर्जन्यः, त्रिष्टुप्

For this Richa, the Rishi is Bhauma in the lineage of Rishi Atri. The Devta is Parjanya. The Chanda is Trishtup. (in Maharshi Dayananda translated Rigveda, Chanda for this Richa is given as Bhurik Pankti)

म॒हान्तं॑ कोश॒मुद॑चा॒ नि षि॑ञ्च स्यन्द॑न्तां कु॒ल्या वि॒षिता॑ः पुरस्तात् ।
घृ॒तेन॒ द्यावा॑पृथि॒वी व्यु॑न्धि सुप्रपा॒णं भ॑वत्व॒घ्न्याभ्यः ॥5/83/8

Meaning of words/combination of words

म॒हान्तं॑ Greatly extended कोश॒मुद॑चा॒ open the treasure नि downwards षि॑ञ्च flow स्यन्द॑न्तां कु॒ल्या वि॒षिता॑ः rivers full of water पुरस्तात् may proceed towards the east घृ॒तेन॒ with water द्यावा॑पृथि॒वी Heaven and Earth व्यु॑न्धि fill up सुप्रपा॒णं high quality water for drinking भ॑वत्व॒घ्न्याभ्यः and for cattle.

This Richa translates to: 'O greatly extended Devta of clouds, raise on high and mighty sheath of rain, pour down its contents, let the rivers flow unimpeded towards the east. Saturate with water, both Heaven and Earth, and let there be abundant water for drinking and for the use of kine'.

The Rishi praises the Devta of clouds by saying that you are large, please carry along with you, great amount of water. Bring forth abundant rain, so that when you empty this water downwards, rivers on Earth flowing eastwards become full and run towards the east. This water may be used by both Devtas in Heaven and men and the cattle on Earth.

R 91 Richa 5/83/9 भौमोऽत्रिः, पर्जन्यः, अनुष्टुप्

For this Richa, the Rishi is Bhauma in the lineage of Rishi Atri. The Devta is Parjanya. The Chanda is Anushtup. (in Maharshi Dayananda translated Rigveda, Chanda for this Richa is given as Nichrat Anushtup)

यत् पर्जन्य॒ कनि॑क्रदत् स्तन॒यन्हंसि॑ दुष्कृतः ।
प्रती॒दं विश्वं॑ मोद॒ते यत् किं च॑ पृथि॒व्यामधि॑ ॥९॥5/83/9

Meaning of words/combination of words

यत् When पर्जन्य clouds कनिक्रदत् thundering and making great noise स्तनयन्हंसिं दुष्कृतं: destroys evil-doers and यत् when प्रतीदं विश्वं किं चं पृथिव्यामधि whatever is there in this world मोदते becomes happy.

This Richa translates to: 'When Parjanya Devta, sounding loud and with thundering clouds, you destroy the wicked ones, the whole world and all that is upon the Earth, rejoices'.

This Richa implies that with the coming of rain, which comes along with the loud noise of thunder, the evil doers, that is bacteria causing diseases, are destroyed and the beings on Earth become happy.

R 92 Richa 5/83/10 भौमोऽत्रि:, पर्जन्य:, त्रिष्टुप

For this Richa, the Rishi is Bhauma in the lineage of Rishi Atri. The Devta is Parjanya. The Chanda is Trishtup. (in Maharshi Dayananda translated Rigveda, Chanda for this Richa is given as Bhurik Pankti)

> अवर्षीर्वर्षमुदु षू गृंभायाऽकर्धन्वान्यत्येतवा उं ।
> अजीजन् ओषधीर्भोजनायु कमुत प्रजाभ्योंऽविदो मनीषाम् ॥5/83/10

Meaning of words/combination of words

अवर्षीर्वर्षमुदु You have rained enough उं now षू गृंभाय pull back your rain कर्धन्वान्यत्येतवा you have made even deserts flow with water अजीजन् ओषधीर्भोजनायु for eating happily you have enabled plants to grow कमुत प्रजाभ्योंऽविदो मनीषाम् and received praises from people, your subjects.

This Richa translates to the following: 'You have rained enough, even the deserts are flowing with water. Now stop the rain. You have given birth to plants so that men can happily feed themselves. You have also obtained praises from the people'.

The purport is that now the rainy season is towards its end and it has rained enough. Even the deserts have become wet. Plants can grow profusely giving ample grain for men to eat. O rain-god, please stop now, otherwise there would be an excess and floods.

Agriculture in Rigveda: Seeds of India's Civilizational Prosperity

Thus, Mandal 5, Sukta 83 is devoted entirely to the rain-Devta, that is Parjanya, and the wind Devtas that is Maruts. In the next two Suktas - 84 and 85, in some of the Richas, this theme is continued.

R 93 Richa 5/84/3 भौमोऽत्रि:, पृथिवी, अनुष्टुप्

For this Richa, the Rishi is Bhauma in the lineage of Rishi Atri. The Devta is Earth that is Prithvi. The Chanda is Anushtup. (in Maharshi Dayananda translated Rigveda, Chanda for this Richa is given as Virat Anushtup)

> दृळ्हा चिद् या वनस्पतीन् क्ष्मया दर्धर्ष्योजसा ।
> यत् ते अभ्रस्य विद्युतो दिवो वर्षन्ति वृष्टय: ॥5/84/3

Meaning of words/combination of words

यत् When ते on you दिवो of the Heaven, stationed in heaven अभ्रस्य clouds विद्युतो वर्षन्ति वृष्टय: persuaded by lightning, rain pours down या then दृळ्हा चिद् क्ष्मया your steadfast strength दर्धर्ष्योजसा sustains with great power वनस्पतीन् trees and plants.

This Richa translates to: 'O Prithvi (Earth) for whom, the showers of the heavenly clouds fall from the shining sky, you sustain with your solid strength and great power, all the trees and plants'.

The purport is that trees and plants have their roots in the solid Earth. When rain falls on the Earth, trees and plants draw nourishment from the Earth remaining firmly rooted.

There is another reference to rains in the next Sukta.

R 94 Richa 5/85/3 भौमोऽत्रि:, वरुण, त्रिष्टुप्

For this Richa, the Rishi is Bhauma in the lineage of Rishi Atri. The Devta is Varuna. The Chanda is Trishtup. (in Maharshi Dayananda translated Rigveda, Chanda for this Richa is given as Nichrat Trishtup)

> नीचीनंबारं वरुण: कवन्धं प्र ससर्ज रोदसी अन्तरिक्षम् ।
> तेन विश्वस्य भुवनस्य राजा यवं न वृष्टिर्व्युनत्ति भूम ॥5/85/3

Meaning of words/combination of words

वरुंण: Lord Varuna रोदंसी अन्तरिक्षम् for the welfare of the Earth and Heaven कवंध्नं clouds प्र संसर्जं नीचीनंबारं opened up in the downward direction वृष्टिर्युनत्ति भूमं watering the soil यवं न and the barley for us तेनं राजा विश्वंस्य् भुवंनस्य् that is why he is the monarch of all the world and the universe.

This Richa translates to: 'Varuna has set free the waters contained in the clouds through their downward opening for the benefit of Heaven and Earth, watering the soil as the rain bedews the barley. That is why, he is the monarch of all the world and the universe'.

The purport is that Varuna Devta works for the welfare of the Earth as well as the entire universe. He has enabled the clouds to gather water and subsequently released them so that they can come down from the skies and wet the soil, enabling barley to grow. It is by facilitating this process of growth and nourishment, that Varuna Devta is the monarch of Heaven and Earth.

In the next Sukta in Mandal 5, there is a request that food be given to those who are deserving, that is those who are pious and who worship Varuna.

R 95 Richa 5/86/6 भौमोऽत्रि:, इन्द्राग्नी, विराट् पूर्व

For this Richa, the Rishi is Bhauma in the lineage of Rishi Atri. The Devtas are Indra and Agni. The Chanda is Virat Poorva.

> एवेन्द्राग्निभ्यांमहांवि हव्यं शूष्यं घृतं न पूतमद्रिभिः ।
> ता सूरिषु श्रवों बृहद्द्वयिं गृणत्सुं दिधृतमिषं गृणत्सुं दिधृतम् ॥5/86/6

Meaning of words/combination of words

एव In this way शूष्यं invigorating, giving strength घृतं न like ghee (clarified butter) पूतमद्रिभिः made pious by preparing through the rubbing of stones हव्यं offering of juice इन्द्राग्निभ्यांमहांवि offered oblation for Indra and Agni ता these two Devtas सूरिषु गृणत्सुं learned and qualified दिधृतम् give, bestow upon श्रवों बृहद्द्रयिं fame and great wealth इष गृणत्सुं दिधृतम् give food to those who praise you.

The Richa may be translated as: 'The invigorating praise has been offered to Indra and Agni. The offering of (Soma) juice has been duly prepared by the rubbing of stones. Both of you, please bestow fame and great riches upon the pious and the learned, and give (ample) food to those who praise you'.

The purport of this Richa is that Devtas like Indra and Agni also draw upon the juices whose production is possible by the process of rains and agricultural growth. As such, these Devtas whose praises are sung by mankind in the Richa should make people satisfied with what they have. All deserving people that is people who are learned and who are able to praise the Devtas in the Yajnas should be able to procure enough food for their needs. In fact, it is because of these Yajnas that by the blessings of the Devtas, food has become available for mankind in general.

In the next Richa, we take note of the recognition by the Rishis, that it is from one seed, abundant crops are grown and mankind is blessed with unlimited food. This acknowledgement comes in Mandal 1, Sukta 25, Richa 15.

In this Sukta, the Rishis are in the lineage of Vishwamitra by the name of Ajigarti (आजीगर्तिः), Shunah (शुनः), Shepah (शेपः), Kritrima (स कृत्रिमो) वैश्वामित्रो who are the descendants of Vishwamitra and Devrata (देवरातः). The Devta for this Richa is Varuna (वरुणः). Shunah-Shepah also refers to a star constellation *(See Bhaty, 2021)*. The specific Richa is given below.

R 96 Richa 1/25/15 आजीगर्तिः शुनः शेपः स कृत्रिमो वैश्वामित्रो देवरातः, वरुणः, गायत्री

For this Richa, the Rishis are Ajigarti, Shunah-Shepah, Kritrima and Devrata in the lineage of Vishwamitra. Devta is Varuna. Chanda is Gayatri.

> उत यो मानुंषेष्वा यशांश्चक्रे असाम्या ।
> अस्माकंमुदरेष्वा ॥1/25/15

Meaning of words/combination of words

उत् यो Who has मानुषेष्वा among men spread out यशं fame चक्रे and accomplished this unparalleled turning of the wheel (the cycle of life or the cycle of creation) अस्माकंमुदरेष्वा similarly, he has made this beautiful construction of our stomachs *[so that food can be digested for our nourishment]*, which also functions like a cycle.

This Richa translates to: 'Who but Varuna Devta has accomplished this unparalleled feat of the turning of the wheel. This cycle pervades the working of our stomachs as well as the whole creation'.

In this Richa, the praise is for Varuna Devta, who runs the wheel of creation. He has given fame to men. He is responsible for the cyclical movements of stomach so that food is digested, and nourishment creates energy. He is also responsible for the cyclicality of rainfall, water running into the oceans, evaporating, and becoming clouds and rainfall again.

With a view to serving Indra, Somaras is to be offered so that Indra ensures ample rains and victory over enemies.

Mandal 1 Sukta 2

R 97 Richa 1/2/4 मधुच्छन्दा वैश्वामित्रः, इन्द्र-वायु, गायत्री

For this Richa, the Rishi is Madhuchanda, son of Vishwamitra. Devtas are Indra and Vayu. The Chanda is Gayatri.

इन्द्रवायू इमे सुता उप प्रयोभिरा गंतम्।
इन्दवो वामुशन्ति हि ॥1/2/4

Meaning of words/combination of words

इन्द्रवायू Devtas Indra and Vayu इमे सुता these praises are for you उप प्रयोभिरा गंतम् flow out in abundance इन्दवो this Soma juice वामुशन्ति हि that awaits for you.

Agriculture in Rigveda: Seeds of India's Civilizational Prosperity

This Richa translates to: 'Indra and Vayu, these preparations are poured out for you. Come to us with food (for us) and the drops (of Soma juice) await you both'.

The purport is that Indra and Vayu Devtas are praised through Yajnas by mankind so that they may come with ample food when they arrive. Upon their arrival, men would serve them with abundant and well-prepared Soma juice.

R 98 Richa 7/22/6 मैत्रावरुणिर्वसिष्ठ:, इन्द्र:, विराट्

For this Richa, the Rishi is Vashishtha. Devta is Indra. Chanda is Virata.

भूरि हि ते सवना मानुषेषु भूरिं मनीषी हवते त्वामित्।
मारे अस्मन्मंघवञ्ज्योक्कं: ॥7/22/6

Meaning of words/combination of words

भूरि हि ते सवना मानुषेषु Among men, there are many places for preparing the Somaras भूरिं मनीषी हवते त्वामित् there are many knowledgeable people who perform Yajnas for you मारे अस्मन्मंघवञ्ज्योक्कं: Hey Maghavan (Indra Devta) therefore do not be far away from us or away from us for long.

This Richa translates to: 'Many are the Yajnas offered, O Maghavan (Indra), to you by mankind. The worshipper constantly invokes you. Therefore, do not be far away from us nor stay away from us for a long time'.

This Richa implies that Indra is the Devta for various blessings but importantly for rainfall and water. Rishis beseech that he may never be far away because communities that live on the banks of river Saraswati are always engaged in performing Yajnas in praise of Indra so that he may remain close to these communities who will always remain blessed by him. All non-believers in Devtas or Yajnas may go away to far distances.

Seasons in Indian Agriculture

In Rigveda as well as Atharvaveda, there is an acknowledgement of different seasons that influence agricultural crops and outputs. The next two Mantras are taken from Atharvaveda.

M 12 Atharvaveda Mantra 12/1/36, अथर्वन्, भूमि, विपरीतपादलक्ष्मापांक्ति:

For this Mantra, the Rishi is Atharvan. The Devta is Bhumi (Earth or land). The Chanda is Vipareetpadalakshmapanktih.

> ग्रीष्मस्ते भूमे वर्षाणि शरद्धेमन्तः शिशिरो वसन्तः।
> ऋतवस्ते विहिता हायनीरहोरात्रे पृथिवी नो दुहाताम् ॥ 12/1/36

Meaning of words/combination of words

ग्रीष्मस्ते भूमे On this land, summer वर्षाणि rains शरद्धेमन्तः Sharad and Hemant (winter and autumn) शिशिरो Shishir वसन्तः Vasant (Spring) ऋतवस्ते these (six) seasons विहिता have been established हायनीरहोरात्रे during day and night पृथिवी O Earth नो दुहाताम् keep us happy and fulfilled.

This Mantra translates to: 'On this land, six seasons namely, summer, rains, pre-winter, winter, autumn, and spring, have been established. May this Earth keep us happy and fulfilled during days and nights of all of these seasons'.

This Richa recognizes that in India, six seasons have been recognized since the Vaidic times. In fact, India is the only country where six seasons have been recognized. The distinction amongst these seasons is important for the choice of crops and the methods or ways through which these different seasonal crops are to be nursed so that output is always abundant and nourishing. This will keep the population happy and satisfied. The variation in the seasons is linked to changes in weather which in turn is linked to changes in the external atmosphere and planetary arrangements. This variability makes the production of different crops possible. The Devta of this Richa, that is land, may enable us to remain happy and well-provided during all the times characterized by these different seasons.

M 13 Atharvaveda Mantra 12/1/42 अथर्वन्, भूमि, स्वरादनुष्टुप्

For this Mantra, the Rishi is Atharvan. The Devta is Bhumi (Earth or land). The Chanda is Swaradunushtup.

> यस्यामन्नं व्रीहियवौ यस्यां इमाः पञ्च कृष्टयः।
> भूम्यै पर्जन्यपत्न्यै नमोः स्तु वर्षमेदसे ॥ 12/1/42

Meaning of words/combination of words

यस्यामन्नं In which land various grains such as व्रीहियवौ rice and barley यस्यां where इमाः पञ्च these five types of people namely, learned people, warriors, traders, people with skills, and workers devoted to service कृष्टयः live भूम्यै पर्जन्यपत्न्यै that land which is nursed by rains वर्षमेदसे where by rains, various grains are produced नमोः स्तु our praise or worship is to that land.

This Mantra translates to: 'Praise be to that land, where different grains such as rice and barley are produced, where five types of people live, which is nursed by the Parjanya Devta, where various grains are produced by rains.

In this Atharvaveda Mantra, that land contained by the run of the ninety plus rivers is praised which is nursed by ample rain and with such rains, grains like rice and barley are produced for the five types of people who reside on this land. In Rigveda and Atharvaveda, often five (not four) types of people are referred to. These are learned people, warriors, traders, workers who do work requiring skills, and workers who are desirous of serving. Alternatively, these refer to five peoples who are descendants of Yayati namely, Puru, Yadu, Turvasa, Anu, and Druhyu.

The seasons of farming, are described in short, in Taitiriya Samhita (7/2,10.2) which may be translated as: *'It (wheat) gets ripe in summer. Without doubt, it must have been sown during the winter season. Similarly, rice gets ripe in autumn while it was sown at the beginning of* the rainy season. 'Mash' (Urad) and 'Til' (sesamum) are sown during rains in the summer season. They get ripe as winter sets in.' These practices continue even in modern India. Other crops are also mentioned in Taitiriya Samhita.

Yajna of Creation: Place of Foodgrains and Rainfall

Rainfall requires divine intervention. In fact, food grains and rainfall are a critical part of the cycle of creation and existence, inseparable from the Brahman, the Supreme Being, the Creator.

G 9 Srimad Bhagvad Gita: Chapter 3, Shloka 14

In Srimad Bhagvad Gita, Sri Krishna says:

> अन्नाद्भवन्ति भूतानि पर्जन्यादन्नसम्भवः।
> यज्ञाद्भवति पर्जन्यो यज्ञः कर्मसमुद्भवः॥ 3-14

This Shloka means: 'From food grains, all living beings are born and sustained. Food grains become possible by rains. Rains come from Yajnas. Yajnas, with which Devtas are propitiated, are performed by the performance of (prescribed) karmas by men'.

G 10 Srimad Bhagvad Gita: Chapter 3, Shloka 15

> कर्म ब्रह्मोद्भवं विद्धि ब्रह्माक्षरसमुद्भवम्।
> तस्मात्सर्वगतं ब्रह्म नित्यं यज्ञे प्रतिष्ठितम्॥ 3-15

This Shloka means: 'Karmas, that is action, result from the energy of Brahman. Brahman himself emanates from the immutable Supreme Being. Therefore, the all-pervading Brahman, is constantly established in all Yajnas'. This process is continued in the next Shloka.

G 11 Srimad Bhagvad Gita: Chapter 3, Shloka 16

> एवं प्रवर्तितं चक्रं नानुवर्तयतीह यः।
> अघायुरिन्द्रियारामो मोघं पार्थ स जीवति॥ 3-16

This Shloka means: 'This is how this circularity of interdependence has been established. That person, who does not acknowledge or pursue this cycle, becomes a slave of his sense-organs, and wastes his life, remaining disconnected from the Brahman'.

Together these three Shlokas in Chapter 3 of Srimad Bhagwad Gita indicate the way in which the wheel of nature operates. The recognition of this cycle which links rainfall, food grains, birth of humans, performance of Yajnas, generation of Karmas, and the presence of Brahman himself emanating from the immutable Supreme being, is essential and valuable for human beings. It uplifts the activity of agriculture to a divine status, the status of a Yajna. Figure 7 describes this process of interlinkage.

Figure 7: Yajna of Creation

Source: Author's presentation

Summary and Key Points

This Chapter has focused on the role of rainfall in agriculture specifically and human life in general. Physical bodies of mankind and in fact, all lifeforms, have water as the main ingredient. This endogenized water content has a spontaneous harmony with water available in different forms in nature. Water is present in oceans, rivers, glaciers, and underground. All of these water bodies are interlinked in a cyclical way. A cycle is created with the interplay of sunlight and water. Sunlight converts water available on Earth into steam and then clouds which are reverted back to Earth through rainfall. This entire cycle is praised as a Devta in Sukta 5/83 of Rigveda. The presiding Devta for this process is Parjanya. It is the recognition of this cycle and the knowledge pertaining to this which can be considered as the Yajna. In this Yajna, life forms are sustained by the interplay of natural forces which leads to edible forms of food through the agricultural activities. The main points of this Chapter are summarized below.

> Parjanya as the Devta of clouds, is to be praised if rainfall is to be aligned with the needs of mankind for his agricultural activities.
> Knowledgeable Rishis such as Parashar (see Appendix 1 A.1) had developed a methodology based on astronomical parameters for predicting the timing and volume of rainfall according to specific areas.
> Yajnas performed in the praise of Parjanya may enable profuse rainfall as and when required.
> Rainfall not only ensures growth of agricultural crops but growth and sustenance of trees and plant life in general which flourishes in the rainy seasons.
> With the coming of rain along with the noise of thunder, bacteria causing diseases are also destroyed. Evil spirits are subdued, and Earth as a whole becomes happier. Along with

Earth, mankind, cattle, and animal life in general become healthier and happier.

In fact, this natural cycle relating to the process of formation of clouds and rainfall has been extended to a bigger cycle of interlinkages for life itself which is interpreted as a Yajna in Srimad Bhagwad Gita.

Chapter 6 Forms of Agri-wealth: Food grains, Cattle, and Land

In this Chapter, we look at the importance of food and food grains as visualized and emphasized by the Rishis. Grains constitute both the input and output of agriculture. Stored safely, these constitute capital stock. That part of output, which is not consumed, becomes next year's investment. Grains carry with them, the necessary genetic information, which enables the seed, when planted into soil and nursed with water and other supporting inputs, to grow back into a plant, which can reproduce the seed with which it started. Food grains are key to giving birth and sustaining the progeny of the population living on the banks of Saraswati and other rivers mentioned in the Rigveda.

Food grains, Cattle, Fertile Land as Forms of Wealth

Food grains are a form of wealth in the Rigvaidic civilization. These are also an important link in the cycle of human effort, agriculture, interface with nature and the animal world, human prosperity, and progress. Land is also a form of agri wealth. Animals used on the farmland are also an important form of agri wealth. Many wars, referred to in Rigveda were fought for fertile land, cattle, horses, and stored up grains. Some of these are referred to below.

R 99 Richa 5/70/4 उरुच्क्रिरात्रेय:, मित्रावरुणौ, गायत्री

For this Richa, the Rishi is Uruchkriratreya. Devtas are Mitra and Varuna. The Chanda is Gayatri.

> मा कस्यांद्भुतक्रतू युक्षं भुंजेमा तनूभि: ।
> मा शेषसा मा तनंसा ॥5/70/4

Meaning of words/combination of words

मा तनूभि: do not consume कस्यादभुतक्रतू you, doers of wonderful deeds युक्षं भुंजेमा somebody else's food मा शेषसा any other's food मा तनंसा food not produced from our own bodily efforts. Consume food produced only by our own effort and share it with our sons, grandsons and descendants.

The Richa translates as: 'Doers of wonderous deeds, let us not depend on the bounty of any persons other than your own self. Let us not consume any other's food either ourselves or with our sons and grandsons, or relatives. Let us consume only that which is earned from our own bodily effort, that is, from our own healthy bodies'.

This praise and plea are to the Devtas Mitra and Varuna. The Rishi says to the Yajna performers that you are doers of wonderful deeds. Please ensure that we ourselves, along with our children, consume only that, which is due to our own bodily efforts and never that which is coming from others' efforts or generosity. There is thus, in the Vaidic values, a clear emphasis on dependence on self-effort and self-reliance. For this purpose, one has to keep one's body healthy so that enough food can be produced for ourselves and our families. This Richa provides a Vaidic endorsement to the value attached to the concept of self-reliance in general and with respect to food grains in particular.

R 100 Richa 6/25/4 बार्हस्पत्यो भरद्वाज:, इन्द्र:, त्रिष्टुप्

For this Richa, the Rishi is Bharadwaj. The Devta is Indra. The Chanda is Trishtup.

> शूरों वा् शूरं वनते शरीरैस्तनूरुचा् तरुषि यत् कृण्वैतें ।
> तोके वा् गोषु तनंयें यदप्सु वि क्रन्दसी उर्वरासु ब्रवैते ॥6/25/4

Meaning of words/combination of words

शरीरैस्तनूरुचा् तरुषि When warriors confront each other with their bodies यत् कृण्वैतें while engaging in battle शूरों वा् शूरं वनते then the warrior defeats the other warrior with his strength तोके वा् गोषु तनंयें यदप्सु वि क्रन्दसी उर्वरासु ब्रवैते they fight for the sake of their sons and grandsons and for cattle, water, and fertile land.

Agriculture in Rigveda: Seeds of India's Civilizational Prosperity

This Richa translates as follows: 'O Indra, the warriors who have been blessed by you, they, with their bodily [strength], destroy the enemy warriors, while they engage with clamour in mutually harmful battle. They fight for [the sake of their] sons, grandsons, cows, water, and fertile land'.

The purport is that wars happen among warriors who have prepared themselves for the battles with strong bodies with the aim of inflicting harm on the opponents for three main reasons namely, fertile land, sources of water, and cattle. Countries must protect their land and sources of water for the sake of their citizens. Bodily strength is part of the preparation for such wars. Societies must ensure enough and healthy food for their warriors.

Some of the important agriculture related Richas where reference is made to agri-assets and other aspects of agricultural practices are in Mandal 1, Sukta 23.

R 101 Richa 1/23/15 मेधातिथिः काण्वः, पूषा, गायत्री

For this Richa, the Rishi is Medhatithi in the lineage of Kanva. Devta is Pusha. The Chanda is Gayatri.

> उतो स महामिन्दुंभिः षड् युक्ताँ अनुसेषिधत् ।
> गोभिर्यवं न चंकृषत् ॥1/23/15

Meaning of words/combination of words

उतो स महामिन्दुंभि and this for my sake, full of Somaras षड् युक्ताँ associated with the six seasons अनुसेषिधत् done repeatedly in the same manner गोभिर्यवं using oxen and the barley plant चंकृषत् like the farmer.

This Richa translates to: 'He has repeatedly brought for my benefit, the six seasons connected fully with the drops of the Soma juice just as a farmer repeatedly ploughs the Earth with oxen for planting barley'.

The Rishi is Meghatithi from the Kanva lineage. The praise is for Devta 'Pusha', who is associated with agriculture and for bringing about the seasons. In this Richa, it is recognized that the main crop in those days was barley. As mentioned earlier, in Rigvaidic days, barley was the main initial crop which was a divine gift. In addition, plough was an agricultural asset which was to be used repeatedly, season after season, and oxen also constituted an important resource for successful agricultural outcomes.

In the Vedas, linked to the two main agricultural seasons, are the two modern day crops namely, Kharif (July to October) and Rabi (November to March/April). Generally, most agricultural crops take three months for completing the production cycle. Hence, four seasonal harvests are mentioned in the Taitariya Samhita. These are the times when ripened crops like barely for summer, medicinal herbs for the rainy season, paddy in autumn, and beans and sesame in winter become available. According to the Kaustaki Brahmana, after one day of Chaitra Amavasya that is, after Chaitra Shukla Pratipada, the winter crops are ready for harvesting.

R 102 Richa 1/127/6 परुच्छेपो दैवोदासिः, अग्निः, अतिधृतिः

For this Richa, the Rishi is Paruchepah from the lineage of Divodas. Devta is Agni. The Chanda is Atidhriti.

> स हि शर्धो न मारुतं तुविष्वणिरप्रंस्वतीषूर्वरांस्विष्टिनिरार्तनास्विष्टनिः
> आदद्भव्यान्यांदुदिर्यज्ञस्यं केतुरुहणां ।
> अधं स्मास्यु हर्षतो हृषींवतो विश्वें जुषन्त पन्थां नरं: शुभे न पन्थाम् ॥
> 1/127/6

Meaning of words/combination of words

स हि शर्धो न मारुतं he, Agni, like strong winds तुविष्वणिरप्रंस्वतीषूर्वरांस्विष्टनिरार्तनास्विष्टनिः worthy of worship, this Agni in Yajna-actions, fertile lands, and in battles, makes thunderous noise आदद्भव्यान्यांदुदिर्यज्ञस्यं that worshippable Agni accepts havi केतुरुहणां symbol of Yajna अधं स्मास्यु हर्षतो making others happy हृषींवतो and himself remaining happy, O Agni विश्वें all Devtas जुषन्त traverse पन्थां the path of Agni नरं: शुभे न पन्थाम् like men traverse the path of their welfare.

This Richa translates to: 'He roars aloud like the thunderous sound of strong winds, this Agni is worthy of worship in performing Yajnas, tending to fertile lands, and amidst battles, that venerable Agni accepts the Havi, he is the symbol of Yajna. All Devtas pursue the path of Agni in the same way as men follow the path of Agni for their welfare. Agni gives happiness to his worshippers, being happy himself'.

Agni is described as the one who bestows happiness on those who worship him and follow his path in all their pursuits, be it the performance of Yajnas, or the pursuit of agriculture in fertile fields, or battles against enemies.

R 103 Richa 1/100/18 वार्षगिराः ऋज्राः श्वाऽम्बरीष-सहदेव-भयमान-सुराधसः; इन्द्रः; त्रिष्टुप्

For this Richa, the Rishi is Suradhasa. The Devta is Indra. The Chanda is Trishtup.

> दस्यूञ्छिम्यूँश्च पुरुहूत एवैर्हत्वा पृथिव्यां शर्वा नि बर्हीत् ।
> सनत् क्षेत्रं सखिभिः श्वित्न्येभिः सनत् सूर्यं सनदपः सुवज्रं: ॥1/100/18

Meaning of words/combination of words

दस्यूञ्छिम्यूँश्च the Dasyus and the Shimyus पुरुहूत who everyone calls for help, such Indra एवैर्हत्वा having destroyed with the help of the warriors पृथिव्यां residing on Earth शर्वा नि बर्हीत् with powerful thunderbolt destroyed them from the roots सनत् क्षेत्रं सखिभिः freed and obtained the lands with his friends श्वित्न्येभिः with white ornaments सनत् सूर्यं freed the sun सनदपः freed the water सुवज्रं: with the powerful Vajra.

This Richa translates to: 'Indra, who is invoked by many, who is attended to by the moving Devtas that is Maruts, having attacked the Dasyus and the Shimyus, and slewing them with his thunderbolt, the thunderer Indra, wearing white ornaments, then divided the fields amongst his friends. He rescued the Sun and set free, the water'.

This Richa refers to a war between Indra and his friends on the one hand, and Dasyus and Shimyus on the other. Indra was accompanied and assisted by the wind Devtas, Maruts. These Dasyus and Shimyus had stopped the flow of water on the mountains by building some massive barrier, thereby blocking the downward flow of the river waters. This barrier must have been quite high because even sunshine was blocked. Indra annihilated these enemies and destroyed the barrier. Thereby, the land was set free, water was allowed to flow downwards, and the land could become fertile and productive again with sunshine.

R 104 Richa 8/21/3 सोभरिः काण्वः, इन्द्रः, ककुप्

For this Richa, the Rishi is Sobhari from the lineage of Kanva. The Devta is Indra. The Chanda is Kakup.

> आ यांहीम इन्दुवोऽश्वपते गोपंतु उर्वरापते ।
> सोमं सोमपते पिब ॥ 8/21/3

Meaning of words/combination of words

आ यांहीम Come, these are for you इन्दुवोऽश्वपते गोपंतु उर्वरापते O owner of horses, of cattle, and of the fertility of land सोमपते O Devta of Soma सोमं पिब Drink the soma juice.

This Richa translates to: 'O Indra, the owner of horses, of cattle, of fertile land, and the Devta of the Soma, these are for you. Come and drink the prepared Soma juice'.

Like the term Kshetrapati used in Rigveda in Sukta 4/57, here the term Urvarapati is being used. This addresses owner of that land which is fertile, the owner of fertile land is thus Indra. Alternatively, Indra, who is the lord of fertility imparts fertility to land on Earth. Indra has gifted this fertility as well as cattle and horses so that a viable agricultural activity can be undertaken on Earth. Fertile land, cattle, and horses are all part of agri-wealth.

It appears, that the use of the word 'Urvarapati' or 'Bhupati' (Rigveda 8/21/3) that is, owner of land, are references to the Paramatman from whom all attributes are derived.

Agriculture in Rigveda: Seeds of India's Civilizational Prosperity

During Vaidic Age, the fertile fields (Urvar Kshetra) were made ready for sowing seeds by the use of a plough. The plough was commonly known as 'Langal', and its front sharp part, was known as 'Fal'. The handle of the plough (Sumatitsakh) used to be very smooth (Atharvaveda, 3/17/3). One long bamboo (Isha) was tied to the plough, over which, one yoke (Yug), was placed. The oxen were tied to this yoke using ropes around their necks. The plough was pulled and drawn by 6, 8 or 12 bullocks, and from this number, we can imagine the heavy weight and the big size of the plough.

The ploughman (Kina) used to drive the bullocks with the help of the pointed iron stick (Toya). Generally, the Vaishyas used to carry out farming in Vaidic age. The fields were generally rich and crop-producing. If they were not capable of producing good crops, manures were used. Cow-dung (Karish) was used for this purpose. The natural waste products of the animals were considered as an important fertiliser for the fields as stated in Atharvaveda 4/2/9.

The farmers had to face a number of calamities. Animals living in the holes of the ground (for example, rats) used to spoil the seeds. This was common in the Vaidic days as it is today. Challenges also arose from birds and serpent-like animals (upakwas, jamya, tard, patang) who damaged the new buds. Excess rainfall as well as drought hampered the crops. Atharvaveda describes auspicious chants for protection from such calamities. As stated in Chhandogya Upanishad, insects called 'Matchi' also destroyed crops to a large extent. There is a reference of one incident where crops in the whole of the Kuru Janpad were destroyed by such insects in Chhandogya Upanishad 1/10/1 *(Matchi hateshu Kurushu)*.

Fruits were also a form of agri-wealth. Fruit trees are referred to in Richa 4 of Sukta 45 in Mandal 4 of the Rigveda (Rigveda 3/45/4).

R 105 Richa 3/45/4 गाथिनो विश्वामित्रः, इन्द्रः, बृहती

For this Richa, the Rishi is Vishwamitra of the lineage of Gathin. Devta is Indra. The Chanda is Brihati.

आ नुस्तुजं र॒यिं भ॒रांशं न प्र॑तिजानते ।
वृ॒क्षं पक्वं फलमङ्कीव धूनु॒हीन्द्रं स॒म्पारणं वसुं ॥3/45/4

Meaning of words/combination of words

आ नुस्तुजं र॒यिं O Indra, grant us riches भ॒रांशं न प्र॑तिजानते (as a father, gives his son) his share upon reaching maturity वृ॒क्षं पक्वं ripened on a tree फलमङ्कीव fruit धूनु॒हीन्द्रं स॒म्पारणं वसुं as a crook brings it down.

This translates to: 'Grant us riches, securing (us against foes), (as a father bestows) his portion on (a son) who reaches maturity. Send down upon us, Indra, wealth adequate (to our desires), as a crook (crooked instrument) brings down the ripe fruit from a tree'.

The purport is that it is best to let a fruit mature while it is still on the tree. Then, when it is ready, it can be plucked off by a skilful person. In that manner, O Indra, when you consider that we have become mature enough, please grant us wealth so that we can nurture it and enjoy it. This is how a father also decides to give the share of his wealth to his son when he comes of age that is, when the father is confident that the son will take care of and manage the wealth and not just enjoy it.

In the Rigvaidic landscape, agriculture, water, and animals are mutually interdependent, forming a productive system for the survival and prosperity of mankind. The most important representatives of the animal world are cattle. Cows are a gift to mankind from the Devtas. Their milk, produced in surplus, over and above the consumption of their calves, has been the main nourishing food for mankind who gains strength and prosperity and remains free from diseases. Oxen are used extensively on the agricultural lands. Both oxens and horses are used to carry grain from farm lands to storehouses and markets by using either horse driven or bullock driven carts. While many Richas are devoted to the cows, one entire Sukta (10/169) portrays the cows as the Devta. This particular Sukta is known as the "Go-Sukta", 'Go' being the Sanskrit name of the cow.

Famous Go-Sukta 10/169/1-4

R 106 Richa 10/169/1 शबरः काक्षीवतः, गावः, त्रिष्टुप्

For this Richa, the Rishi is Shabarah of the family of Kakshivata. The cows are the Devta. The Metre is Trishtup.

> मयोभूर्वातों अभि वांतूस्रा ऊर्जस्वतीरोषधीरा रिंशन्ताम् ।
> पीवंस्वतीर्जीवर्धंन्याः पिबन्त्ववुसायं पुद्वतें रुद्र मृळ ॥10/169/1

Meaning of words/combination of words

मयोभूर्वातों अभि वांतूस्रा May the wind blow towards the cows making them comfortable ऊर्जस्वतीरोषधीरा the nutritious, life-sustaining waters रिंशन्ताम् पीवंस्वतीर्जीवर्धंन्याः पिबन्त्ववुसायं let them drink पुद्वतें रुद्र मृळ May Rudra have compassion on these sources of food (nourishment) that have feet.

This Richa translates to: 'May the refreshing wind blow upon the cows, may they consume the juicy grass, let them drink the nutritious, life-sustaining (waters). May Rudra have compassion upon this source of food (milk) which have feet, (namely cows)'.

In this Richa, in praise of the cows, the Rishi acknowledges that among their other virtues, they do serve as a source of food, that is, the milk that they yield. The quality and quantity of this milk depends on their being comfortable in the setting of nature with gentle breeze and access to health and nutritious feedstock and ample drinking water of good quality. With these inputs for their own selves, cows will produce very nutritious food for us.

R 107 Richa 10/169/2 शबरः काक्षीवतः, गावः, त्रिष्टुप्

For this Richa, the Rishi is Shabarah of the family of Kakshivata. The cows are the Devta. The Metre is Trishtup.

> याः सरूपा विरूपा एकंरूपा यासामग्निरिष्ट्या नामानि वेदं ।
> या अङ्गिरसस्तपसेह चक्रुस्ताभ्यः पर्जन्य महि शर्म यच्छ ॥10/169/2

Meaning of words/combination of words

याः These are सरूपा of similar forms विरूपा (and of) different forms एकंरूपा (and of a) single form यासामग्निरिष्ट्या नामानि वेदं Agni knows their (individual names) through the process of Yajna या अङ्गिरसस्तपसेह चक्रुस्ताभ्यः those (cows) who Rishi Angiras created through Tapas in this world पर्जन्य महि शर्म यच्छ O Parjanya, please provide these cows, great comfort.

This Richa translates to: 'Grant great comfort, O Parjanya, to those cows who are of similar forms, of different forms, or of a single form, whose names Agni knows through the Yajna, or those whom (Rishi) Angiras created in this world by Tapasya'.

In this Richa, an acknowledgement is made that the cows of different forms were brought on this Earth by Rishi Angiras through his Tapasya, whose names became known to Agni Devta through the performance of Yajnas. May Parjanya, who is Devta of rain and winds, grant comfort to the cows who are blessed through Yajnas so that Agni Devta knows them individually by their names.

R 108 Richa 10/169/3 शबरः काक्षीवतः, गावः, त्रिष्टुप्

For this Richa, the Rishi is Shabarah of the family of Kakshivata. The cows are the Devta. The Metre is Trishtup.

> या द्रेवेषु तन्वश्मैरयन्त यासां सोमो विश्वां रूपाणि वेदं ।
> ता अस्मभ्यं पयसा पिन्वमानाः प्रजावंतीरिन्द्र गोष्ठे रिरीहि ॥10/169/3

Meaning of words/combination of words

Agriculture in Rigveda: Seeds of India's Civilizational Prosperity

या देवेषुं These cows for the Devtas तन्वश्मैरयन्तु provide milk from their own bodies यासां सोमो विश्वां रूपाणि वेदं of whose milk and other forms are known to Soma ता those cows अस्मभ्यं पयसा पिन्वमानाः who have milk for our consumption प्रजावतीरिन्द्र गोष्ठे रिरीहि and who have calves. May Indra bring them to our cowhouses.

This Richa translates to: 'May Indra bring to our cow-house, these cows who offer the milk from their bodies to the Devtas. Soma knows all the properties of their milk and other products, those that nourish us with their milk and those that have calves'.

The purport is that cows are blessed since they produce milk for the Devtas. In that way, their bodies become performers of Yajnas. Devtas prefer the milk mixed with Somaras. Somaras knows the properties of the milk of the cows who have calves. Somaras is ready to be mixed with such milk. Indra is known to bring the cows to the cow-houses (cowsheds) built by men. In this Richa, the interdependence of men, cows and Devtas is highlighted. This relationship is conceptualized as a Yajna.

R 109 Richa 10/169/4 शबरः काक्षीवतः, गावः, त्रिष्टुप्

For this Richa, the Rishi is Shabarah Kashivat. The Devta is Cow. The Metre is Trishtup.

प्रजापंतिर्मह्यमेता रराणो विश्वैर्देवैः पितृभिः संविदानः ।
शिवाः सतीरुपं नो गोष्ठमाकुस्तासां वयं प्रजया सं संदेम ॥10/169/4

Meaning of words/combination of words

प्रजापंतिर्मह्यमेता May Prajapati रराणो विश्वैर्देवैः in accordance with the wishes of all the Devtas पितृभिः and the Pitars (ancestors) संविदानः bestow these cows for us शिवाः सतीरुपं of the auspicious form of Shiva and Sati नो गोष्ठमाकुस्तासां bring those cows to our cow-sheds वयं प्रजया with their calves सं संदेम so that we may be in possession of them.

This Richa translates to: 'May Prajapati in accordance with the wishes of all the Devtas and Pitars bestow these cows upon us, and bring these auspicious welfare enhancing cows, with the form and attributes of Shiva and Sati, with their calves, to our cow-sheds, so that we may be enriched with them in our possession'.

Cows are a gift from the Devtas and the Pitars to men, the descendants of Manu. May Prajapati ensure that all the cows along with their progeny reach the cow-sheds that we have built for them and add to our welfare.

In Sukta 68 of the tenth Mandal, cows are described along with their various qualities.

R 110 Richa 10/68/3 अयास्य आंगिरसः, बृहस्पतिः, त्रिष्टुप्

For this Richa, the Rishi is Angiras. The Devta is Brihaspati. The Metre is Trishtup.

> साध्वर्या अंतिथिनींरिषिराः स्पार्हाः सुवर्णां अनवद्यरूपाः ।
> बृहस्पतिः पर्वतेभ्यो वितूर्यां निर्गा ऊपे यवमिव स्थिविभ्यं: ॥ 10/68/3

Meaning of words/combination of words

साध्वर्या अंतिथिनींरिषिराः Auspicious givers of milk, always given to moving about स्पार्हाः सुवर्णां अनवद्यरूपाः desirable, attractively colured, beautiful, giving milk like rain बृहस्पतिः पर्वतेभ्यो Brihaspati frees them (from their captivity) in the mountains वितूर्यां निर्गा ऊपे यवमिव स्थिविभ्यं: like a farmer takes out barley for sowing from the accumulated (stored up) grains and takes them to the Devtas.

This Richa translates to: 'Brihaspati brings to the Devtas, after extricating them from the mountains, the cows that are yielders of pure milk. (These cows are) ever in motion, the objects of search and of desire, well-coloured and of unexceptionable form, as men bring barley from the granaries (for sowing)'.

Thus, cows were not only given by the Devtas to men, but also restored to them by the Devtas from the mountains where they were kept in hiding by the villains or enemies of men. These cows are beautiful, and yielders of pure milk. They always move about, being full of energy. They are as attractive or useful as barley which is sown in the agricultural fields, which yields sumptuous crops. Thus, both barley and the cows are gifts from the Devtas to men for their sustenance and growth.

In Richa 4 of the first Mandal of the Rigveda, cows are praised along with the horses.

R 111 Richa 1/29/4 आजीगर्तिः शुनःशेप स कृत्रिमो वैश्वामित्रो देवरातः, इन्द्रः, पंक्ति

For this Richa, the Rishi is Ajigarti Shunah Shepah, Kritrim and Devrat. The Devta is Indra. The Metre is Pankti.

> ससन्तु त्या अरांतयो बोधन्तु शूर रातयं: ।
> आ तू नं इन्द्र शंसय गोष्वश्वेषु शुभ्रिषुं सहस्त्रेषु तुवीमघ ॥1/29/4

Meaning of words/combination of words

शूर O brave warrior ससन्तु त्या अरांतयो May our enemies remain in slumber बोधन्तु रातयं: may our friends be awake इन्द्र तुवीमघ O Indra, owner of multiple riches गोष्वश्वेषु शुभ्रिषुं सहस्त्रेषु including thousands of excellent cows and horses आ तू नं शंसय may we be enriched by you.

This Richa translates to: 'O Indra, the brave warrior, may our enemies remain in slumber, and our friends, remain awake. O Indra, of boundless wealth, may we be enriched by thousands of excellent cows and horses'.

The purport is that Indra, who is the Devta of wealth and riches as also the Devta of wars and victories, may he ensure that our enemies keep sleeping and our friends remain fully awake and conscious, so that we may always emerge victorious. May Indra also ensure that we get the best kind of wealth including excellent cows and horses since these animals are a significant contributor to human prosperity.

In Mandal 6, Sukta 47, Richa 20, a reference is made to the incident relating to the search for the cows who had been abducted and hidden by the enemies of men. This search is by men who are being helped by the Devtas.

R 112 Richa 6/47/20 गर्गो भारद्वाजः, इंद्रः, देव–भूमि-बृहस्पतीन्द्रा, त्रिष्टुप्

For this Richa, the Rishi is Garga from the lineage of Bharadwaj. The Devtas are Earth, Brihaspati and Indra together. The Metre is Trishtup.

> अग॒व्यूति क्षेत्रमागंन्म देवा उ॒र्वी स॒ती भूमिरंहू॒रणाभूत् ।
> बृहस्पते॒ प्र चिकित्सा॒ गविष्टावि॒त्था स॒ते जरित्र इन्द्र पन्थाम् ॥6/47/20

Meaning of words/combination of words

अग॒व्यूति क्षेत्रमागंन्म Here, we have arrived and we are wandering about in an area without cows while we keep searching for them देवा O Devtas उ॒र्वी स॒ती भूमिरंहू॒रणाभूत् Here, this large area has become a protector of sinful enemies बृहस्पते॒ प्र चिकित्सा॒ गविष्टावि॒त्था once we locate the cows, O Brihaspati, take good care of them स॒ते जरित्र इन्द्र पन्थाम् O Indra, please guide us, men, the Yajna-performers, by a good path towards the cows.

This Richa translates to: 'O Devtas, we have arrived into an area where there is no trace of (or clear track leading to) the cows. The area is large, it serves to protect our sinful enemies. O Indra, please direct us, through a good path, towards the cows. O Brihaspati, please take good care of the health of the cows, once we, your worshippers, locate them'.

This Richa refers to a situation where men are searching for stolen cows who are being hidden in a large area. Men have arrived in this area, but they are lost. They plead to Indra Devta to help them locate the cows and win them back. Men also suspect that the cows may not be in good health. Therefore, they request Brihaspati Devta to ensure that their health is restored once they are found.

In another important Richa in Mandal 3, there is reference to the importance of cows for mankind. This Richa is discussed below.

Agriculture in Rigveda: Seeds of India's Civilizational Prosperity

R 113 Richa 3/45/3 गाथिनो विश्वामित्रः, इन्द्रः, बृहती

For this Richa, the Rishi is Gathin in the lineage of Vishwamitra. The Devta is Indra. The Metre is Brihati.

> गम्भीराँ उद्धीँरिव क्रतुं पुष्यसि गा इव ।
> प्र सुंगोपा यवसं धेनवों यथा हृदं कुल्या इंवाशत ॥3/45/3

Meaning of words/combination of words

[O Indra, you take care of the Yajna-performer], गम्भीराँ उद्धीँरिव like a deep ocean क्रतुं पुष्यसि गा इव प्र सुंगोपा like a careful herdsman nurses the cows into good health यवसं धेनवों like the cows eat barley यथा हृदं कुल्या इंवाशत like the small rivers flow into a large reservoir, similarly all the Soma juice comes to you.

This Richa translates to: 'O Indra, you take care of the Yajna-performer, like you fill the deep seas (with water) or like a careful herdsman who nurses the cows into good health, or like the cows eat barley. All the Soma-juice reaches you like small rivers flow into a large reservoir'.

This Richa is devoted to Indra. Indra takes care of his devotees who perform Yajna and prepare the Soma-juice. Indra is well-known as a herdsman for taking care of the cows and it is also known that cows keep themselves in good health by eating barley. The Yajna-performers are bestowed with wealth and good health while the Soma-juice is accepted by Indra Devta.

In the next Richa given below, pertaining to Sukta 36 of Mandal 1, cows and horses are mentioned together in appreciation of their role to serve as an asset to mankind.

R 114 Richa 1/36/8 कण्वो घौरः, अग्निः, प्रगाथः

For this Richa, the Rishi is Ghaur of the lineage of Kanva. The Devta is Agni. The Chanda is Pragath meaning that it alternates for Chandas with odd and even numbers. For odd, it is Brihati, and for even it is Satobrihati except for Chanda 13 where it is Uparistadbrihati.

घ्नन्तों वृत्रमंतर॒न् रोद॑सी अ॒प उ॒रु क्ष॒याय॑ चक्रिरे ।
भुव॒त् कण्वे॒ वृषा॑ द्युम्न्याहु॑तः क्रन्द॒दश्वो॒ गविष्टिषु ॥1/36/8

Meaning of words/combination of words

घ्नन्तों वृत्रमंतर॒न् The attacking warriors have destroyed Vritra रोद॑सी अ॒प उ॒रु क्ष॒याय॑ चक्रिरे and expanded the Earth, Heaven and space substantially to accommodate water भुव॒त् कण्वे॒ वृषा॑ द्युम्न्याहु॑तः strong and bright Agni has received *Ahutis* in Yajnas. In the same manner, Agni became a benefactor of the Kanvas who are performing the Yajnas क्रन्द॒दश्वो॒ गविष्टिषु as neighing horses help in battles for winning cattle.

This Richa translates to: 'The destroying warriors (such as Indra and Agni) have slain Vritra. They have expanded Earth, Heaven and space enough to accommodate abundant water for the living creatures. May Agni, owner of wealth, having received the invocations, be a benefactor to the Kanvas, like a neighing horse ensures victory in battles for possessing cattle'.

Devtas have ensured that there is enough water on Earth, Heaven and other planets in space where living creatures exist. They have expanded these planets to accommodate substantial water. Through Yajnas, Devtas bestow benefits on mankind just like when battles are waged for the possession of cattle. Active and aggressive horses make a lot of noise to ensure victory so that cattle can be won. Implicitly, this Richa asserts that the universe is expandable, water is critical for life, and Devtas shower benefits for mankind. Yajnas are the link between mankind and Devtas. Horse and cattle are mutually supportive of each other. Wars often happen to win over cattle.

Agriculture in Rigveda: Seeds of India's Civilizational Prosperity

This mutual dependence of horses and cows is also described in Mandal 6, Sukta 39.

R 115 Richa 6/39/5 बार्हस्पत्यो भरद्वाज:, इन्द्र:, त्रिष्टुप

For this Richa, the Rishi is Bharadwaj from the lineage of Brihaspati. The Devta is Indra. The Chanda is Trishtup.

नू गृणानो गृणते प्रत्न राज॒न्निषं: पिन्व वसुदेयाय पूर्वीः ।
अप ओषधीरविषा वनानि गा अर्वतो नृनृचसें रिरीहि ॥6/39/5

Meaning of words/combination of words

नू गृणानो गृणते Upon being praised, you give to the worshipper प्रत्न राज॒न्निषं: पिन्व वसुदेयाय and to whom affluence is due पूर्वीः sovereign of ancient times अप water ओषधीरविषा poison-less plants वनानि and woods गा cattle अर्वतो horses नृनृचसें रिरीहि grant for those men.

This Richa translates to: 'Sovereign of ancient times, may you, when praised, bestow upon your worshippers, who deserve affluence, abundant food, water, woods, poison-less plants, cattle and horses'.

This praise is for Indra, who is one of the ancient Devtas. After his glorification, the worshippers ask for those things that they need namely, water, plants, food, cattle, and horses. Together, these consist of the full and integrated system of agriculture.

The subject of horses is pursued in Mandal 6 further.

R 116 Richa 6/63/10 बार्हस्पत्यो भरद्वाज:, अश्विनौ, त्रिष्टुप

For this Richa, the Rishi is Bhardwaj from the lineage of Brihaspati. The Devtas are Ashwini Kumars. The Metre is Trishtup.

सं वां शता नासत्या सहस्राऽश्वानां पुरुपन्थां गिरे दात् ।
भरद्वाजाय वीर नू गिरे दाद्धता रक्षांसि पुरुदंससा स्युः ॥6/63/10

Meaning of words/combination of words

नांसत्या O Ashwini Kumars पुरुपन्थां गिरे King Purupantha who praises you सं वां शता सहस्राऽश्वानां दात् has given hundreds and thousands of horses भरद्वाजाय for Bhardwajas also वीर् नू गिरे who praise you दाद्धृता may these be given रक्षांसि पुरुदंससा स्युः now that Rakshasas have been slain.

This Richa translates to: 'O Nasatyas, achievers of great deeds, King Purupantha, who praises you, has given hundreds and thousands of horses. May these also be given to the Bharadwajas, who praise you, now that the Rakshasas have been slain.

In this Richa, Rishi Bharadwaj praises the Ashwini Kumars and asks for the gifts of many horses for himself and his descendants who have become available after the Rakshasas have been killed in the battle where these horses were brought by King Purupantha.

R 117 Richa 7/18/1 मैत्रावरुणिर्वसिष्ठः, इन्द्रः, त्रिष्टुप्

For this Richa, the Rishi is Vashishtha from the lineage of Mitra and Varuna. The Devta is Indra. The Metre is Trishtup.

> त्वे ह यत्पितरश्चिन्न इन्द्र विश्वां वामा जरितारो असन्वन् ।
> त्वे गावः सुदुघास्त्वे ह्यश्वास्त्वं वसुं देवयते वनिष्ठः ॥7/18/1

Meaning of words/combination of words

इन्द्र O Indra त्वे ह यत्पितरश्चिन्न our forefathers, by glorifying you विश्वां वामा जरितारो असन्वन् obtained all desirable riches त्वे गावः सुदुघास्त्वे you have the cows who give excellent milk ह्यश्वास्त्वं you have the horses वसुं देवयते वनिष्ठः and you give ample wealth to those devoted to the Devtas.

This Richa translates to: 'Indra, by praising you, our forefathers, have obtained all desirable riches. You have the cows who give excellent milk and the horses, and you give ample wealth to those devoted to the Devtas'.

In this Richa, Rishi Vashishtha praises Indra and says that from the times of their forefathers, they have been glorifying Indra and beseeching him for the gift of various forms of wealth relevant for mankind. These include cows and horses. The implication is that the worship of Devtas was in vogue much before the time of Vashishtha. This Richa indicates that the history of the Vaidic civilization goes much farther back than the time when this Richa was visualised.

R 118 Richa 7/27/5 मैत्रावरुणिर्वसिष्ठ:, इन्द्र:, त्रिष्टुप्

For this Richa, the Rishi is Vashishtha from the lineage of Mitra and Varuna. The Devta is Indra. The Metre is Trishtup.

नू इन्द्र रा॒ये वरि॑वस्कृधी नु॒ आ ते॒ मनो॑ ववृत्याम मु॒घायं᳴ ।
गोमदश्वांव॒द्रथं॑व॒द्व्यन्तों यू॒यं पा॑त स्व॒स्तिभि॒: सदा॑ न: ॥7/27/5

Meaning of words/combination of words

नू इन्द्र O Indra रा॒ये वरि॑वस्कृधी नु॒ for our enrichment, please grant us wealth quickly आ ते॒ मनो॑ ववृत्याम मु॒घायं᳴ enable us to please you so that you may grant us गोमदश्वांव॒द्रथं॑व॒द्व्यन्तों cattle, horses, and chariot, यू॒यं पा॑त स्व॒स्तिभि॒: सदा॑ न: please always cherish us with your blessings.

This Richa translates to: 'O Indra, for making us prosperous, grant us wealth without delay. May we always attract your favour by our adoration. Please give us wealth consisting of cattle, horses, and chariots. May you always cherish us with blessings'.

In this Richa also, cattle, horses, and vehicles driven by them are recognized as forms of wealth for the mankind.

Summary and Key Points

There are three main forms in which agri-wealth is retained and accumulated by men. The first form is grain, which in terms of modern economic parlance serves as both a 'stock' and 'flow'. The second form is cattle and animal wealth including cows, oxen, and horses who had an integral role in India's ancestral farming. The third form in which wealth can be held is fertile land where fertility of the soil is the key attribute of land which is worth preserving and sustaining. It is notable that horses helped to acquire and preserve agri-wealth through a series of battles, which took place from time to time.

Grains contain the required genetic information to enable the seed to grow back into a plant, capable of reproducing the seed with which it began when planted in soil and nurtured with water and other supporting inputs. Food grains were recognized as essential for the birth and sustenance of the progeny of the people who lived along the banks of river Saraswati and other Rigvaidic rivers. Some of the key messages of this Chapter are summarized below.

- In the Vaidic values, there is a clear emphasis on self-reliance in food production for families and communities.

- Among cattle, cows and oxen are recognized as the most important for an agricultural society and economy.

- Cows ensure production of highly nutritious milk for mankind if they are themselves fed with nutritious feedstock, good quality air and water, and kept happy. From this milk, different kinds of healthy and nourishing milk-products could then be produced.

- Countries must protect their land, even if wars are to be waged for this ownership. This is called for to ensure that land and sources of water which are key to self-reliance of the citizens are protected. This is also the main reason why many small and big wars happened in the Vaidic times. One example of a major war is the Dashrajna Yuddha described in detail in Sukta 18 of Mandal 7. Bodily strength and disease-free status were required for the warriors for waging such wars. Societies therefore were required to ensure enough and healthy food for their warriors. They also needed adequate knowledge of diseases and plants and specialized waters which could play a key role in combating diseases. Such plant life therefore was also recognized as a form of wealth. This is discussed in detail in the next Chapter.

Chapter 7 Rigveda's Aushadhi Sukta: praising medicinal plants

A discussion on the Vaidic discourse on agriculture would not be complete without recognizing and discussing the broad group of trees, roots, herbs, seeds and other medicinal plants. In fact, Rigveda has devoted a complete set of Mantras to the praise of such a group of plants. In Mandal 10, Sukta 97 which we may refer to as the 'Aushadhi Sukta', there are twenty-three Mantras devoted to plant-based medicines. Reference is made here, not only to trees but to smaller plants, herbs and plants that largely grow under the soil whose roots may be used for their medicinal properties. Specific plants that have been named in these Suktas are Peepal, Palasha, Ashwavati, Somavati, Urjayanti, and Udojas.

For some of these, modern botanical names are available. 'Ficus religiosa' or sacred fig is a species of fig native to the Indian subcontinent and Indochina that belongs to Moraceae, the fig or mulberry family. It is also known as the Bodhi tree or Peepal tree which is also spelt as Pipal tree. In Sanskrit, it is named as the Ashwattha tree.

Similarly, the Palasha tree has the botanical name 'Butea monosperma'. It is a species of Butea native to tropical and sub-tropical parts of the Indian subcontinent and Southeast Asia, ranging across India, Bangladesh, Nepal, Sri Lanka, Pakistan, Myanmar, Thailand, Laos, Cambodia, Vietnam, Malaysia, and western Indonesia. Common names include 'flame-of-the-forest', 'palash', and 'bastard teak'.

Rishis recognize that medicinal properties may be obtained from flowers, fruits, trunks, roots, seeds, and juices drawn from any of these. The Soma plant is recognized as the leading plant, which was brought down from Dyulok, the land of Devtas, for the benefit of mankind. It is important for deriving the maximum benefit from these plants that Yajnas are performed in praise of these plants so that their curative and strength-giving properties are invoked to have full effect. It is recognized in this Chapter that plants have a mind of their own and they need to be pleased so as to fully benefit mankind. It may also be realized that often different plants or medicines derived from them would need to be used together so as to take advantage of their different properties in overcoming difficult diseases. Men need to develop enough expertise to recognize individual plants and their specific medicinal or beneficial properties. Their medicinal values may be relevant not only for men but also for animals who are domesticated by men. The lesson that is to be drawn from this Chapter is that men must endeavour to identify beneficial plant life and the plant life with medicinal value and sustain all of these plants in a manner such that they grow and prosper. Thus, the Vaidic message is that mankind, agriculture, trees and plants, and animals together with nature constitute one integrated self, full of varied life forms. To derive the full benefit of this interdependence, mankind must not organize his activities in a manner that would disturb this interdependence or harm either nature or animal or plant life. Rigveda's Aushadhi Sukta may be considered as the beginning of the Ayurveda and in fact, mankind's search for deriving medicines extracted from plants. All modern medicinal systems make use of the ingredients derived from medicinal plants in different ways.

The Rishi for all the Mantras in this Sukta is Bhishaj who is from the lineage of Atharvan. Atharvan is the main Rishi for the Atharvaveda. In Atharvaveda, an extensive treatment of health issues, role of viruses and bacteria and the role of medicinal plants is also given in detail. In this Volume however, our focus is largely on the Rigveda. From the word 'Bhishaj', the word 'Bhaishaj' is derived which also means 'Vaidya' or physician. The Metre in all the Mantras is Anushtup and the Devtas in all the Mantras are the medicines or the medicinal plants themselves.

Mandal 10 Sukta 97 Aushadhi Sukta

R 119 Richa 10/97/1 आथर्वणो भिषग्, ओषधयः, अनुष्टुप्

For this Richa, the Rishi is Bhishaj (the physician), the son of Atharvan. Medicinal plants or herbs are the Devtas. The Metre is Anushtup.

> या ओषधीः पूर्वा जाता देवेभ्यंस्त्रियुगं पुरा ।
> मनै नु बभ्रूणामहं शतं धामांनि सप्तं च ॥10/97/1

Meaning of words/combination of words

या This ओषधीः medicinal plants or medicinal juices पूर्वा जाता which were born or made earlier देवेभ्यंस्त्रियुगं पुरा even before the three earlier ages that is Satyug, Tretayug and Dwaparyug by the Devtas मनै नु I think of बभ्रूणामहं शतं धामांनि सप्तं च these hundred and seven applications or uses of these brown coloured plants.

This translates to: 'I or we think of the hundred and seven applications (that is, many applications) of the brown-shaded medicinal plants, which are ancient and were created by the Devtas even before the three ages implying the three ages of Satyug, Tretayug and Dwaparyug'.

The message is that these medicinal plants have been created by the Devtas early in the process of creation for the use of mankind or in fact, all living beings so that they can be protected from diseases and ailments and their bodies can remain in good health.

R 120 Richa 10/97/2 आथर्वणो भिषग्, ओषधयः, अनुष्टुप्

For this Richa, the Rishi is Bhishaj (the physician), the son of Atharvan. Medicinal plants or herbs are the Devtas. The Metre is Anushtup.

> शतं वों अम्ब धामांनि सहस्त्रमुत वो रुहः ।
> अधा शतक्रत्वो यूयमिमं मे अगदं कृत ॥10/97/2

Meaning of words/combination of words

शतं वो अम्ब O hundreds of medicines, you are like our mother धामानि सहस्रमुत वो रुहः you have thousands of birthplaces or places of origin and you spread out in the form of many plants and branches अर्धा शतक्रत्वो यूयमिमं and you have the capacity to fulfil many tasks में अगदं कृत you may please make me disease-free.

This translates to: 'O hundreds of medicinal mothers (of mankind), you have your origins in thousands of places, and you branch out in the form of many plants and you grow manifold. You have the capacity to fulfil hundreds of functions. Please make me and my people disease-free'.

The implication is that these medicinal plants are of many varieties and they have many applications. Their origins are in different places and they propagate or multiply themselves very fast so that their availability never falls short. Their role is like the mother of mankind and they have the capacity to keep mankind disease-free. It is now up to us to recognize the medicinal values of these special plants and protect and utilize these for our welfare. For this purpose, we have to ensure that we do not pollute them with artificially created or unnatural chemicals and let them retain their original healing properties.

R 121 Richa 10/97/3 आथर्वणो भिषग्, ओषधयः, अनुष्टुप्

For this Richa, the Rishi is Bhishaj (the physician), the son of Atharvan. Medicinal plants or herbs are the Devtas. The Metre is Anushtup.

> ओषधीः प्रति मोदध्वं पुष्यंवतीः प्रसूवरीः ।
> अश्वां इव सजित्वरीर्वीरुधः पारयिष्ण्वः ॥10/97/3

Meaning of words/combination of words

ओषधीः O medicines, you प्रति मोदध्वं पुष्यंवतीः प्रसूवरीः be pleased towards the sick person and grow with many flowers and high quality fruits अश्वां इव सजित्वरी you win over the disease as speedily as a war horse wins over the enemy वीरुधः पारयिष्ण्वः be the medium for letting the ill person get over his disease, pain and discomfort.

This translates to: 'O medicinal plants, please be happy and therefore prosper. You bear abundant flowers and fruits, enabling overcoming the diseases with such speed as can be obtained by a horse victorious in a war. Please keep growing and enable men to overcome disease, illness and discomfort'.

The prayer is to the medicinal plants to remain in a pleasant state all the time so that they can grow spontaneously, producing flowers and fruits which may be used by mankind so as to overcome the illnesses and discomforts that they undergo in the natural process of existence. Thus, Devtas had ensured, before mankind was created or brought on Earth, that there would be adequate means by which they would be protected from the frequent diseases that they may encounter while existing on Earth. Some of these diseases may be of their own creation, but in their generosity, Devtas have tried to provide us with a protection against our own excesses.

R 122 Richa 10/97/4 आथर्वणो भिषग्, ओषधय:, अनुष्टुप्

For this Richa, the Rishi is Bhishaj (the physician), the son of Atharvan. Medicinal plants or herbs are the Devtas. The Metre is Anushtup.

ओषधीरिति मातरस्तद्वो देवीरुपं ब्रुवे ।
सुनेयमश्वं गां वासं आत्मानं तवं पूरुष ॥ ॥10/97/4

Meaning of words/combination of words

ओषधीरिति O medicines, you are मातरस्तद्वो देवीरुपं like our mother in the form of a Devi that is blessed with many divine qualities ब्रुवे I say this to you सुनेयमश्वं गां that I will give horses, cows, वासं आत्मानं clothes and even myself तवं पूरुष for you, O healer.

This Richa translates to: 'O mother-like plants, you are bestowed with divine qualities. To please you and to ensure that you prosper and grow, I will give for you, O healer, horses, cows, clothes and even myself'.

The implicit meaning is that the medicinal plants have the same status and quality as that of Devtas. These medicinal plants need to be protected and served and for this purpose, we will ensure their nourishment and care by making use of our animal wealth, and the products that we have created such as clothes or garments, and if we have to sacrifice our own interests for the welfare of these plants, we will do so because these plants have the status of a physician or a healer.

R 123 Richa 10/97/5 आथर्वणो भिषग्, ओषधयः, अनुष्टुप्

For this Richa, the Rishi is Bhishaj (the physician), the son of Atharvan. Medicinal plants or herbs are the Devtas. The Metre is Anushtup.

> अश्वत्थे वों निषदनं पर्णे वों वसतिष्कृता ।
> गोभाज् इत्किलासथ यत्सनवथ पूरुषम् ॥10/97/5

Meaning of words/combination of words

अश्वत्थे वों निषदनं Your residence is on the 'Peepal' or Ashwattha tree पर्णे वों वसतिष्कृता you reside on the leaves of the Palasha tree गोभाज् इत्किलासथ you nourish all the cows यत्सनवथ पूरुषम् at the same time when you ensure the nourishment and growth of men.

This Richa translates to: 'Your residence is on the Ashwattha tree. You live on the leaves of the Palasha tree. You ensure the welfare of the cattle while ensuring nourishment and growth of men'.

In this Richa, there is a confirmation of the medicinal qualities of two types of trees found in India namely, the Peepal tree and the Palasha tree. These medicinal properties are embedded in these trees in their trunks, branches and leaves. There is thus an abundance of the medicinal products which can be made out of these trees not only for mankind, but also for animals who are under their care.

The importance of the Ashwattha tree is recognized in Srimad Bhagwad Gita where Sri Krishna identified himself as the tree of Ashawattha (Peepal).

G 12 Srimad Bhagvad Gita: Chapter 10, Shloka 26

> अश्वत्थः सर्ववृक्षाणां देवर्षीणां च नारदः ।
> गन्धर्वाणां चित्ररथः सिद्धानां कपिलो मुनिः ॥ 10-26

Meaning of words/combination of words

In this Shloka, Sri Krishna, in the context of narrating those beings or forms where he is most easily identifiable because he is present as a 'Vibhuti' that is, specialized form, says that amongst the trees, he is present in the Peepal tree, among the Devarishis, he can be seen as Narad, among the Gandharvas, he is recognizable as their King, Chitraratha, and among accomplished sages, he can be seen in Kapil Muni.

Peepal is a tree which releases oxygen during the night-time while other trees release oxygen during the day time (phenomenon of photosynthesis) and carbon dioxide during the night time (phenomenon of respiration). It means that processes of photosynthesis and respiration were known to our Rishis. In Atharvaveda, 300 varieties of various trees have been listed.

In Atharvaveda, one entire Sukta of Kanda 3 is devoted to Ashwattha. This Sukta contains eight Mantras. Of these, we have taken two for reference here.

M 14 Atharvaveda Mantra 3/6/3 जगद्बीजं पुरुषः, वानस्पत्योऽश्वत्थः, अनुष्टुप्

For this Mantra, the Rishi is Jagadbeejam Purusha. Devta is Ashwattha of the family of Vanaspati or trees. Metre is Anushtup.

> यथांश्वत्थ निरभंनोऽन्तर्महृत्यऽर्णवे ।
> एवा तान्त्सर्वान् निर्भङ्ग्धि यानुहं द्वेष्मि ये च माम् ॥ 3/6/3

Meaning of words/combination of words

यथांश्वत्थ Like the Peepal tree निरभनोऽन्तर्महृत्यऽर्णवे breaks into the powerful flood of air एवा तान्त्सर्वान् in that manner, you break all those निर्भङ्ग्धि यानहं द्वेष्मि ये च माम् whom I hate or who hate me.

This Mantra translates to: 'As you break forth, O Ashwattha, into the great abundance (of air), similarly, you break up all those whom I hate and those who hate me'.

The implication is that the powerful exhalation of the Peepal tree drives away, all influences in the contaminated air around us that are inimical or harmful for mankind. The reference is to enemies who may be men or ailments which may be physical or psychological because all of these elements are eliminated by the cleaner air. By invoking the Ashwattha tree and by taking benefits endowed by this tree for the welfare of mankind, we can keep our enemies at bay.

M 15 Atharvaveda Mantra 3/6/8 जगद्बीजं पुरुष:, वानस्पत्योऽश्वत्थ:, अनुष्टुप्

For this Mantra, the Rishi is Jagadbeejam Purusha. Devta is Ashwattha of the family of Vanaspati or trees. Metre is Anushtup.

> प्रैणान् नुद्वे मनसा प्र चित्तेनोत ब्रह्मणा ।
> प्रैणान् वृक्षस्य शाखंयाश्वत्थस्यं नुदामहे॥ 3/6/8

Meaning of words/combination of words

प्रैणान् नुद्वे मनसा I remove these enemies out of my mind प्र चित्तेनोत ब्रह्मणा from out of my consciousness or thought and knowledge प्रैणान् वृक्षस्य शाखंयाश्वत्थस्यं नुदामहे using the branch of the Ashwattha tree, I remove all of these enemies using my mind, consciousness or thought and knowledge.

This translates to: 'I drive them out with my mind, drive them out with my thought, and also with my incantation. We drive them out with a branch of the Ashwattha tree'.

The purport is that using the praise or incantation of the Peepal tree, men remove all harmful or inimical elements from their mind, thought, consciousness and knowledge. Thus, Peepal tree is recognized as the basic plant bestowed upon mankind for fighting against all kinds of challenges to life so that on Earth, mankind may prosper, leading a healthy and disease-free life.

R 124 Richa 10/97/6 आर्थवणो भिषग्, ओषधयः, अनुष्टुप्

For this Richa, the Rishi is Bhishaj (the physician), the son of Atharvan. Medicinal plants or herbs are the Devtas. The Metre is Anushtup.

> यत्रौषधीः समग्मंत॒ राजा॑न॒ः समिंताविव ।
> विप्र॒ः स उंच्यते भिषग्रंक्षो॒हामीं॑वृचात॑न॒ः ॥10/97/6

Meaning of words/combination of words

यत्रौषधीः Where the medicines समग्मंत॒ राजा॑न॒ः समिंताविव congregate together just as many kings join together in a battle विप्र॒ः स the knowledgeable उंच्यते is so spoken of भिषग्रंक्षो॒हामीं॑वृचात॑न॒ः when he is the destroyer of all pains and diseases.

This Richa translates to: 'Where the medicinal plants, you are gathered together like many kings who assemble in a battle, there the wise person, who is designated as the physician is able, with the help of these medicines, to become the destroyer of all pains and diseases'.

The purport is that often different medicines may have to be combined together for a successful cure of complicated pains and diseases. This feat is achieved by a knowledgeable physician who understands the different properties of these different medicines derived from the plants and use them in a proper and effective combination just as many kings join hands to defeat the enemy army.

R 125 Richa 10/97/7 आथर्वणो भिषग्, ओषधयः, अनुष्टुप्

For this Richa, the Rishi is Bhishaj (the physician), the son of Atharvan. Medicinal plants or herbs are the Devtas. The Metre is Anushtup.

> अश्वावतीं सोमावतीमूर्जयन्तीमुदोजसम् ।
> आविन्ति सर्वा ओषधीरस्मा अरिष्टतातये ॥10/97/7

Meaning of words/combination of words

अश्वावतीं Medicines who are known as Ashwavati सोमावतीमूर्जयन्तीमुदोजसम् and similarly, Somavati, Urjayanti, and Udojas आविन्ति सर्वा ओषधीरस्मा and I know other such medicines also अरिष्टतातये for the purpose of defeating this disease.

This Richa translates to: 'The Ashwavati, the Somavati, the Urjayanti, and the Udojas, and similarly, various other medicinal plants - I know these plants and I praise them with a view to overcoming this disease'.

In this Richa, four major medicinal plants have been identified as the Ashwavati, the Somavati, the Urjayanti, and the Udojas. Theirproperties and those of similar other medicinal plants are worth knowing if they are to be effectively used for curing the diseases. Their effectiveness increases when they are praised through Mantras by a knowledgeable physician such as Bhishaj, who is the Rishi of this Mantra.

A detailed list of medicinal plants recognized through the ancient times in India is given in Appendix 3 where their Sanskrit names along with modern botanical names are given.

A number of works have traced the practice of agriculture in Rigvaidic times. A comprehensive work is that of Majumdar (1927) which gives detailed references to Rigveda and other Vedas as also other ancient Indian texts on the subject of plant life.

Agriculture in Rigveda: Seeds of India's Civilizational Prosperity

R 126 Richa 10/97/8 आथर्वणो भिषग्, ओषधयः, अनुष्टुप्

For this Richa, the Rishi is Bhishaj (the physician), the son of Atharvan. Medicinal plants or herbs are the Devtas. The Metre is Anushtup.

> उच्छुष्मा ओषधीनां गावों गोष्ठादिवेरते ।
> धनं सनिष्यन्तीनामात्मानं तव पूरुष ॥10/97/8

Meaning of words/combination of words

उच्छुष्मा ओषधीनां गावों गोष्ठादिवेरते Like the cows come out of the cowshed, similarly medicines self-emanate different kinds of healing properties धनं सनिष्यन्तीनामात्मानं different kinds of wealth will be given for the benefit of your body by these medicines तव पूरुष for you, O mankind.

This Richa translates to: 'The properties or healing strengths of the plants emanate from them as spontaneously as cows come out of the cowshed as soon as the gate is opened. These medicines are desirous of bestowing upon you, O mankind, different kinds of wealth in the form of a disease-free body and mind for you'.

The purport is that the medicinal properties of the plants flow from them spontaneously for keeping the mankind in good health. In this sense, the health status of a person is like enjoyment of wealth for him. This is the reason why the Devtas have created different kinds of medicinal plants for the benefit of mankind so that his body and mind can be kept in disease-free status. In acknowledgement of this gift from the Devtas, mankind is supposed to perform Yajnas and prayers of the medicinal plants and of the Devtas who govern their properties.

R 127 Richa 10/97/9 आथर्वणो भिषग्, ओषधयः, अनुष्टुप्

For this Richa, the Rishi is Bhishaj (the physician), the son of Atharvan. Medicinal plants or herbs are the Devtas. The Metre is Anushtup.

> इष्कृतिर्नाम वो माताऽथो यूयं स्थ निष्कृतीः ।
> सीराः पतत्रिणीः स्थन यदामयति निष्कृथ ॥10/97/9

Meaning of words/combination of words

इष्कृंतिर्नामं वो मातांऽथों The name of your mother is Ishkriti, which means the one who keeps you disease-free यूयं स्थ निष्कृंतीः therefore, you also become capable of keeping the diseases away सीराः पंतत्रिणीः you become capable of going or descending fast (into the disease to overcome it) स्थन् यदामयंति निष्कृंथ to overcome the disease of the person who is ill so as to cure him.

This translates to: '(O Medicines), Ishkriti is the name of your mother. This itself means the one who is capable of keeping the diseases away. Therefore, O medicines, you also become able to inherit the same capability of keeping the diseases away. In this endeavour, you be fast and effective like a flowing or falling stream so that you may cure the disease of an ill person speedily and completely'.

Here, there is a recognition that the medicinal plants have inherited the properties of their generic mother known in the Vedas as 'Ishkriti'. Her name literally means the mother who keeps the diseases away. Therefore, from your mother, O medicinal plants, you are entitled to inherit the same properties and you may exercise these in a manner such that your capabilities can work with great speed and success in curing an ill person. This way, you will do justice to the name of your mother.

R 128 Richa 10/97/10 आर्थवणो भिषग्, ओषधयः, अनुष्टुप्

For this Richa, the Rishi is Bhishaj (the physician), the son of Atharvan. Medicinal plants or herbs are the Devtas. The Metre is Anushtup.

अतिं विश्वांः परिष्ठा स्तेन इंव व्रजमंक्रमुः ।
ओषंधीः प्राचुंच्यवुर्यत्किं चं तन्वोंऽ३ रपंः ॥10/97/10

Meaning of words/combination of words

स्तेन इंव Like a thief अतिं विश्वांः परिष्ठा attacks the cowshed व्रजमंक्रमुः ओषंधीः similarly, medicines comprehensively attack on a disease प्राचुंच्यवुर्यत्किं चं तन्वोंऽ३ रपंः and overcome whatever may be the reasons for pain and illness.

This Richa translates to: 'The all-encompassing disease-defeating capacities of the medicinal plants quickly overcome the illness from out of the body of the diseased person just as a thief attacks a cowshed in order to speedily drive away all the cows'.

The purport is that the medicinal plants have universal and comprehensive properties to overcome all diseases faced by mankind and their effect takes place with considerable speed. As such, the understanding of the properties of the medicinal plants and performance of Yajnas in recognition of such a gift to mankind by the Devtas will ensure keeping mankind disease-free provided his behaviour remains consistent with the maintenance and sustenance of all the beneficial plant life.

R 129 Richa 10/97/11 आथर्वणो भिषग्, ओषधयः, अनुष्टुप्

For this Richa, the Rishi is Bhishaj (the physician), the son of Atharvan. Medicinal plants or herbs are the Devtas. The Metre is Anushtup.

> यदिमा वा॒जय॑न्त्र॒हमोष॑धी॒र्हस्तं आद॒धे ।
> आ॒त्मा यक्ष्म॑स्य नश्यति पुरा जीवगृ॒भों यथा ॥10/97/11

Meaning of words/combination of words

यदिमा वा॒जय॑न्त्र॒हमोष॑धी॒र्हस्तं आदधे When the strength-giving medicines are taken in my hand आ॒त्मा यक्ष्म॑स्य नश्यति पुरा जीवगृ॒भों यथा then diseases run away from the body like animals run away from a tiger. (In this way) Diseases are destroyed from their very source and men are restored to their normal self.

This Richa translates to: 'As soon as I take these strength-giving medicinal plants in my hand for application on to the ill person, the source of the illness runs away from him like animals run away from a tiger and quickly, the man is restored to his normal self'.

In this Richa, the Rishi assures all mankind that medicinal plants of great healing properties have been gifted to mankind and when the knowledgeable physician takes these in his hand, diseases run away fast and from the source so that the original health of the ill person is restored. It is important to identify the knowledgeable physician who knows the different properties of the medicinal plants.

R 130 Richa 10/97/12 आथर्वणो भिषग्, ओषधय:, अनुष्टुप्

For this Richa, the Rishi is Bhishaj (the physician), the son of Atharvan. Medicinal plants or herbs are the Devtas. The Metre is Anushtup.

> यस्यौषधीः प्रसर्पथाङ्गमङ्गं परुष्परुः ।
> ततो यक्ष्मं वि बाधध्व उग्रो मध्यमशीरिव ॥10/97/12

Meaning of words/combination of words

यस्यौषधीः For that person, O medicines, प्रसर्पथाङ्गमङ्गं परुष्परुः in whom the diseases have spread out from limb to limb and joint to joint ततो यक्ष्मं वि बाधध्व you drive away all the illness from his body उग्रो मध्यमशीरिव like a strong intermediary person.

This translates to: 'From him, O medicinal plants, in whom diseases have crept from limb to limb and joint to joint, you drive away even such a disease like a mighty intermediary king who is stationed in the midst of the body of the host'.

In praise of the strength of the medicinal plants, the Rishi says that these plants have such curative effectiveness that they can fight out from the body of the diseased person, even such diseases which may have spread out from limb to limb and joint to joint within the ill person.

R 131 Richa 10/97/13 आथर्वणो भिषग्, ओषधय:, अनुष्टुप्

For this Richa, the Rishi is Bhishaj (the physician), the son of Atharvan. Medicinal plants or herbs are the Devtas. The Metre is Anushtup.

> साकं यक्ष्मं प्र पत चाषेण किकिदीविना ।
> साकं वातस्य ध्राज्या साकं नश्य निहाकया ॥10/97/13

Meaning of words/combination of words

यंक्ष्म् O disease, साकं प्र पत् चार्षेण किकिदीविनां you speedily fly away like the birds named Chasha and Kikidivi साकं वातंस्य् ध्राज्यां you get destroyed fast with the speed of wind साकं नंश्य निहाकंया you get destroyed with speed like the animal named iguana.

This translates to: 'O sickness, fly away quickly with the speed of birds named Jay and blue Jay, that are named in Sanskrit as Chasha and Kikidivi, and similarly run away with the velocity of the wind, and perish along with the iguana'.

This Richa directly addresses the disease itself and says that it is not welcome in the body of men. It must speedily depart as a result of the use of medicines derived from medicinal plants and herbs and by the repeated chants of the Mantras. The implication is that the diseases themselves have a mind and intent of their own and when it is clarified to them that they are not welcome, that they are to be treated as an enemy, they must gather speed and fly away.

R 132 Richa 10/97/14 आथर्वणो भिषग्, ओषधयः, अनुष्टुप्

For this Richa, the Rishi is Bhishaj (the physician), the son of Atharvan. Medicinal plants or herbs are the Devtas. The Metre is Anushtup.

> अन्या वों अन्यामवत्वन्यान्यस्या उपावत ।
> ताः सर्वाः संविदाना इदं मे प्रावता वचं: ॥10/97/14

Meaning of words/combination of words

अन्या वों अन्यामवत्वन्यान्यस्या उपावत Let one medicine go to another and let the second go to the third medicine ताः सर्वाः and like that, all the medicines work together संविदाना इदं speaking to each other, sharing their thoughts, becoming of one mind मे प्रावता वचं: and in that manner, protect the prayer of my pleading.

This Richa translates to: 'Let one plant approach another and the second plant approach a third, and in that manner, let them mutually interact and become of one mind and in this way, let them defend my prayer'.

The purport is that different medicines may be used together in a manner such that they can have a combined impact on the disease and their different properties may come together in order to completely overcome the illness. This is our pleading to the medicines so that they may join hands and harmonize their effects. The Rishis show recognition of the value of combining different medicines drawn out from different medicinal plants. It is also implied that they have studied in depth, the properties of individual plants and the manner in which these can be combined.

R 133 Richa 10/97/15 आर्थवणो भिषग्, ओषधयः, अनुष्टुप्

For this Richa, the Rishi is Bhishaj (the physician), the son of Atharvan. Medicinal plants or herbs are the Devtas. The Metre is Anushtup.

> याः फ़लिनीर्या अफ़ला अंपुष्पा याश्चं पुष्पिणीः ।
> बृहस्पतिप्रसूतास्ता नों मुञ्चन्त्वंहसः ॥10/97/15

Meaning of words/combination of words

याः Those फ़लिनीर्या अफ़ला that bear fruits and those that do not bear fruits अंपुष्पा याश्चं पुष्पिणीः and those that produce flowers and those that do not बृहस्पतिप्रसूतास्ता all of these plants have been created by Devta Brihaspati नों मुञ्चन्त्वंहसः and let them all join together to free us from sins and diseases.

This translates to: 'Whether bearing fruit or not bearing fruit, whether flowering or not bearing flowers, all of these progenies of Brihaspati, may they liberate us from sins and illnesses'.

The purport is that all the plants have been created by Brihaspati, the Guru of all Devtas. These plants may have different features. Some of these may bear fruits and some flowers. Some may not either bear fruits or flowers. But they all have beneficial properties for the welfare of mankind. Once the plants are recognized as the progeny of Devtas, they must be valued, protected and used for the welfare of mankind.

Agriculture in Rigveda: Seeds of India's Civilizational Prosperity

R 134 Richa 10/97/16 आर्थवणो भिषग्, ओषधय:, अनुष्टुप्

For this Richa, the Rishi is Bhishaj (the physician), the son of Atharvan. Medicinal plants or herbs are the Devtas. The Metre is Anushtup.

> मुञ्चन्तु मा शप॒थ्या॒३दथो वरुण्यांदुत ।
> अथो यमस्य पड़बींशा॒त्सर्वस्माद्देवकिल्बिषात् ॥10/97/16

Meaning of words/combination of words

मुञ्चन्तु You save us (O medicines) मा शप॒थ्या॒३दथो sins that are generated out of taking vows वरुण्यांदुत from sins caused by Varuna अथो यमस्य and similarly from Yama पड़बींशा॒त्सर्वस्माद्देवकिल्बिषात् and similarly, from all sins and diseases which may have arisen from displeasing the Devtas.

This Richa translates to: 'May you (O medicines) save me from the sins resulting from curses and from the sins due to displeasing Varuna and from the fetters of Yama, and from any guilt induced by the Devtas'.

In this Richa, there is an acknowledgement that ailments may be generated because of any curses or due to displeasure of Devtas or they may have induced us into sins, and some Devtas like Yama have strong fetters. The Rishi says that the medicinal plants have enough strength even to overcome the ill-effects of ailments that may be caused by the Devtas which may otherwise be incurable. This is so because the medicines have also been created by the Devtas themselves.

R 135 Richa 10/97/17 आर्थवणो भिषग्, ओषधय:, अनुष्टुप्

For this Richa, the Rishi is Bhishaj (the physician), the son of Atharvan. Medicinal plants or herbs are the Devtas. The Metre is Anushtup.

> अ॒वुपतं॒न्तीरवदन्न्दिव ओषधय॒स्परि ।
> यं जी॒वमश्रवांमहै न स रिष्याति पूरुष: ॥10/97/17

Meaning of words/combination of words

अ॒वप॑तं॒न्तीरव॑दन्दि॒व ओष॑धय॒स्परि॑ Descending from Dyulok, that is the land of the Devtas, the medicinal plants said यं जी॒वम॒श्नवा॑महै॒ न स रि॑ष्याति॒ पूरु॑षः that person whom we protect will remain disease-free.

This translates to: 'The plants, descending from Dyulok, announced that the person whom we protect by pervading him, he is assured of remaining free from illnesses'.

In this Richa, first it is reasserted that the medicinal plants have been brought down from the land of the Devtas for the benefit of mankind. These plants have a self and a will of their own. When they are pleased with a person, they may assure him of a life which remains disease-free. They may do so by pervading his body and spreading their beneficial effect throughout their being.

R 136 Richa 10/97/18 आथर्वणो भिषग्, ओषधयः, अनुष्टुप्

For this Richa, the Rishi is Bhishaj (the physician), the son of Atharvan. Medicinal plants or herbs are the Devtas. The Metre is Anushtup.

> या ओष॑धीः॒ सोम॑रा॒ज्ञीर्ब॒ह्वीः॒ श॒तवि॑चक्षणाः ।
> तासां॑ त्व॒मस्यु॑त्त॒मारं॒ कामा॑य॒ शं हृ॒दे ॥10/97/18

Meaning of words/combination of words

या ओष॑धीः॒ सोम॑रा॒ज्ञी These medicines of whom the Soma plant is the king ब॒ह्वीः॒ श॒तवि॑चक्षणाः have hundreds and in fact, innumerable positive properties तासां॑ त्व॒मस्यु॑त्त॒मारं॒ of these, O Soma, you are the supreme one कामा॑य॒ शं हृ॒दे you be pleased to enable me to attain all my heart's desires.

This translates to: 'Of these plants, Soma is the king. Each of these plants have hundreds and in fact, innumerable properties and even among these, you, Soma plant, are the supreme. Please be generous enough to fulfil all my heart's desires'.

In this Richa, the Rishi praises the unique place and qualities of the Soma plant. Soma has the capacity not only to cure all diseases but also to fulfil all desires of mankind as well as Devtas. The entire ninth Mandal of

Agriculture in Rigveda: Seeds of India's Civilizational Prosperity

Rigveda is devoted to the worship of and enumeration of the qualities of the Soma plant where time and again, it is indicated that the Soma plant was brought to Earth from Dyulok, that is from the abode of Devtas.

R 137 Richa 10/97/19 आर्थवर्णो भिषग्, ओषधयः, अनुष्टुप्

For this Richa, the Rishi is Bhishaj (the physician), the son of Atharvan. Medicinal plants or herbs are the Devtas. The Metre is Anushtup.

> या ओषधी: सोमंराज्ञीर्विष्ठिताः पृथिवीमनु ।
> बृहस्पतिंप्रसूता अ्स्यै सं दंत्त वीर्यम् ॥10/97/19

Meaning of words/combination of words

या ओषधी: सोमंराज्ञीर्विष्ठिताः These medicines of whom Soma is the king पृथिवीमनु who are stationed in many places on the Earth बृहस्पतिंप्रसूता have all emanated from Brihaspati, the Guru of Devtas अ्स्यै सं दंत्त वीर्यम् and they may all give the strength generated by Brihaspati to this ill person.

This Richa translates to: 'O plants, you have Soma as your king, and you have been established in different places over the Earth. All of you are the offspring of Brihaspati. May you give vigour to the (infirm body) of this ill person'.

In this Richa, it is reasserted that the Soma plant should be considered at the apex of all beneficial plants. Devtas having brought these plants from their own abode ensured that they may be scattered and established all across the Earth so as to become available for mankind at large. These plants are the progeny of Brihaspati and derive their strength from him. May they give that same strength to the body of this ill person so as to cure him.

R 138 Richa 10/97/20 आर्थर्वणो भिषग्, ओषधय:, अनुष्टुप्

For this Richa, the Rishi is Bhishaj (the physician), the son of Atharvan. Medicinal plants or herbs are the Devtas. The Metre is Anushtup.

मा वों रिषत्खनिता यस्मैं चाहं खनांमि व: ।
द्विपच्चतुंष्पदुस्माकं सर्वमस्त्वनातुरम् ॥10/97/20

Meaning of words/combination of words

O medicinal plants मा वों रिषत्खनिता let that person who digs you out may not himself be destroyed यस्मैं चाहं खनांमि for whose cure I am digging you व: द्विपच्चतुंष्पदुस्माकं सर्वमस्त्वनातुरम् let all our bipeds and quadrupeds become free from disease.

This Richa translates to: 'Let the person who digs out the medicinal plants may himself not be hurt and let not that sick person be hurt for whom I am digging you up. May all our bipeds and quadrupeds be cured from disease'.

Here the reference is to medicinal roots which grow under the soil. The person who digs them out has the welfare motive of using these medicinal roots for men and for other domestic animals. Therefore, let him not be punished for the act of digging the plant up which may otherwise be considered a sin. Let the person also be careful enough to dig the medicinal plant in a manner such that the plant is not damaged. Thus, the Rishi is showing recognition of the medicinal value not only of trees or other plants who bear fruit or flowers above the ground but also of thoseplants who have medicinal value in their roots.

R 139 Richa 10/97/21 आर्थर्वणो भिषग्, ओषधय:, अनुष्टुप्

For this Richa, the Rishi is Bhishaj (the physician), the son of Atharvan. Medicinal plants or herbs are the Devtas. The Metre is Anushtup.

याश्चेदमुंपशृण्वन्ति याश्चं दूरं परांगता: ।
सर्वा: संगत्यं वीरुधोऽस्यै सं दंत्त वीर्यम् ॥10/97/21

Agriculture in Rigveda: Seeds of India's Civilizational Prosperity

Meaning of words/combination of words

याश्चेदमुपशृण्वन्ति Those medicines who hear these, our praises याश्च दूरं परागताः and those medicines who are located far away (and therefore unable to hear directly, our praises) सर्वाः संगत्यं let them all get together वीरुधोऽस्यै सं दत्त वीर्यम् to give strength and capacities to this suffering body.

This Richa translates to: 'Let the plants that hear this prayer, and those that are located far away, come together to give strength and necessary capacities to this infirm body'.

The purport is that prayers are being offered to invoke the medicinal properties of the plants. Let such properties be invoked not only in those plants that are located in the vicinity of the place where the Yajnas are being performed but also let all medicinal plants be able to access their medicinal properties and let them all come together, communicating as it were, with each other in a manner such that their properties can become jointly effective in curing the person and giving him strength.

R 140 Richa 10/97/22 आथर्वणो भिषग्, ओषधयः, अनुष्टुप्

For this Richa, the Rishi is Bhishaj (the physician), the son of Atharvan. Medicinal plants or herbs are the Devtas. The Metre is Anushtup.

ओषंधयः सं वंदन्ते सोमेंन सुह राज्ञां ।
यस्मैं कृणोतिं ब्राह्मणस्तं रांजन्पारयामसि ॥10/97/22

Meaning of words/combination of words

ओषधयः सं वदन्ते सोमेन These medicines together with their king, the Soma plant, make out this declaration सह राज्ञा यस्मै कृणोति ब्राह्मणस्तं together with the king, the person whom the physician treats रांजन्पारयामसि we take him beyond sickness.

This translates to: 'All these plants, together with their king, the Soma plant, make this assertion - O king, we take that person beyond disease whom the physician has undertaken to treat'.

Here, there is reference to a commitment by the medicinal plants in the presence of their leading plant namely, the Soma plant that when a physician undertakes to treat a person with our help, we will ensure that he gets fully cured. This Richa indicates that the Rishis recognize plants as having their own mind and entity. They guarantee mankind as endorsed by their leading Soma plant that it is their duty and commitment to ensure that mankind would be fully cured when knowledgeable physicians utilize the properties of the medicinal plants for treating diseases in a proper manner.

R 141 Richa 10/97/23 आथर्वणो भिषग्, ओषधयः, अनुष्टुप्

For this Richa, the Rishi is Bhishaj (the physician), the son of Atharvan. Medicinal plants or herbs are the Devtas. The Metre is Anushtup.

> त्वमुत्तमास्योषधे तवं वृक्षा उपस्तयः ।
> उपस्तिरस्तु सो३ऽस्माकुं यो अ॒स्माँ अभिदासति ॥10/97/23

Meaning of words/combination of words

त्वमुत्तमास्योषधे You are the best of all of us plants, O Soma तवं वृक्षा उपस्तयः all of us plants prostrate to you or bow down to you, honouring you उपस्तिरस्तु सो३ऽस्माकुं यो अ॒स्माँ अभिदासति let all our enemies who attack us also bow down to us.

This Richa translates to: 'O Soma plant, you are the best amongst us all trees and we prostrate before you. Similarly, let those who attack us, also prostrate before us'.

The purport is that mankind has been blessed with a number of medicinal trees including the Soma plant. The medicinal trees themselves acknowledge the great beneficial value of the Soma plant for mankind who performs Yajnas in their praise and in the praise of the Soma. Since he does so, let all his enemies get defeated and let them therefore submit to mankind. Here, indirectly, enemies may refer to diseases that attack mankind or the animals under his care. Let all such diseases be defeated because he performs Yajnas in the praise of Devtas.

Summary and Key Points

A narration of Vaidic understanding of agriculture would not be complete without a recognition and acknowledgement of the role that different trees, plants, and herbs play in supporting mankind and in fact, all life forms. Rigveda's Sukta 10/97 which we have referred to as the 'Aushadhi Sukta' is devoted to the role of medicinal plants and herbs for the benefit and upkeep of the health of men. The Richas here may be considered as the origin of Ayurveda. Some of the key points highlighted in this Chapter are indicated below.

- Medicinal plants were brought from Dyulok, that is the land of the Devtas to the Earth for the benefit of mankind.
- These plants, in all their forms, that is fruits, flowers, trunks, branches, seeds and leaves may all have medicinal roles.
- These plants often need to be combined for maximizing their medicinal benefits.
- It is not only the medicinal plants that grow above the Earth but also herbs and roots that grow below the Earth or have growth of seeds below Earth which are also highly useful for medicinal and health purposes.
- Some of the beneficial medicinal plants named in this Sukta include Peepal, Palasha, Ashwavati, Somavati, Urjayanti, and Udojas. The Soma plant is recognized as the king of such beneficial plants both for Devtas and mankind.
- An understanding of the medicinal properties of individual plants is critical for their optimal application. Their properties require to be invoked through performance of Yajnas using Mantras such as those given in this Sukta.

Chapter 8 Agriculture and Industry

Agriculture and industry were closely inter-linked in the Rigvaidic times. Industrial activities were required for producing agricultural implements, means of storage and transport. Alongside as trade developed both within the nation and internationally, mainly through the river and sea routes, boats and ships were also required. Grain had to be processed, stored, transported to markets using a variety of implements and vehicles. Industrial products were also needed for taking care of the animals like cows and horses that were critical for successful agriculture. The interrelationship between industry and agriculture is brought out in an elaborate way in Sukta 101 of Mandal 10.

Mandal 10 Sukta 101: Agriculture-Industry Interface

In the tenth Mandal, the 101st Sukta is mainly devoted to agriculture and the use of industrial inputs into agriculture. The Rishi for this Sukta is Somputra Budh and Devtas are the Vishvedevas, that is, all the Devtas or Ritvij. The Metre is Trishtup for most of the Richas.

R 142 Richa 10/101/1 बुधः सौम्यः, विश्वे देवा ऋत्विजो वा, त्रिष्टुप्

For this Richa, the Rishi is Somputra Budh and Devtas are Vishvedevas, that is, all the Devtas. The Chanda is Trishtup.

> उद्बुध्यध्वं समनसः सखायः समग्निमिन्ध्वं बहवः सनीळाः ।
> दधिक्रामग्निमुषसं च देवीमिन्द्रांवृतोऽवसे नि ह्वये वः ॥ 10/101/1

Meaning of words/combination of words

सखायः Friends समनसः thinking similarly, being of the same mind उद्बुध्यध्वं please get up. Implicitly, the description is that of the morning समग्निमिन्ध्वं बहवः सनीळाः getting several of you together, please light up the fire दधिक्रामग्निमुषसं च देवीमिन्द्रांवृतोऽवसे नि ह्वये वः । request three Devis/Devtas, Dadhika, Agni, and Usha (goddess of early morning) together with Lord Indra for our protection.

This Richa may be translated as 'Friends (who will perform the Yajna), wake up with same mind (or thoughts), gathering together in one place, ignite the fire. I will invoke Indra with Dadhika, Agni, and Usha Devi for our protection'.

This Richa portrays an early morning setting where a small community of men is present and is about to wake up to get ready for performing the Yajna and then to proceed for their daily occupations. There is an emphasis on harmony in thoughts for the performance of the works during the day. Preparations are being made for igniting the fire.

R 143 Richa 10/101/2 बुधः सौम्यः, विश्वे देवा ऋत्विजो वा, त्रिष्टुप्

For this Richa, the Rishi is Somputra Budh and Devtas are Vishvedevas, that is, all the Devtas. The Chanda is Trishtup.

> मन्द्रा कृणुध्वं धियु आ तनुध्वं नावमरित्रपरणीं कृणुध्वम् ।
> इष्कृणुध्वमायुधारं कृणुध्वं प्राञ्चं यज्ञं प्रणयता सखायः ॥ 10/101/2

Meaning of words/combination of words

मन्द्रा कृणुध्वं Friends sing happliy for the Yajna धियु आ तनुध्वं expand our great works नावमरित्रपरणीं कृणुध्वम् build the boat with oars and the anchor that will take us across the river इष्कृणुध्वमायुधारं build many weapons skillfully in large quantities प्राञ्चं यज्ञं प्रणयता perform the auspicious Yajna.

This Richa may be translated as: 'Friends, singing happily, expand our good works, build the ship that has oars and an anchor, capable of taking us across. Build many weapons skillfully, in sufficient quantities which can carry out strikes. Let us organize an auspicious Yajna'.

In this second Richa, there is reference to the industrial activities and skills. There is recognition of skills for building boats/ships and weapons. There is emphasis on the expansion of industrial activities for making weapons and ships. The setting is of a community of people possibly on the banks of a large river or a coastal town, where the community wakes up early in the morning, lights up fire, performs Yajna, and then happily

Agriculture in Rigveda: Seeds of India's Civilizational Prosperity

gets engaged in skillful activities such as building of ships and making of weapons. Some of the community members also engage in agricultural activities, as indicated in the next Richa.

R 144 Richa 10/101/3 बुधः सौम्यः, विश्वे देवा ऋत्विजो वा, त्रिष्टुप

For this Richa, the Rishi is Somputra Budh and Devtas are Vishvedevas, that is, all the Devtas. The Chanda is Trishtup.

> युनक्त सीरा वि युगा तनुध्वं कृते योनौ वपतेह बीजंम् ।
> गिरा चं श्रुष्टिः सभंरा असंन्नो नेदीय इत्सृण्यंः पक्रमेयांत् ॥ 10/101/3

Meaning of words/combination of words

युनक्त सीरा Get the ploughs ready युगा तनुध्वं apply the yoke कृते योनौ in the well prepared field वपतेह बीजंम् plant the seeds गिरा चं श्रुष्टिः सभंरा असंन्नो from our well considered prayer, let the grains fully mature नेदीय इत्सृण्यंः पक्रमेयांत् and let the sickle be applied to the ripened dhan (rice).

This Richa translates to: 'Friends, prepare the ploughs for applying on the field, expand or apply the yoke, plant the seeds in this well-prepared field. From our praiseworthy prayer, let the grains mature fully, let the sickle be applied to the ripened grain (rice)'.

Thus, in addition to Yava (barley), there is reference to rice or dhan. The plough and yoke are industrial products. In this Richa, the full cycle of an agricultural product is described from sowing of the seeds, ploughing of the field, maturing of the grains and then using implements to reap the crop.

R 145 Richa 10/101/4 बुधः सौम्यः, विश्वे देवा ऋत्विजो वा, त्रिष्टुप

For this Richa, the Rishi is Somputra Budh and Devtas are Vishvedevas, that is, all the Devtas. The Chanda is Trishtup.

> सीरां युञ्जन्ति कवयों युगा वि तन्वते पृथक् ।
> धीरां देवेषुं सुम्नया ॥ 10/101/4

Meaning of words/combination of words

देवेषु धीरां कवयों सुम्नया Wise people sing in praise of Devtas with a happy or harmonious mind सीरां युञ्जन्ति while ploughs are applied on the field युगा वि तन्वते पृथक् many others separate the yoke from the oxen when the day's work is over.

Thus, the Richa translates to: 'Wise people sing in praise of Devtas with a happy mind while ploughs are applied on the field, and other active people separate the yoke from the oxen'.

This Richa indicates that sowing was a pleasuarable activity carried out while singing and chanting was going on. The description in this Richa is possibly that of the end of a fruitful day when the yoke is to be taken off and the daily activity is being wound up. Oxen are to be given relief as soon as the day's work is done.

R 146 Richa 10/101/5 बुधः सौम्यः, विश्वे देवा ऋत्विजो वा, बृहती

For this Richa, the Rishi is Somputra Budh and Devtas are Vishvedevas, that is, all the Devtas. The Chanda is Brihati.

निरांहावान्कृणोतन् सं वंरत्रा दंधातन ।
सिञ्चामंहा अवृतमुद्रिणं वृयं सुषेकमनुंपक्षितम् ॥10/101/5

Meaning of words/combination of words

निरांहावान्कृणोतन् For cows and other animals, many places may be made for drinking water वंरत्रा सं दंधातन tie up the ropes वृयं let us सिञ्चामंहा be able to irrigate our land अवृतमुद्रिणं सुषेकमनुंपक्षितम् inexhaustible wells which draw water from great streams.

Thus, the Richa may be translated to: 'Friends, make many places for drinking water for cows and other animals. Join together the ropes, let us irrigate our land with adequate and inexhaustible wells that may be fed by auspicious [great] streams'.

The purport is that both land and animals must be provided with ample quantity of good quality water for which some construction of suitable places or water storage devices for drinking water should be made and ropes should be used for the requisite purposes of drawing water from the wells and of tying up the animals. These references indicate that construction activities and making of ropes were prevalent in the Vaidic period.

R 147 Richa 10/101/6 बुधः सौम्यः, विश्वे देवा ऋत्विजो वा, गायत्री

For this Richa, the Rishi is Somputra Budh and Devtas are Vishvedeva, that is, all the Devtas. The Chanda is Gayatri.

> इष्कृताहावमवृतं सुवरत्रं सुषेचनम् ।
> उद्रिणं सिञ्चे अक्षितम् ॥10/101/6

Meaning of words/combination of words

इष्कृताहावमवृतं Having made arrangements सुवरत्रं good ropes सुषेचनम् good source of water उद्रिणं सिञ्चे अक्षितम् from an inexhaustible source, I draw water for irrigation.

This Richa may be translated to: 'Having made arrangements for animals, whereby water has been made available in plenty and good ropes have also been made available. We irrigate from the inexhaustible source full of water that is made ready for drawing water'.

This Richa describes activities of drawing water using ropes from a well, supplied by ample water, both for the animals and for irrigating the fields. Arrangements have also been made for providing shelter for the animals. In this Richa, industrial products such as ropes and wells and related activities are also being referred to.

R 148 Richa 10/101/7 बुधः सौम्यः, विश्वे देवा ऋत्विजो वा, त्रिष्टुप्

For this Richa, the Rishi is Somputra Budh and Devtas are Vishvedevas, that is, all the Devtas. The Chanda is Trishtup.

> प्रीणीताश्वान्हितं जयाथ स्वस्तिवाहं रथमित्कृणुध्वम् ।
> द्रोणाहावमवृतमश्मचक्रमंसंत्रकोशं सिञ्चता नृपाणम् ॥ 10/101/7

Meaning of words/combination of words

प्रीणीताश्वान्हितं Please or satisfy the horses and oxen with water and feedstock स्वस्तिवाहं रथमिकृणुध्वम् must make the Ratha or vehicle which can easily carry the foodgrains नृपाणंम् appropriate for men's drinking द्रोणाहावमवुतमश्मंचक्रमंसंत्रकोशं सिञ्चता covered like an armour, joined with a wheel made of stone, accompanied by a vessel made of wood (containing a defined volume of water), having obtained a well with ample water, use it for irrigation.

The Richa translates to: 'Satisfy horses and bullocks with feedstock and water. This container of water for the animals will be of (thirty-two) seers. In this, there is an axle made of stone. Gather grain from the field. Do make comfortable vehicles for carrying grain easily. For drinking by men, the water may be contained or kept in well-like structures (tanks). Fill these up with water'.

In this Richa, quite a number of industrial tools are described: a water-container with an exactly specified volume, an axle made of stone, vehicles for carrying grains, and well-like structures for storing water.

R 149 Richa 10/101/8 बुधः सौम्यः, विश्वे देवा ऋत्विजो वा, त्रिष्टुप्

For this Richa, the Rishi is Somputra Budh and Devtas are Vishvedevas, that is, all the Devtas. The Chanda is Trishtup.

व्रजं कृणुध्वं स हि वों नृपाणो वर्मं सीव्यध्वं बहुला पृथूनि ।
पुरः कृणुध्वमायंसीरधृष्टा मा वः सुस्रोच्चमसो दंहता तम् ॥ 10/101/8

Meaning of words/combination of words

व्रजं कृणुध्वं Make properly, places for accomodating the cattle स हि वों नृपाणो वर्मं सीव्यध्वं बहुला पृथूनि make many large armour पुरः कृणुध्वमायंसीरधृष्टा make cities using iron that are invincible to the enemies सुस्रोच्चमसो दंहता तम् your vessel made of leather should also be strong so that water should not seep through.

This Richa translates to: 'Make suitable and proper places for cows. Similarly, make places that should be suitable for making food available for people. Weave together, many large sheaths [kavach] or armours. Make cities using iron so that these are invincible to the enemies. Equip these cities with many weapons. Make water containers such that water should not seep through these containers made of leather, make them strong'.

This Richa makes reference to a number of industrial activities useful for setting up a township or city which is well-protected from enemies. Also, within the city, suitable arrangements such as cowsheds are provided which require construction skills. Similarly, for fighting the enemies, both defensive and offensive weapons have to be provided for. Clearly, in the Rigvaidic times, considerable industrial activities to manufacture all of these must have been available. In those days, there was also a developed leather industry which was used for making water containers. In Mandal 9, which is devoted to Somaras, it is described that in the processing of the Soma plant, leather and a sieve made from woollen fabrics were required. Clearly, all of these skills were available in the Rigvaidic times.

R 150 Richa 10/101/9 बुधः सौम्यः, विश्वे देवा ऋत्विजो वा, त्रिष्टुप्

For this Richa, the Rishi is Somputra Budh and Devtas are Vishvedevas, that is, all the Devtas. The Chanda is Trishtup.

आ वो धियं यज्ञियां वर्त ऊतये देवां देवीं यंजतां यज्ञियामिह ।
सा नों दुहीयद्ध्वंसेव गत्वी सहस्रंधारा पयंसा मही गौः ॥ 10/101/9

Meaning of words/combination of words

देवां O Devtas आ वो धियं यज्ञियां वर्त ऊतये I seek the protection of your intellect capable of seeking the divine (Parmeshwar) देवीं यंजतां यज्ञियामिह Please bear this sharp intellect in this place for Yajna सा नों दुहीयद्ध्वंसेव this intellect may fulfill our desires गत्वी सहस्रंधारा पयंसा मही गौः just like our cows give milk through thousand streams after eating only grass and other feedstock.

This Richa translates as: 'I persuade the Devtas, so that they may facilitate the meditation by the Ritviks (people performing the Yajnas). Just like cows give good quality milk in thousand strands after eating only grass and other feedstock, similarly, Devtas, you may adorn/occupy this shining and sacred Yajna-place. Let our intellect and meditation fulfill our desires'.

The purport of the Richa is that by praising the Devtas, the performers of the Yajnas ensure that the Devtas agree or be pleased to arrive at the place where Yajnas are being performed. Let the Yajna-performers have enough capacity and devotion in their meditation so that the Devtas bless them with the means to fulfil all their desires. The metaphor is drawn with the cows who eat only grass and some other feedstock, but they yield in return, plentiful and high-quality milk. Similarly, the Devtas may respond to the limited praises through Mantras by giving in return, abundant food and riches so that all the desires of the Yajna-performers are fulfilled.

R 151 Richa 10/101/10 बुधः सौम्यः, विश्वे देवा ऋत्विजो वा, त्रिष्टुप्

For this Richa, the Rishi is Somputra Budh and Devtas are Vishvedevas, that is, all the Devtas. The Chanda is Trishtup.

आ तू षिञ्च हरिमीं द्रोरुपस्थे वाशीभिस्तक्षताश्मन्मयीभिः ।
परिष्वजध्वं दशं कक्ष्याभिरुभे धुरौ प्रति वहिं युनक्त ॥ 10/101/10

Meaning of words/combination of words

आ तू And you षिञ्च हरिमीं द्रोरुपस्थे water this green Soma kept in the wooden vessel वाशीभिस्तक्षताश्मन्मयीभिः using stone implements, prepare a vessel परिष्वजध्वं दशं कक्ष्याभि using ten fingers and ropes, shake the vessel धुरौ प्रति वहिं युनक्त tie the oxen with the two axles of the vehicle.

The Richa translates to: 'Take out this green coloured Soma kept in the wooden vessel. Prepare these vessels using stone implements. Using ten fingers and ropes, shake the vessel well. Prepare the vehicle [Ratha] by tying the oxen to the two axles'.

Agriculture in Rigveda: Seeds of India's Civilizational Prosperity

This Richa describes various activities pertaining to the preparation of the vessel in which the Somaras can be made and kept, and a vehicle on which it can be carried. The processing of grains after they have ripened and harvested is described by using a metaphor from the battlefield. Such a metaphor serves two purposes. Killing enemies in the battlefield is as spontaneous as threshing of grains so that the chaff can be separated from the genuine grain.

R 152 Richa 10/101/11 बुधः सौम्यः, विश्वे देवा ऋत्विजो वा, त्रिष्टुप्

For this Richa, the Rishi is Somputra Budh and Devtas are Vishvedevas, that is, all the Devtas. The Chanda is Trishtup.

उभे धुरौ वह्निरापिब्दंमानोऽन्तर्योनेव चरति द्विजानिः ।
वनस्पतिं वन् आस्थांपयध्वं नि षू दंधिध्वमखंनन्त उत्संम् ॥
10/101/11

Meaning of words/combination of words

उभे धुरौ Both wheels and axles वह्निरापिब्दंमानोऽन्तर्योनेव make noise चरति द्विजानिः while the oxen are moving वनस्पतिं वन् आस्थांपयध्वं establish this piece of Soma-wood well in the forest दंधिध्वमखंनन्त उत्संम् stabilize the Somaras in that and with proper effort, draw out the superlative liquid.

This Richa translates to: 'Making noise with the two wheels (and axles), these animals are enjoying themselves, similar to men who own or who are endowed with two wives. Set this piece of Soma wood properly, stabilize it and draw with (little) effort, the superlative Soma liquid'.

The purport is that the vehicle carrying the Soma juice is so well made that the animals who are driving it do so effortlessly and happily because the wheels and axles are properly aligned and they move together so smoothly just like life becomes comfortable for a manwhen his two wives carry on and perform all the required work, coordinating with each other, without any strife.

R 153 Richa 10/101/12 बुधः सौम्यः, विश्वे देवा ऋत्विजो वा, जगती

For this Richa, the Rishi is Somputra Budh and Devtas are Vishvedevas, that is, all the Devtas. The Chanda is Jagati.

> कृपृंन्नरः कपृथमुद्दधातन चोदयंत खुदत् वाजंसातये ।
> निष्टिग्र्यः पुत्रमाच्यांवयोतय् इन्द्रं सुबाधं इह सोमंपीतये ॥ 10/101/12

Meaning of words/combination of words

O इन्द्रं (Indra Devta) कपृंन्नरः give happiness to men (narah) उद्दधातन to uplift him चोदयंत खुदत् वाजंसातये who (men) may persuade him (Indra) for giving foodgrains and strength सुबाधं you that is men, who are full of constraints/ sorrows निष्टिग्र्यः पुत्रमाच्यांवयोतय् may overcome these with the help of the son of Aditi that is Indra (Nishtigra) सोमंपीतये for whom we offer Somaras for drinking.

The Richa translates to: 'O men, Indra Devta is the giver of happiness. Establish him in your heart, persuade him to give prosperity and strength obtained from food, praise him to obtain peace and happiness. In this world, O Indra, the son of Aditi, obtain, by all means, Somaras, which is being offered by men troubled by sorrows'.

Thus, the key to overcoming all constraints is to praise Indra Devta who may be pleased by drinking the Somaras. The purport of this Richa is to emphasise that it is the performance of Yajnas in praise of Indra that will enable to achieve prosperity and strength along with the means of livelihood and the needed peace and happiness for living a satisfying life.

In the next Richa which is being quoted here, there is a reference to a metaphor that involves threshing of grains and the context is killing of enemies in a war. Both threshing and conduct of warfare with weapons involve industrial products. This Richa is taken from Sukta 48 of Mandal 10.

Agriculture in Rigveda: Seeds of India's Civilizational Prosperity

R 154 Richa 10/48/7 वैकुण्ठ इन्द्र:, इन्द्र:, त्रिष्टुप्

For this Richa, the Rishi is Vaikuntha Indra. The Devta is Indra. The Chanda is Trishtup.

> अ॒भी३दमेक॒मेकों अस्मि नि॒ष्षाळ्भी द्वा किमु॒ त्रयं: करन्ति ।
> खले॒ न प॒र्षान्प्रतिं हन्मि॒ भूरि॒ किं मां निन्द॒न्ति शत्रंवो ऽनिन्द्रा:
> ॥10/48/7

Meaning of words/combination of words

अ॒भी३दमेक॒मेकों अस्मि I can defeat one enemy नि॒ष्षाळ्भी द्वा किमु॒ foeless, I can defeat even two enemies त्रयं: करन्ति or even three enemies खले॒ न प॒र्षान्प्रतिं हन्मि॒ भूरि॒ like a farmer threshing grains on the threshing floor, I kill these (numerous) villanous enemies किं मां निन्द॒न्ति शत्रंवो ऽनिन्द्रा: why should these enemies who do not know Indra, decry me?

This Richa translates to: 'By myself, I overcome my single adversary, overpowering them, I overcome two foes, what effect can three (enemies) have against me. I smite numerous adversaries like sheaves of grain on the threshing floor. Can my enemies, who do not know Indra, revile me?'

The worshipper of Indra has become as skillful in killing enemies on the battlefield as processing grains on the threshing floor. Both activities have become possible by the blessings of Indra. In both cases, industrial products are required. For the battles, many weapons are required and for the processing of grains, suitable threshing tools are required.

The ripened crops were cut or processed using a hacksaw which was referred to as Datra or Sruni. These were then stored in godowns or Khal from which the word 'Khalihan' is derived. Further, cleaning was done by processing through sieves or by using a jerky motion with the help of 'Soop'. There is an indirect reference to this process in Mandal 10 of Rigveda in Richa 2 of Sukta 71 (Rigveda 10/71/2).

R 155 Richa 10/71/2 बृहस्पतिरांगिरसः, ज्ञानम्, त्रिष्टुप्

For this Richa, the Rishi is Brihaspati of the family of Angira. Devta is Gyanam. The Chanda is Trishtup.

> सक्तुमिव तितंउना पुनन्तो यत्र धीरा मनसा वाचमक्रत ।
> अत्रा सखायः सख्यानि जानते भद्रैषां लक्ष्मीर्निहिताधि वाचि
> ||10/71/2

Meaning of words/combination of words

सक्तुमिव तितंउना Winnow their speech as if through a sieve पुनन्तो then यत्र where धीरा wise men मनसा by their wisdom वाचमक्रत create speech अत्रा सखायः सख्यानि friends जानते know भद्रैषां लक्ष्मीर्निहिताधि वाचि good fortune is associated with their words.

This translates to: 'When the wise men create speech (that is, construct their sentences to express a thought), they use their wisdom as if men winnow barley with a sieve to clean it up. Then the friends of these wise men understand that good fortunes will be associated with the words of these wise men'.

The purport is that wise men are careful in expressing their thoughts through speech. They construct their sentences in a manner such that anything unnecessary is weaned out. In their friend circle or their associates, when they are advised by these wise men, there is an assurance that good fortune would follow by taking their advice or thoughts.

Some of the tools used in agriculture and the related specialized jobs in the processing of grains as mentioned in Rigveda are discussed in detail in Appendix 1 A.4.

Summary and Key Points

Agriculture is the mother of industry. By producing enough surplus, it left the Vaidic community, enough spare manpower and resources, facilitating conceptualization and production of industrial products.

Agriculture in Rigveda: Seeds of India's Civilizational Prosperity

Agriculture also tied up communities to specific locations. With the growth of population, townships and urban activities developed. Alongside, trade and commerce also developed. In Rigveda, in many places, there are references to large boats or ships, travelling across the high seas, indicating that the community in those Vaidic times engaged extensively in global trade (Rigveda 1/56/2; 1/97/8; 1/181/5 and 7; 4/55/6; 6/58/3).

Rigvaidic agriculture and industry were tightly intertwined. Industrial activities provided agricultural implements, means of storage, and transport. For maintaining large animal stock including cattle and horses, facilities for storing water for their drinking were also developed in an elaborate manner. Trade developed both within the nation and internationally, mainly through the seas. For this purpose, identification of suitable routes and maps, methods of locating directions, and boats and ships were required. In these endeavours, relevant astronomical knowledge, and development of precision tools and industrial products played a key role. Industrial products were also needed for maintaining livestock and ensuring their growth, which was considered an indispensable and an organically integrated part of agriculture. Cows, oxen and horses were required for this purpose. Various equipment and vehicles were needed to harvest, store and market the grain. The main points of this Chapter are summarized below.

- ➢ The essence of industrial development was working together that is, for people to join hands with a view to working with the same mind and objective. This ensured efficiency by harmonious cooperation of men who may have different skills or expertise.
- ➢ Industrial townships developed particularly on the coastal belt wherefrom ships and large boats could be launched. Often towns developed in the place where large rivers flowed into the sea. The surrounding areas served as a junction to link domestically produced output from various inland towns that may be brought over the rivers which can then be loaded on to larger ships for global trade.

- Industry developed mainly to serve agriculture in the first place and trade of agricultural output which became available in surplus.
- For travel over the seas, various astronomical inputs were required for which necessary precision tools were also developed.
- Considerable emphasis was given on storage of water for serving the large animal stock.
- Various containers were developed to store foodgrains, both for sowing in the next seasons and for transport to markets through ships.
- Efficiency was ensured by developing specialization in identified activities. In this context also, a number of Richas in Rigveda emphasise this.

About the author

D.K. Srivastava

Dr. D. K. Srivastava's education took place in two traditions: first, in India's traditional and yogic lineage of Guru Shishya Parampara, and second, in the modern mode of schooling and higher education which largely follows the western conventions.

In the yogic tradition, learning takes place by being with and spending time with one's Guru. Dr. Srivastava received his Diksha from his Guru, Swami Bimalananda way back in 1972. His Guru's life and message are described in a Volume entitled "Guru Smriti: Swami Bimalananda and his Yoga Teaching" published in 2018 by Academic Foundation, New Delhi. This Volume which is edited by Dr. Srivastava, contains contributions from many of the prominent disciples of Swamiji, giving their reminiscences over a lifetime of learning. Dr. Srivastava was blessed enough to receive his Diksha in the holy cave of Amarnath in Kashmir, India. His learning continued in various Ashramas where his Guru resided from time to time. This includes Prayagraj (Allahabad) where his Guru's Ashram was located first in Daragunj and later, on Jawaharlal Nehru Road. Swamiji spent nearly six months in the year in Pahalgam, Kashmir for a number of years. He also spent considerable time in Goalpara in Assam where he had a large following. Dr. Srivastava was privileged enough to spend considerable time in all these places, getting constant guidance from his Guru.

It is easier to capture the landmarks in the more contemporary tradition of learning as described below. Dr. Srivastava's understanding of the life and related issues took shape from both modes of learning.

Dr. D. K. Srivastava was Professor of Economics at Banaras Hindu University during 1984-1995, Senior Fellow at the National Institute of Public Finance and Policy, New Delhi during 1996-2005, and Director, Madras School of Economics during 2005-2012. Since then, he is associated with Ernst and Young, India as their Chief Policy Advisor. Earlier in his career, he taught in the University of Allahabad, University of St. Andrews, United Kingdom, and the University of the West Indies, Jamaica.

Dr. Srivastava holds an M.A. in Economics from the University of Allahabad, and M.Litt. and Ph.D degrees from the University of St. Andrews, United Kingdom. He was a National Scholar and a Commonwealth Scholar. He was given the Stanley Smith Fellowship at the University of St. Andrews.

Dr. Srivastava received the Tassie Medallion of Adam Smith for outstanding performance at the University of St. Andrews. The Uttar Pradesh and Uttarakhand Economic Association conferred on him, the Kautilya Samman in October 2011. In February 2019, he was given Prof. J. K. Mehta Award for excellence in the field of Public Finance by the Allahabad University Department of Economics Alumni Association.

Dr. Srivastava was the Economic Advisor to the Tenth Finance Commission, Principal Consultant to the Eleventh Finance Commission, and Member of the Twelfth Finance Commission. More recently, he was Member of the Advisory Council to the Fifteenth Finance Commission.

Dr. Srivastava has been associated with a number of committees set up by the central and state governments and by the RBI. He was the Chairman of the Working Group on States' Financial Resources for India's Twelfth Plan and Chairman of the RBI Working Group on 'State Fiscal Responsibility Legislations: The Next Phase'. He was a member of the High-level Expert Committee on Efficient Management of Public Expenditure constituted by the erstwhile Planning Commission. He was Member Secretary, Advisory Group of the RBI-MSE Macro Econometric Modelling Project. More recently, he was Chairman of the Committee on Fiscal Statistics set up by the National Statistical Commission in 2017.

Dr. Srivastava is the author of numerous scholarly articles and books. His recent books include 'Federalism and Fiscal Transfers in India' in co-authorship with Dr. C. Rangarajan, published by the Oxford University Press in 2011. He is the co-editor of 'Development and Public Finance: Essays in Honour of Raja J. Chelliah' (2012) and 'Environment and Fiscal Reforms in India' (2014), both published by Sage India. His articles have been published in well-known national and international journals including Indian Journal of Economics, Indian Economic Journal, Economic and Political Weekly, Journal of International Economics and Finance, Modern Economy, Journal of Advanced Studies in Finance, Business and Economics Journal, Global Business Review, Public Finance/ Finances Publique, Journal of Policy Modelling, and Artha Vijnana.

Dr. Srivastava is the lead author of the EY Economy Watch, a monthly overview of the Indian economy in a global context. This document has established itself as a thought leadership publication, providing valuable inputs to policymakers in the central and state governments, academicians, and industry. It has received significant attention in the media over the years. By May 2022, 67 issues of the Economy Watch have been published.

Dr. Srivastava has guides, while at Benaras Hindu University, a number of research scholars, for their Ph.D. degree. Dr. Srivastava has also guided numerous projects commissioned by the World Bank, UNDP, ADB, Forum of Federations, DFID, Reserve Bank of India, erstwhile Planning Commission, Ministry of Finance, Government of India and various state governments. These include a number of international studies covering countries such as Nepal, Sri Lanka, Kuwait, Romania, Indonesia and Jamaica.

References

1. Agrawal, D. P. (2002). Medicinal Properties of Neem. (*Neem findings http://www. infinityfoundation. com/ma ndala/test/esag raw neem-framset. htm.*)

2. Agrawal, D.P. Surapala's Vrikshayurveda: an Introduction (Accessed in 22 March 2022; https://www.infinityfoundation.com/mandala/t_es/t_es_agraw_sura pala_frameset.htm)

3. Bakshi, G. (2020). The Saraswati Civilization: A Paradigm Shift in Indian History. Garuda Prakasan.

4. Balkiwal, P.C. and Grover, A.K. (1988). Signatures and migration of Saraswati River in Thar Desert, Western India, Record Geol. Survey Ind., 116, 77–86.

5. Bhadra, B.K., Gupta, A.K. and Sharma, J.R. (2006). Subsurface water oozing at Kalayat village, Jind district, Haryana in December 2005: Possible connection with Saraswati palaeochannel, Jour. Geol. Soc. India, 68, 946–948.

6. Bhadra, B.K., Gupta, A.K. and Sharma, J.R. (2009). Saraswati Nadi in Haryana and its linkage with the Vedic Saraswati — integrated study based on satellite images and ground-based information, Jour. Geol. Soc. India, 73, 273–288.

7. Bhaty, Rupa (2020). 'Sangamtalks' (posted on YouTube on 29 February). Accessed 20 February 2022 :https://www.youtube.com/watch?v=fRhO-y9NgjI

8. Chatterjee, A., Ray, J.S., Shukla, A.D. et al. (2019). On the existence of a perennial river in the Harappan heartland. Sci Rep 9, 17221. https://doi.org/10.1038/s41598-019-53489-4

9. Dalal, R. (2010). Hinduism: An alphabetical guide. Penguin Books India.

10. Danino, M. (2010). The lost river: On the trail of the Sarasvati. Penguin Books India.

11. Department of AYUSH, Ministry of Health and Family Welfare, Government of India New Delhi. (2008). A Manual for Doctors on Mainstreaming of AYUSH under NRHM.

12. Hastings, James (published in 1908 and digitized in 2007). Encyclopaedia of Religion and Ethics at Google Books, Vol. 7, Harvard Divinity School, TT Clark, pp. 51–56.

13. Heritage Amruth. (December 2015). Published by the medplan conservatory society, Bangalore.

14. Howard, S. A., & CIE, M. A. (1950). An agricultural testament. Prabhat Prakashan.

15. Jamieson, S. W. (2014). Rigveda. Texas: Oxford University Press.

16. Jamison, S. W., & Brereton, J. P. (Eds.). (2014). The Rigveda: the earliest religious poetry of India (Vol. I, II and III). Oxford University Press, South Asia Research.

17. Kalyanraman, S. (2018). http://bharatkalyan97.blogspot.com/2018/08/metaphors-of-rastri-suktam-rgveda-10125.html.

18. Maddison, A. (1995). Monitoring the world economy, 1820-1992 (p. 238). Paris: Development Centre of the Organisation for Economic Co-operation and Development.

19. Maddison, A. (1995). Explaining the economic performance of nations. *Books*.

20. Maddison, A. (2006). The World Economy. Volume 1 and 2. Development Centre Studies, OECD. (https://www.stat.berkeley.edu/~aldous/157/Papers/world_economy.pdf)

21. Maddison, A. (2007). Contours of the world economy 1-2030 AD: Essays in macro-economic history. OUP Oxford.

22. Majumdar, G. P. (1927). Vanaspati: Plants and Plant-life as in Indian Treatises and Traditions. University of Calcutta. (https://www.rarebooksocietyofindia.org/book_archive/196174216674_10151216246831675.pdf)

23. Malhotra, R. and Satyanarayana Dasa Babaji (2020). Sanskrit Non-Translatables: The Importance of Sanskritizing English. Amaryllis, An Imprint of Manjul Publishing House.

24. Manu Smriti, Chapter VII, Suktas 155,156 and 157; *[https://www.sacred-texts.com/hin/manu/manu07.htm; accessed on 6 May 2022]*

25. Mukundananda, Swami (2014). Bhagavad Gita - The Song of God (https://www.holy-bhagavad-gita.org/index)

26. Mukundananda, S. (2020). https://www.holy-bhagavad-gita.org/chapter/15 (Accessed on 19 November).

27. Mukundananda, S. (2020). https://www.holy-bhagavad-gita.org/chapter/9- (Accessed on 26 November).

28. Naishthik, Acharya Agnivrat (2017). Ved Vigyan Alok. A Vaidic Theory of Universe. published by Vaidic Swasti Pantha Nyas, Jodhpur.

29. National Health Systems Resource Centre, National Rural Health Mission. Ministry of Health & Family Welfare, Government of India. New Delhi. (2009). Mainstreaming AYUSH & Revitalizing Local Health Traditions under the National Rural Health Mission- A Health Systems Perspective.

30. National Health Systems Resource Centre, National Rural Health Mission Ministry of Health & Family Welfare, Government of India, New Delhi. (2010). Status and role of AYUSH and Local health

Traditions under the National Rural Health Mission-Report of a Study.

31. Oak, N. (2011). When did the Mahabharata War Happen? – The Mystery of Arundhati. Subbu Publications.

32. Oak, N. (2019). 12209 BCE Rama Ravana Yuddha. Om Publications.

33. Oak, N. N., & Bhaty, R. (2018). Ancient updates to Surya-siddhanta. Presented in Oxford Coffee Table Conference.

34. Oak, N. (2014). The Historic Rama: Indian Civilization at the End of Pleistocene. CreateSpace Independent Publishing Platform

35. Parthasarathi, Srinidhi K. (2020). "Ancient Science of Mantras – Wisdom of the Sages." International Journal of Yoga vol. 13,1: 84–86. doi:10.4103/ijoy.IJOY_81_19

36. Prime, R. (2002). Vedic ecology: Practical wisdom for surviving the 21st century. Mandala Publ.

37. Sadhale, Nalini (Tr.). (1996). Surapala's Vrikshayurveda (The Science of Plant Life by Surapala). Agri-History Bulletin No.1. Asian Agri-History Foundation, Secunderabad 500 009, India; http://www.infinityfoundation.com/mandala/t_es/t_es_agraw_surapala_frameset.htm

38. Saraswati, Swami Dayananda. Satyarth Prakash (97th edition, 2019). Arsh Sahitya Prachar Trust. Delhi-110006. (first edition was published in 1875 by Israr Mahal inside Rampur in Kashi).

39. Sarasvati, S. D. (1908). An English translation of the Satyarth Prakash.

40. Sanyal, S. (2012). Land of seven rivers: History of India's Geography. Penguin UK.

41. Shiva, V. (1991). Ecology and the politics of survival: conflicts over natural resources in India. United Nations University Press.

42. Shiva, V. (1991). Biodiversity: Social and Ecological Perspectives. Zed Press, United Kingdom.

43. Shiva, V. (1993). Monocultures of the mind: Perspectives on biodiversity and biotechnology. Palgrave Macmillan.

44. Shiva, V. (1997). Biopiracy: the Plunder of Nature and Knowledge, South End Press, Cambridge Massachusetts, I ISBN 1-896357-11-3.

45. Shiva, V. (2000). Stolen Harvest: The Hijacking of the Global Food Supply, South End Press, Cambridge Massachusetts, ISBN 0-89608-608-9.

46. Shiva, V. (2008). Soil Not Oil, South End Press ISBN 978-0-89608-782-8.

47. Shiva, V. (2011). Biopiracy: The Plunder of Nature & Knowledge, Natraj Publishers, ISBN 978-8-18158-160-0.

48. Shiva, V. (2011). Monocultures of the Mind: Perspectives on Biodiversity, Natraj Publishers, ISBN 978-8-18158-151-8.

49. Shiva, V. (2019). "Foreword". In Extinction Rebellion (ed.). This Is Not a Drill: An Extinction Rebellion Handbook. Penguin Books. pp. 5–8. ISBN 9780141991443.

50. Singh, O. R., Das, B., Padhi, M. M., & Tewari, N. S. (2003). Common herbs used in different skin disorders as described in ayurvedic classics. Ancient science of life, 22(3), 88.

51. Srikanth, N., Tewari, D., & Mangal, A. K. (2015). The science of plant life (Vrikshaayurveda) in archaic literature: an insight on botanical, agricultural and horticultural aspects of ancient India. World J Pharm Pharm Sci, 4(6), 388.

52. Srivastava, D. K. (2018). Guru Smriti: Swami Bimalananda and His Yoga Teaching. Gurugram, Haryana, India: Academic Foundation Press.

53. Swaminathan, S. (2015, April 14). Ships in the Rig Veda Retrieved from speakingtree.in (https://www.speakingtree.in/blog/ships-in-the-rig-veda)

54. Trivedi, R. G. (1954). Hindi Rigveda. Allahabad: The Indian Press.

55. University Maharshi Mahesh. (20 November 2020). https://maharishi-programmes.globalgoodnews.com/vedic-agriculture/programmes.html.

56. Valdiya, K. S. (2002). Saraswati: the river that disappeared. Universities Press.

57. Valdiya, K. S. (2016). Prehistoric River Saraswati, Western India. Springer International Pu.

58. Valdia, K. S., Bisht, R. S., Tandon, S. K., Sinha, R., Bhadra, B. K., Kar, A., & Prabhakar, V. N. (2016). Palaeochannels of North West India: Review and assessment. Report of the expert committee to review available information on palaeochannels.

59. Vedic Heritage, Indira Gandhi National Centre for the Arts, Ministry of Culture, Government of India (Access link: https://vedicheritage.gov.in/)

60. Witzel, M. (1995, updated 2001). Rigvedic History, Poets, Chieftains and Polities, Academia.edu 1995, updated 2001.

Appendix 1: Notes on Krishi Parashar and other Ancient Indian Texts on Agriculture and related aspects

Apart from Rigveda and Atharvaveda, some important sources in Sanskrit literature where agriculture is mentioned in detail, may be taken note of in order to highlight the continuity of work and thinking relating to agriculture amongst Indian Rishis and other important thinkers from Rigveda onwards. Some of the important milestones in this context are listed below

1. Krishi Parashar
2. Kashyapiya Krishi
3. Vrikshayurveda, (Charaka, Shushruta, Vagbhata)
4. Brihatsamhita – Varahmihir
5. Tarkasangraha
6. Kadambini
7. Upavanvinod
8. Vrikshavallabha
9. Roopchandrika

Amongst these, we have provided brief notes on Krishi Parashar, Kashyapiya Krishi Sukti and Vrikshayurveda. Krishi Parashar is an elaborate Treatise(s) on agriculture by Rishi Parashar. This appendix provides, very briefly, a flavour of its rich contribution to the practical applications of the Vaidic principles in agriculture. These notes are based, among other sources, on:

1. Krishi Parashar by Prof. Ramchandra Pandey, Hindi Translation, Motilal Banarasi Das, 2002, available at Google Books
2. https://udaybhanuojha.blogspot.com/2014/03/an-introduction-tovedic-farming-methods.html
3. https://www.hinduscriptures.com/vedic-sciences/ancient-vedic-agriculture/2142/

A.1 Notes on Krishi Parashar

A key reference for the roots of Indian agriculture is 'Krishi Parashar.' Maharshi Parashar, son of Muni Shakti, was Maharshi Vashishtha's grandson. Maharshi Vedvyas was his son. He wrote extensively about rain, rain forecasting, rain measurement, agricultural crops and agricultural tools in Krishi Parashar. There are two hundred and forty-three verses in this Treatise that are mostly composed in Anushtup Metre. Other Metres that are used include Vasant-tilika, Malini, Shardulavikridita, Upendravajra, Indravajra, and Upajati.

This ancient treatise on agriculture is divided into three parts: Khand 1 (Introduction), Khand 2 (Vrishti Khand, pertaining to rainfall) and Khand 3 (Krishi Khand, pertaining to agriculture). A limited number of selected Shlokas are cited below.

In the introduction, the key role of food grains is praised (Shloka 1/6).

> अन्नं प्राणा बलं चान्नमन्नं सर्वार्थ साधनम् ।
> देवासुर मनुष्याश्च सर्वे चान्नोपजीवनम्॥ **(Prastavikam, 1/6)**

Meaning of words/combination of words

अन्नं प्राणा Food is life बलं चान्नमन्नं food is strength सर्वार्थ साधनम् and it is the means for accomplishing all objectives देवासुर for Devtas as well as Asuras मनुष्याश्च as also for all mankind सर्वे चान्नोपजीवनम् for each one of them, food is the livelihood for all beings.

This translates to: 'Food is life, food is strength, food is the reason for all pursuits. Food is for the livelihood of all, that is Devas, Asuras, and mankind'.

The purport is to highlight the importance of food which is the source of energy for all beings including Devtas, Asuras and mankind. It is by the intake of food that generation of energy becomes possible which is essential for any pursuits or for achieving any objectives. Agriculture is the approved means consistent with the Vaidic message and knowledge for the production of food. This is why agriculture is a key economic pursuit for mankind in coordination with Devtas as described in the Rigveda and other Vedas.

Part 2 of Krishi Parashar is devoted to a discussion of rainfall and the role that clouds play in causing rainfall. Clouds are classified into four groups. These are Avarta, Samvarta, Pushkar, and Drona (आवर्त, संवर्त, पुष्कर, द्रोण).

The cloud Avarta ensures rain in a specific location. Samvarta ensures rainfall that is widely spread all over the country. In Pushkar, very scant rain is experienced while in Drona, bountiful rain is the norm.

Rishi Parashar also indicates that rainfall over oceans is most plentiful, somewhat less on mountain tops, and relatively less, on the plains. In fact, the exact ratio is given as 10:6:4. This is specified in the Vrishti Khand of Krishi Parashar in Shloka 20 as given below.

> समुद्रे दशभागांश्च षड्भागानि पर्वते ।
> पृथिव्याम् चतुरोभागान् सदावर्षति वासवः ॥ **(Vrishti Khand, 2/20)**

Meaning of words/combination of words

समुद्रे In oceans दशभागांश्च in the ratio of ten षड्भागानि in the ratio of six पर्वते on mountains पृथिव्याम् on land चतुरोभागान् in the ratio of four सदावर्षति वासवः it always rains in this way on the Earth.

This Shloka translates to: 'The Devta of rains, Indra, always causes ten parts of rainfall over oceans, six parts over mountains, and four parts over plains'.

This implies that of the total rainfall on Earth, the maximum rainfall is on the surface of oceans which is fifty per cent of the total rainfall, followed by thirty per cent on mountains and hills and twenty per cent on plains. Thus, the ratio of the incidence of rainfall is 5:3:2 on oceans, mountains, and on plains. In this way, a full circuit of flow of water is created across oceans, mountains, and land. Whatever rains on oceans, is replenished in the form of clouds, back to the oceans through rainfall. Whatever rains on mountains, flows back to the oceans through the rivers which flow down from the mountains. Whatever is absorbed in the soil on the mountains and on plains, becomes useful for the pursuit of agriculture. Through agriculture, food grains are produced which are consumed by mankind and which are also used in the Yajnas performed by the mankind for the Devtas including Indra. Indra then ensures that rainfall happens in a manner benefitting mankind and in fact, all life forms on Earth.

In this Chapter devoted to rains, Rishi Parashar gives a clue as to when to expect the rainfall to occur almost instantaneously. Rains may be invoked by reciting appropriate Mantras by knowledgeable sages under the circumstances indicated below.

> जलस्थो जलहस्तो वा निकटेऽथ जलस्यं वा ।
> प्रष्टा पृच्छति वृष्ट्यर्थं वृष्टिः संजायतेऽचिरात् ॥ (Vrishti Khand, 2/56)

Meaning of words/combination of words

जलस्थो Standing in water जलहस्तो holding water in one's hand वा निकटेऽथ or standing close to जलस्यं water वा प्रष्टा पृच्छति or if somebody asks वृष्ट्यर्थं regarding the possibility of rain वृष्टिः संजायतेऽचिरात् rainfall happens instantaneously.

This translates to: 'If stationed (or standing) in water, holding water in one's hand, or being close to a water body, if a question is asked about the likelihood of rains, it rains almost immediately'.

In this Shloka, Muni Parashar indicates that it was possible to invoke rainfall through Mantras when urgently required for some legitimate purpose and in order to succeed in this endeavour, Rishis in those days had accomplished Siddhi of the Mantras. This process was facilitated by being close to water, holding water, standing in water and talking about water.

Muni Parashar developed a full-fledged science of clouds and rainfall. "Adhaka" was specified as the rain unit. He advanced several methods and theories of forecasting rainfall. His main technique of rain forecasting was based on the position of the moon and the sun. In Table A1.1, different volumes of rainfall are linked to the configurations of the moon and the sun.

Table A1.1: Predicted quantity of rainfall based on astronomical considerations by Muni Parashar

Sign of the Moon	Sign of the Sun	Predicted total rainfall of the year
Gemini, Aries, Taurus, or Pisces	Cancer	100 adhakas
Gemini, Aries, Taurus, or Pisces	Leo or Sagittarius	50 adhakas
Gemini, Aries, Taurus, or Pisces	Virgo or Leo	80 adhakas
Gemini, Aries, Taurus, or Pisces	Cancer, Aquarius, Scorpio, or Libra	96 adhakas

In the Krishi Khand, that is Part 3 of this Treatise, Muni Parashar says that close care and supervision ensures good crops and lack of effort and care leads to poor results. For example, in Shloka 1 of the third Chapter of Krishi Parashar, these ideas are clearly delineated.

> फलत्यवेक्षिता स्वर्णं दैन्यं सैवान वेक्षिता ।
> कृषिः कृषिपुराणज्ञ इत्युवाच पराशरः ॥ (Krishi Khand, 3/1)

Meaning of words/combination of words

फलत्यवेक्षिता That land which is properly supervised yields fruitful outcomes स्वर्णं resulting in prosperity characterized by acquisition of gold दैन्यं सैवान वेक्षिता कृषिः that agriculture which is not properly supervised or taken care of, results in poor crops and therefore poverty कृषिपुराणज्ञ इत्युवाच पराशरः this is what the agricultural scientist, that is Muni Parashar, says.

This Shloka translates to: 'Close care and supervision ensures golden crops. Lack of effort and lack of care leads to poverty. This is said by Parashar, the agricultural scientist, about agriculture'.

The message of this Shloka is that successful agriculture requires close and constant supervision throughout the year or throughout the agricultural cycles if agriculture is to yield its expected outcomes. Prosperity results from careful and close supervision of the agricultural operations in all its stages. Any laxity or carelessness results in misery and disaster. Agriculture responds to close human interaction. In fact, even plants and trees that are close to human habitats and therefore subject to active and passive supervision, yield maximum and healthiest fruits when properly supervised and taken care of. This is emphasized in Shloka 6 of Chapter 3.

> कृषिं च तादृशीं कुर्यात् यथा वाहान्न पीडयेत्।
> वाह पीडार्जितं शस्यं गर्हितं सर्वकर्मसु ॥ **(Krishi Khand, 3/6)**

Meaning of words/combination of words

कृषिं च तादृशीं कुर्यात् Agriculture should be carried out in this manner यथा such that वाहान्न पीडयेत् the oxen who are employed in agriculture are not caused any discomfort वाह पीडार्जितं if these oxen are caused any pain or discomfort शस्यं गर्हितं सर्वकर्मसु that field will not yield satisfactory grain.

This translates to: 'Oxen should be so employed as to not give them discomfort. If pain or discomfort is caused to the oxen, the grain that would be so earned is criticised among all actions'.

The purport is that if the oxen employed in the process of agriculture are overworked or used in unsatisfactory ways, causing them discomfort or pain, negative vibrations would be generated which would be received by the field on which the crop is being sown and that field will not cooperate with the farmer responsible for causing pain or discomfort to the animals employed on the farmland.

Agriculture in Rigveda: Seeds of India's Civilizational Prosperity

In Krishi Parashar, there is also an extensive discussion about the scale of agricultural activities. In fact, the implements used tended to be of large and efficient sizes which required the association of a number of oxen. A large number of oxen also ensured that no single animal was unduly stressed apart from reaping the benefits of economies of scale.

> हलमष्टगवं प्रोक्तम् षड्गवं व्यवहारिकं।
> चतुर्गवं नृशंसानाम् द्विगवं तु गवाशिनाम्॥ **(Krishi Khand, 3/18)**

Meaning of words/combination of words

हलमष्टगवं With one plough, eight oxen should be used प्रोक्तम् षड्गवं व्यवहारिकं it would still be practical to use at least six oxen with one plough चतुर्गवं नृशंसानाम् it would however be cruel if only four oxen are used with one plough द्विगवं तु गवाशिनाम् using only two oxen with one plough is sure to invite disaster.

This translates to: 'With one plough, eight oxen are required. If only six oxen are employed, it is still practical. Cruel people use only four oxen. Most cruel people, intent on harming the oxen, use only two oxen'.

The message is that efficiency requires that one plough should be pulled by eight oxen. This would be ideal. Clearly, these ploughs could have been relatively larger in size than what is typically seen in modern days. If eight oxen are used with one plough, this will not only be the most comfortable for the oxen but also would be the most efficient in terms of digging and overturning the soil and would therefore ensure maximum yield and maximum return on the investment of planting seeds to the farmer. Using up to six oxen is still permissible but less than six oxen with one plough is not at all prescribed. Thus, in ancient days, India's agricultural prosperity depended on extensive use of oxen and animal wealth, but they were used in a manner consistent with what was approved in the Vaidic Mantras. This required causing no pain to the oxen and looking after their health. If they remained pleased, the crop could be ensured to be plentiful.

On the number of ploughs that should be employed by a farmer also, Rishi Parashar gives guidance.

> नित्यं दशहले लक्ष्मी नित्यं पंचहले धनं।
> नित्यं तु त्रिहले भक्तं नित्यमेकहले ऋणं ॥ **(Krishi Khand, 3/19)**

Meaning of words/combination of words

नित्यं दशहले लक्ष्मी Regularly ten ploughs should be used to ensure prosperous outcomes नित्यं पंचहले धनं using at least five ploughs regularly would still result in wealth नित्यं तु त्रिहले भक्तं using only three ploughs would be just enough for food नित्यमेकहले ऋणं using only one plough is sure to result in debt.

This translates to: 'Having ten ploughs on a regular basis are considered most desirable for one farmer, leading to great wealth. Regularly employing five ploughs will lead to prosperity. Using only three ploughs is just enough for getting meals. Using only one plough will result in debt (due possibly to the inability to recover costs)'.

The intention is to convey the message that in general, farmers engaged in agriculture were quite rich. They used to engage five to ten ploughs on a regular basis. This provided them with what is known in modern economic terms as economies of scale in the operations on the field as also for maintaining the agricultural assets including farm animals. If a farmer has been forced to use only one plough, it was a signal that he was not able to cover his costs and therefore, he was incurring debt, season after season.

In Shloka 3/34 of the Krishi Khand, different parts of the plough are specified with a view to facilitating the construction of an efficient plough in which the size and length of different parts are so worked out as to lead to an optimal construction. These details are given in the subsequent Shlokas.

Agriculture in Rigveda: Seeds of India's Civilizational Prosperity

> ईषायुगहलस्णुर्नियोलस्य पाशिकाः।
> अङ्डु चल्लश्च शौलश्च पच्चनी च हलष्टकम् ॥ **(Krishi Khand, 3/34)**

Meaning of words/combination of words

ईषा Wooden rod connecting the yoke with the blades युग yoke हलस्णुर्नियोलस्य the blade of the plough and its lagan or hold पाशिकाः ropes used in the plough अङ्डु चल्लश्च शौलश्च wooden handle and Addachal पच्चनी luga च हलष्टकम् these are the eight parts of the plough.

This translates to: 'Eight parts of the plough are specified. These parts are called 'Isha' (rod used in the plough), 'Yug' (yoke), 'Hal' (blade), 'Niryol' (lagan), 'Pashika' (rope), 'Addachal', 'Shaul' (wooden handle), and 'Pacchani' (luga)'.

The basic idea of this Shloka in the Krishi Parashar is to comprehensively define the fabrication of a plough such that it can operate in the most efficient way. Most modern images are of ploughs with a small number of blades. However, in Parashar's description, the number of blades could be much more than these, indicating the relatively large size of ploughs that were in vogue in the early days of agriculture as it developed in the Saraswati valley. Some images of the plough and the yoke are given below (Figure A1.1). These are not related to any particular time period. These may be considered as illustrative only. Here, the plough is shown to have four blades but it could easily have a much larger number of blades.

Figure A1.1: Images of plough and yoke

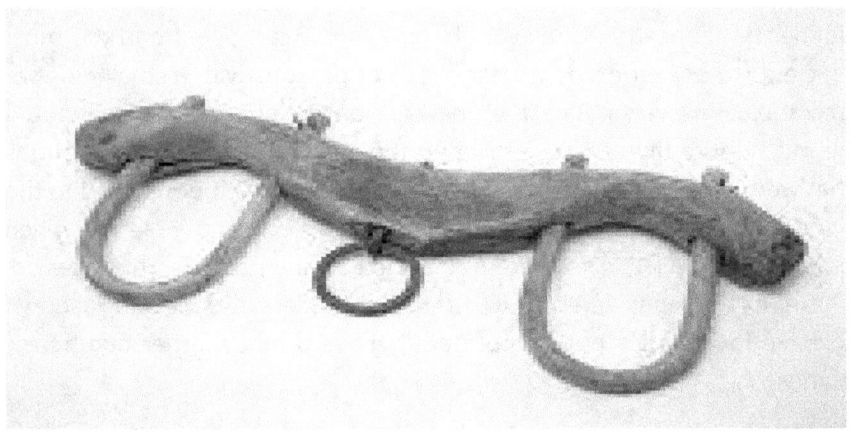

Source: http://bitly.ws/qBxl

In the next Shloka (3/35 of Krishi Khand; *not given here*), the prescribed length of each part has been specified. Exact lengths and specifications of all the parts of the plough are provided to facilitate the fabrication of a plough.

Detailed guidance is also given for constructing and maintaining 'Goshalas' (cowsheds) in Krishi Parashar. On the best method of preserving and sowing seeds also, practical guidance is provided. One example is Shloka 79 of the Krishi Khand.

> एकरूपं तु यद्बीजं फलं फलति निर्भरम्।
> एकरूपं प्रयत्नेन तस्माद्बीजं समाचरेत्॥ **(Krishi Khand, 3/79)**

Meaning of words/combination of words

एकरूपं Homogenous तु where यद्बीजं the seeds फलं फलति yield best crops निर्भरम् एकरूपं प्रयत्नेन effort should be made to use seeds which are of the same kind, same size etc. तस्माद्बीजं समाचरेत् in this manner, seeds should be preserved.

This translates to: 'Seeds that are homogenous give best crops. Therefore, effort should be made to use seeds that are uniform, preserved under uniform conditions'.

The idea conveyed in this Shloka is that the best crops are generated when seeds which are homogenous in quality and size are used. The crops that come up as a result require similar kinds of attention and conditions for best results. If the seeds are heterogenous, then their growth would require different kinds of treatment and different measures of inputs such as water, fertilizers etc., making the whole process more difficult. So, Muni Parashar recommends that efforts should be made to segregate seeds initially in a manner such that similar kinds of seeds are used in a given patch of land.

In Krishi-Parashar, Muni Parashar has also described in detail, the seed treatment of paddy, nursery preparation, transplanting of seedlings and threshing. He said that the farmer should make pillar made of nyagrodha, saptaparna, gambhari, silk cotton tree or audambari for threshing. In the absence of vata, wood for the pillar should be produced from a tree bearing a feminine name. It should be protected by neem leaves and mustard and should be equipped with a flag.

Before taking up the final harvesting, peasants should celebrate. After meals, unguents (ointments) and perfumes containing four items namely sandal, camphor, saffron and musk should be offered to the farmers. Thus, clearly, sandal, camphor and saffron were cultivated and grown during those days.

In Krishi Parashar, great care has been taken for quantification of various inputs and outputs related to agriculture. Earlier, in the Vrishti Khand, Muni Parashar has given detailed measures and methodology for quantification of the volume of rainfall. An 'Adhaka', a unit of measuring food grains is also defined by Muni Parashar in Verse 3/238. It is twelve human fingers in width. However, the depth of the vessel is not defined although 'twelve fingers' can be taken to mean the diameter of a circular vessel or a square of that measurement. Some other details which have been used in later times in India are given below.

The importance of Adhaka as a unit of measurement has been recognized in many works. Its usage has continued even in modern times. Adhaka (आढक) is the Sanskrit name for a weight unit corresponding to 2.56 kilograms used in Ayurvedic literature, according to the Sodasangahrdayam. Adhaka is also known as Patra (cup or pot). A single Adhaka unit corresponds to 4 Prastha units (a single Prastha unit equals 640 grams). One needs 4 Adhaka units to make a single Droṇa unit (1 Droṇa equals 10.24 kilograms)[13].

---

[13] https://www.wisdomlib.org/definition/adhaka

A.2 Notes on Kaashyap Krishi Sukti

Muni Kashyap is known to be one of the original seven Rishis from whom the entire lineage of mankind in the current Manvantara follows. This list is given in Brihadaranyaka and other ancient texts. For the current Manvantara, the Saptarishis are Kashyap, Atri, Vashishtha, Vishwamitra, Gautama, Jamadagni and Bharadwaja. Kashyap Muni has prepared a detailed Treatise on the subject of agriculture for the welfare of mankind. This Volume is known as 'Kaashyap Krishi Sukti' which is divided into four parts.

धान्यदिकृषिक्रमकथन (description of grains in agriculture)

शाकादिकृषिक्रमकथन (description of vegetation in agriculture)

भोज्याभोज्यक्रमकथन (description of eatables and non-eatables)

विविध हव्य निवेदनक्रमकथनात्मक (about materials that can be used in Yajnas)

Part I has 606 shlokas. Part II has 178 Shlokas. In Part III, there are 42 Shlokas. In Part IV, there are 30 Shlokas.

A Hindi translation of Kasyapiya Krishi Sukti is available by Dr. Sri Krishna 'Jugnu', first published in 2013 in the Haridas Sanskrit Series 383. The publisher is Chowkhambha Sanskrit Office, Maidagin, Varanasi.

Part 1, which is the most elaborate, has fourteen sub-chapters or statements. It gives a detailed description of forms in which land and sources of water may be available on Earth such as mountains, rivers, large and small forests, ponds and wells. Some selected Shlokas describing the qualities of desirable farmland are given below.

> सुस्निग्धामल्परक्ताम् च कृष्ण वर्णाम् तथैव च।
> तुषकाचविहीनां च सारां रससमुज्जवलाम् ||34 (Part I, Kashyap Sukti)

This Richa translates to: 'Land should be smooth, soil should be mildly red or black, it should be devoid of straws and glass pieces, good land would be full of substance, clean, and moist'.

> बीजवृद्धिकरीं वेगात् सीता सौख्यप्रदायिनीम्।
> वृषफेनाक्तकां वापि सत्वजन्तुसमन्विताम्॥37 (Part I, Kashyap Sukti)

This Richa translates to: 'For rapid growth of seeds, for smooth ploughing of the blades on soil, the selected land should be treated with the urine of oxen, and other cattle should also be tied on that land'.

> शुभलक्षणसंयुक्ता सर्वेषां शुभदा धरा।
> कुटम्बारोग्यदा शश्वत् धनगोधान्यवृद्धिदा॥ 55 (Part I, Kashyap Sukti)

This Richa translates to: 'Land that is characterized by auspicious features is benevolent for everybody. It gives a disease-free status to the entire family for all times and leads to the growth of cattle, prosperity and food grains'.

Kashyap Muni advises farmers not only to grow grains and pulses on their land but also supplement their nourishment value by growing vegetables.

> शालि क्षेत्रे यथाकालं शाल्यादीन् कलयेत् क्रमात्।
> तारक्षेत्रेषु तद्वच्च चणकादींश्च वर्धयेत्॥2 (Part II, Kashyap Sukti)

This Richa translates to: 'Agricultural scientists should select crops to be grown based on quality of land and season or time. Rice should be grown on land that is suitable for rice. Similarly, pulses may be grown'.

Kashyap Muni says that just grains and pulses are not enough. These should be supplemented by vegetables for taste and nourishment.

> शाकादिकृषिकार्यं च फलदं च विनिश्चितम् ।
> वसन्तकाले ग्रीष्मे वा हैमन्ते वापि वा क्वचित् ॥21॥

This Richa translates to: 'Sowing of vegetables as part of agriculture is always fruitful. This should be done in all seasons, be it spring, summer, winter or any other season'.

A.3 Notes on Vrikshayurveda

Trees were acknowledged to play a major role in the comprehensive interlinkages of nature, mankind, water, environment and Earth. Trees played both a medicinal role and a role in capturing and holding water in the soil with the help of their roots apart from maintaining a cycle of oxygen and carbon dioxide through their exhaling and inhaling cycles over days and nights. India's Rishis developed full-fledged treatise(s) on cultivating, maintaining, and developing agglomerations of trees in various forms including gardens, and forests, over hills, mountains, and plains. Both timber and non-timber products coming from trees played a significant role in the economic prosperity of rural and urban life. Among India's inherited literature, Surpala's Vrikshayurveda holds a special place. Prior to this treatise(s), Brihatsamhita of Varahamihira is also known to contain a Chapter on Vrikshayurveda.

Not much was known about the major contribution by Surpala on this subject of trees, their role and methods by which these are to be taken care of until Y L Nene (Chairman, Asian Agri-History Foundation) procured a manuscript of Surpala's Vrikshayurveda from the Bodleian Library, Oxford, UK. Later, Sadhale undertook a translation of the text at Nene's request. Surpala's manuscript consisted of sixty pages with each page containing six lines in general (occasionally five or seven). It provides a systematic composition on plantation, growth, and care of trees. He starts with the glorification of trees and tree planting. He discusses with authority, the science of plant life including **procuring, preserving, and treating of seeds before planting.** He pays detailed attention to preparing of pits for planting saplings, selection of soil, and methods of watering. Equally important are the discussions on nourishments and fertilizers. Perhaps the most important aspect of his prescriptions relates to treatment of plant diseases and plant protection from internal and external threats. These topics are treated in separate sections and are internally correlated in Surpala's Vrikshayurveda which also contributes to the subject of intercropping and production of various medicinal plants.

Agriculture in Rigveda: Seeds of India's Civilizational Prosperity

A limited number of Surpala's guidance on various aspects of growth of trees are given below based on the contribution of D. P. Agrawal[14] on the subject. In the context of suitable soil, Surpala had observed the following. The number of the Sutra is given in brackets.

- *Arid, marshy, and ordinary are the three types of land. It is further subdivided into six types by colour and savour (35)*

- *Black, white, pale, dark, red, and yellow are the colours and sweet, sour, salty, pungent, bitter, and astringent are the tastes by which land is subdivided (36).*

- *Land, which is even, has accessibility to water, and is covered with green trees is good for growing all kinds of trees (39).*

- *Panasa, lakuca, tala, bamboo, jambeera, jambu, tilaka, vata, kadamba, amrata, kharjura, kadali, tinisa, mrdvi, ketaki, narikela, etc. grow on a marshy land (41).*

- *Sobhanjana, sriphala, saptaparna, sephalika, asoka, sami, karira, karkadhu, kesara, nimba, and saka grow well on an arid land (42).*

- *Bijapuraka, punnaga, champaka, amra, atimuktaka, priyangu, dadima, etc. grow on an ordinary type of land (43).*

With reference to propagation of trees, Surpala observed:

- *Vanaspati, druma, lata, and gulma are the four types of plants. They grow from seed, stalk, or bulb. Thus, planting is of three kinds (45).*

- *Those which bear fruits without flowers are vanaspati (types); those which bear fruits with flowers are druma (types) (46).*

- *Jambu, champaka, punnaga, nagakesara, tamarind, kapittha, badari, bilva, kumbhakari, priyangu, panasa, amra, madhuka, karamarda, etc. grow from seeds. Tambuli, sinduvara, tagara, etc. grow from stalks (49).*

---

[14] https://www.infinityfoundation.com/mandala/t_es/t_es_agraw_surpala_frameset.htm

- *Patala, dadimi, plaksa, karavira, vata, mallika, udumbara kunda, etc. grow from seeds as well as from stalks (50).*
- *Kumkuma, ardra, rasona, alukanda, etc. grow from bulbs. Ela, padma, utpala, etc. grow from seeds as well as from bulbs (51).*
- *After the ash is naturally cooled and removed, kunapa water (liquid manure) should be sprinkled and the pits should be filled with good earth (68).*
- *In fertile lands, which are used excessively, seeds of trapusa or of other vegetables are sown intermittently (70).*
- *Bulbs should be planted in pits measuring one forearm-length, breadth, and depth-and filled with mud mixed with thick sand (81).*
- *Ksirika, tuta, dadimi, bakula, etc. should be planted in the month of Sravana (midst of rainy season). Rajakosa, amra, lakuca, etc. should be planted in the month of Bhadrapada (when rains are receding) (87).*

On treatment of plant-related diseases, Surpala makes many valuable observations. The following are only an illustrative subset of these observations (which are based on Agrawal, D. P.[15])

- *The diseases of the kafa type can be overcome with bitter, strong, and astringent decoctions made out of panchamula (roots of five plant species – sriphala, sarvatobhadra, patala, ganikarika, and syonaka) with fragrant water (187).*
- *For warding off all kafa type of diseases, the paste of white mustard should be deposited at the root and the trees should be watered with a mixture of sesame and ashes (188).*
- *A wise person should treat all types of trees affected by the pitta type of diseases with cool and sweet substances (190).*

---

[15] https://www.infinityfoundation.com/mandala/t_es/t_es_agraw_surapala_frameset.htm

- When watered by the decoction of milk, honey, yastimadhu, and madhuka, trees suffering from pitta type of diseases get cured (191).
- Watered with the decoctions of fruits, triphala, ghee (clarified butter), and honey the trees are freed of all diseases of the pitta type (192).
- To remove insects both from the roots and branches of the trees, wise men should water the trees with cold water for seven days (193).
- The worms can be overcome by the paste of milk, kunapa water, and cow dung mixed with water and also by smearing the roots with the mixture of white mustard, vaca, kusta, and ativisa (194).
- A wound caused by insects heals if sprinkled with milk after being anointed with a mixture of vidanga, sesame, cow's urine, ghee (clarified butter), and mustard (198).
- Trees suffering from (damage due to) frost or scorching heat should be externally covered. Sprinkling with kunapa water and milk is also advisable (199).
- Trees watered continuously with the liquid of triphala, barley, mango seed, and indigo; and also filled at the root with the powder of the same mixture produce fruits resembling collyrium (241).
- Trees treated with water and paste containing the mixture of barley, kimsuka, manjista, turmeric, and sesame and also smeared with the same paste bear red fruits (242).
- All types of flowering plants produce excellent fragrance if earth strongly scented by their own flowers is filled around the base (of the trees) and then fed with water mixed with musta, mura, nata leaves, and wine (249).
- The same treatment used in the evening at their blossoming time along with fat, milk, blood, and kusta intensifies the natural fragrance of the blossoms of punnaga, naga, bakula, etc (250).
- A tamarind plant is grown into an excellent tree if fed with water, mixed with the powder of triphala (253).

A.4 Notes on other ancient texts pertaining to agricultural implements, land categories, and practices

Among the Brahmans, the Shatapath Brahmana gives a clear description of four important stages of agricultural crop production. These are (i) act of tilling or ploughing a land (karsana), (ii) sowing of seeds (vapana), (iii) reaping or harvesting a ripened crop (lavana) and (iv) threshing (mardana) of corns or other crops for getting the grains. Different categories of farmers, cultivation, agricultural land, ploughing with bulls, sowing the seeds of best quality, irrigation, fertilizers or manure, agricultural implements and preservation of crops in granaries etc. are described in detail in the Shatapath Brahmana and other ancient texts. Garga Muni dealt with various agricultural practises.

Bhumivargaha, an Indian Sanskrit text, considered to be 2500 years old, classifies agricultural land into 12 categories namely, urvara (fertile), ushara (barren), maru (desert), aprahata (fallow), shadvala (grassy), pankikala (muddy), jalaprayah (watery), kachchaha (contiguous to water), sharkara (full of pebbles and pieces of limestone), sharkaravati (sandy), nadimatruka (watered from a river), and devamatruka (rainfed).

Two Vaidic terms[16] referring to farmers in the Vedas namely Karsivana and Kinasa (कर्सीवान, किनास) provide the linguistic basis of the term Kisana (किसान) which is used even today. Different types of farmers are recorded in the Vedas. They are named according to their work or profession. Thus, karsivana refers to a 'cultivator', kinasa refers to a 'farmer', sirapati refers to a 'ploughmen', vapa refers to a 'sower', dhanyakrit refers to a 'sower of paddy seeds' and idava refers to 'somebody who carries ripened corns or grains to a granary'. This can also be seen as the beginning of division of labour or recognition of efficiency emanating from specialization.

---

[16] http://vedicheritage.gov.in/vedic-heritage-in-present-context/agriculture-2/

Agriculture in Rigveda: Seeds of India's Civilizational Prosperity

Different types of food grains referred to in the Vaidic literature include Brihi (rice), Yava (barley), Masa, Tila, Mudga, Khalva, Priyangu, Anu (fine rice), Syamaka, Nivara, Godhuma and Masura (dhal).

The plough which is a key tool in the conduct of agriculture has been referred to in the Vaidic parlance and other ancient Indian literature as Langala, Sira, Phala. In fact, eight different components of a plough have been identified in Krishi Parashar as discussed earlier. The Kathaka Samhita prescribes deep ploughing for the rich production of paddy and barley.

Other tools for agriculture include Astra and Tottra which denote a goad. These were used for controlling the yoked oxen. Srini and Datra or 'sickle' continue to be used for reaping the harvest. Khanitra (shovel) has been referred to in the Vedas as a tool for digging the soil. The Vedas record the use of Supa for winnowing the corn like paddy, barley, etc. and Titau for clearing the flour made of barley. The two terms Sira and Laya are used conjointly for two functions of furrowing and harrowing a field respectively. Some other useful instruments for agriculture and allied activities included the Axe (Kulhadi). Axe has resemblance with Parshu of Bhagwan Parshuram, while plough is the main weapon of Balram.

For processing of cotton, ginning process was developed to separate seed from lint but also the spinning wheel (Charkha) was invented for spinning and making the thread. Looms were constructed to weave yarn and make cloth. Needle was the main instrument to stitch the clothes and for doing different kinds of embroidery.

Varahmihir explained the techniques of rain forecasting at length in his 'Varah Samhita'. He explained the unit of rain measurement as 'Drona'. Techniques of rain forecasting given in Varah Samhita may be applicable even today. Kautilya in his 'Arthashastra' also gave crop yield forecasting methods and described agriculture as the basis of business and trade.

Appendix 2: Vaidic Agriculture in Modern Times

In many modern economies including western economies as well as recent initiatives in India, have focused on maximizing agricultural output as well as poultry and livestock in a manner which is highly detrimental to the fertility of the soil, conditions in which livestock are maintained, and eventually the outcomes of these activities. The chemicals used as fertilizers and the inhuman conditions in which livestock are kept result in extensive damage to the life forms that live in sub soil strata and maintain the fertility of the soil. The negative vibrations generated from the commercially produced livestock and the inputs that they are fed on eventually do massive harm to the final consumers located in these countries.

Government policies in India have encouraged a distortionary subsidy regime which results in a long-term damage in the fertility of the soil although in the short-run, output and yield per acre increases. Focus has to shift from maximization of short-term output to optimization of the nourishing value of sustainable output which can be maintained over a long period of time. In fact, the entire concept of maximization of output or output growth requires to be re-examined in the context of sustainability. Ignoring Vaidic values not only with respect to agriculture but also in regard to the overall economic pursuits is the cause of massive proliferation of diseases, periodic and long-term climate disasters, unanticipated shocks emanating from surges of new viruses and bacteria and increase in conflicts amongst nations resulting in avoidable loss of human welfare. The entire economic paradigm needs to be urgently revisited in the light of available knowledge that mankind has inherited from the Vedas. In this context, some initiatives with respect to Vaidic agriculture may prove to be highly valuable.

Vaidic agriculture uplifts a routine economic activity to the status of a Yajna where Devtas and Rishis are involved. Vaidic agriculture is comprehensive as it looks at the entire cycle of agricultural activities including the role and sources of water, role and sources of energy, role of land, soil, and fertility. It describes in detail, the interface of humans with animals particularly cows, oxen, and horses. The production and recycling of seeds, output of agriculture as a form of wealth, and the link of grains to human population and fertility are also discussed in detail in various Rigvaidic Richas. Performance of Yajnas, recitation of Richas, and playing of music can have a significant positive impact on agricultural output and productivity.

In Vaidic agriculture, the following underlying principles emerge as distinguishing features:

1. Underlying divinity
2. Symbiotic relationship with nature and seasons
3. Importance of organic cultivation practices
4. Recognition of cyclicality of inputs and outputs
5. Role of natural inputs such as water and sunshine
6. Symbiotic relations with animals like cows, oxen and horses
7. Importance of soil and fertility, and various sub soil life forms
8. Role of Yajnas and importance of sound waves based on Mantra recitations

In modern times also, some experiments have been initiated where efforts are being made to revive the Vaidic values and practices in agriculture. One such initiative has been organized by Maharshi Mahesh Yogi University[17]. They are attempting to combine the organic and the Vaidic principles into agricultural practices in modern times.

They argue that according to the principles of Vaidic economics, one is considered to be a rich man by the strength of his store of grains and cows. With only these two, humanity can comprehensively address the issues of food security. Indian indigenous cow was worshiped in India

---

[17] https://www.vedicorganic.org/

since ancient times due to many scientific reasons. It is said that there is a Suryaketu nerve on the back of the indigenous or desi Indian cow which absorbs medicinal essences from atmosphere and makes milk, urine and cow dung. Their milk is more nourishing and disease-resistant than milk from other varieties of cows. When their urine and cow dung are used along with the seeds, it makes soil more productive while the output is enriched with medicinal qualities. This soil contains micro-organisms which can balance the nutrients present in soil for the growth of seeds.

In the experiments being carried out at the Maharshi University, considerable importance is attached to the Mantra-based Vaidic vibrations which initiate creative impulses of the Laws of Nature. Vaidic Vibrations carry the nourishing influence of the evolutionary quality of the Laws of Nature fundamental to the growth of the plant and the nutrients within it.

Maharshi traditions have distinguished between forty fundamental structures of sound, that is forty kinds of the Vaidic Sounds that constitute every aspect of the structural and functional aspects of the plant including the plant's physiology and the intelligence that creates it and functions through it. It is argued that these forty values of intelligence are the Laws of Nature that are alive in their concentrated form in the seed of the plant. As the seed sprouts, these forty values of Creative Intelligence together promote the evolution of every fibre of the plant for all its material values.

According to the principles enunciated by Maharshi Mahesh Yogi, these forty values constitute the essence of intelligence, the information that is carried in the finest fibre of the plant as it expresses its material value emerging from the abstract, unmanifest intelligence of the sapling, evolving from its unmanifest value to its manifest value. These forty values of pure intelligence, of Veda, will be enlivened for their fully blossomed potential when these melodies are sung in the fields. The healing and nourishing influence of Vaidic Sound is well documented by scientific research, not only with respect to human life, but also for the animal and plant kingdoms.

When the natural sounds of nature consistent with the sounds of Natural Law, that is the sounds of the Vaidic Mantras are recited, they resonate with the structured sound in Nature, enlivening and revitalizing life from its source and influencing every level of evolution from the individual to the Cosmic.

The Vaidic melodies, that is Vaidic recitations, are so organized that at each stage of the growth of the plant, there are suitable melodies to bring about the full blossoming of that stage of development, so that at each stage, the plant develops in the fullness of its structure and function, for its full nutritional and life-supporting values.

The Vaidic element added to organic agriculture is a phenomenon of intelligence, a phenomenon of consciousness, which is also referred to as a phenomenon of the creative intelligence of nature, directly applied to support different stages of evolution of the plant and the nutrients within it.

In modern times, it is important to recognize the value of organic agriculture and then supplement it with Vaidic principles. This adds a more nourishing dimension to the output of agriculture because of the positive vibrations generated from the Vaidic Mantras along with the pursuit of the Vaidic values of organic interdependence amongst men, farm animals, sub soil life forms and nature.

Maharishi Vaidic Organic Agriculture[18] goes beyond the most rigorous existing standards for pure, organic food. By using the ancient Vaidic agricultural technologies, farmers rise to higher consciousness and live life in harmony with all the laws of nature. The Mantra based Vaidic sounds are used to enliven the inner intelligence of the plants to produce food bursting with the vitality of nature's intelligence, and at the same

---

[18] https://maharishi-programmes.globalgoodnews.com/vedic-agriculture/

time, create a healthy environment for the farmer to cultivate an abundance of pure and nourishing food.

Linked to this initiative is also Maharishi's Poverty Removal Programme, the objectives of which are stated as follows:[19]

'We will establish a Vedic Agriculture University in order to introduce the knowledge of Natural Law that has been scientifically researched in many universities and research institutions in different parts of the world, and we will also introduce the knowledge of the nutritious and life-giving value of naturally grown foods....

...The whole process of the plant sprouting from the seed and growing into leaves, flowers, and fruits, has been found to gain nourishment from soothing music and melodies; from enhanced seasonal influences of Sun, Moon, planets, and stars, and from increased qualities of harmony and pleasantness in the environment. This is now quite well established through worldwide scientific research. To produce this effect, we will have the Vedic Experts from India whose traditional melodies and Vedic Recitations are most effective.' (Maharishi, Maharishi's Poverty Removal Programme)

A similar initiative has also been undertaken at the Sri Sri Institute of Agriculture, Sciences and Technology Trust under the aegis of Art of Living. They have organized different and innovative agricultural farming and training programs which are based on the principles of Vaidic agriculture. In their case also, bio-fertilizers and pesticides are made by using cow dung, urine and ghee (clarified butter) of desi cows. This is considered more eco-friendly and harmless to mother Earth. Similar initiatives have been taken by the Patanjali Ashram and Yogic Institute. In some of these places, Goshalas are also being maintained according to Vaidic principles. Vandana Shiva, in a number of contributions (Shiva,

---

[19]https://maharishi-programmes.globalgoodnews.com/vedic-agriculture/programmes.html

V. 1991, 1993, 1997, 2000, and 2008), has highlighted the importance of various life forms that thrive in the sub soil and the role that they play in maintaining the fertility of soil. Also see 'Vedic origin of organic farming by Vandana Shiva, 3 February 2020[20]'.

The Isha Foundation under the guidance of Sadhguru has taken up a major initiative to make Indian policymakers and farmers aware of agriculture according to principles that are consistent with overall sustainability especially for maintaining the quality of soil. The Isha Foundation has been closely involved in improving farmers' situations and the general state of agriculture in Tamil Nadu for many years. Considering its past experience in agroforestry, creation of herbal gardens and collaboration with other agricultural NGOs, Isha Foundation was asked by the Small Farmer's Agribusiness Consortium (SFAC), Department of Agriculture, Government of India to support and guide the farmers of Thondamuthur block, Coimbatore, in forming an FPO and carrying out collective activities[21].

---

[20] https://www.youtube.com/watch?v=IxEb2XmiljE
[21] https://www.ishaoutreach.org/en/action-rural-rejuvenation/blog/isha-indian-farming-agriculture

Appendix 3: Notes on medicinal plants

In modern times, many of the trees or plants mentioned in Rigveda (10/97) are not available or identifiable anymore. This includes the Soma plant. Sing, et. al. (2002) in their article on the role of herbs for treating skin disorders observe "*The antiquity of Indian materia medica goes back to the period of Vedas when Vedic samhitas mention the use of many herbs. Rigveda the oldest literary document presents the knowledge about the medicinal herbs in Osadhi Sukta (Rigveda 10/ 97.1-23). It also mentions with due prominence the four miraculous herbs namely: Samavati, asavavati, urjayanti and udojas. (Rigveda 10/97.7). More elaborate descriptions are available in Athervaveda.*" They have provided an elaborate list of herbal plants in India giving both their Sanskrit and botanical names (Table A3.1).

Table A3.1: List of Medicinal Plants

S.No	Sanskrit Name	Botanical Name
01.	Aguru	Aquilaria agallocha
02.	Ahifena	Papaver somniferum
03.	Aksota	Juglans regia
04.	Amalaki	Phyllanthus emblica
05.	Amra	Magnifera indica
06.	Apamarg	Achyranthus aspera
07.	Aparajita	Clitoria ternatea
08.	Aragbadha	Casiafistula
09.	Arimeda	Acacia leucoph loea
10	Arka	Calotropis gigantean
11	Asvattha	Ficus religiosa
12	Atasi	Linum usitattissinum
13	Ati -Visha	Aconitum heterophyllum
14	Avarttaki	Cassia auriculata
15	Barbari	Oscimum besilicum
16	Barbur	Acacia nilotia

Agriculture in Rigveda: Seeds of India's Civilizational Prosperity

S.No	Sanskrit Name	Botanical Name
17	Bhandir	Clerodendrum infortunatum
18	Bhringraj	Eclipta alba
19	Bhumyamalaki	Phyllanthus niruri
20	Bhunimba	Andrographis paniculata
21	Bola	Comiphora myrrha
22	Brahmi	Bacopa monnieri
23	Chakramarda	Cassia tora
24	Champaka	Michelia champaka
25	Chandrasura	Lipidium sativum
26	Changeri	Oxalis corniculata
27	Chirbilva	Holoptelia intergrefolia
28	Chitrak	Plumbago rosea
29	Damanak	Artemisia vulgaris
30	Danti	Baleospermum montanum
31	Daruharidra	Berberis asistata
32	Darbha	Eragrostis cynosuroides
33	Decodaru	Cedrus deodara
34	Dhatura	Datura metal
35	Dugdhika	Euphorbia thymifolia
36	Durva	Cynodon dactylon
37	Ha	Elettaria cardmomum
38	Gambhari	Gmelina arborea
39	GhritKuman	Aloe vera
40	Guggulu	Commiphora mukul
41	Gunja	Abrus precatorius
42	Haridra	Curcuma longa
43	Indravaruni	Cucumis trigonus
44	Jalapippali	Phyla nodijlora
45	Jambiri	Citrus Limon
46	Japa	Hibiscus rosa-sinensis
47	Jati	Jasmine officinale

S.No	Sanskrit Name	Botanical Name
48	Jatiphala	Miristika Fragrans
49	Jatamamsi	Nordostachys jatamamsi
50	Jyotismati	Celastrus panniculatus
51	Kampiilak	Mallotus ph ilipinessis
52	Kantaki karanja	Caesalpinia crisis
53	Kanchanar	Bauhinia variegata
54	Karira	Capparis decidua
55	Karpura	Cinnamomum camphora
56	Kasamarda	Cassia oxidentalis
57	Katabh	Careya arborea
58	Kapikachhu	Mucuna pruriens
59	Karvir	Neirum indicum
60	Katuka	Picrorhiza kurroa
61	Karanja	Pongamia pinnata
62	Karpura - Haridra	Curcuma amada
63	Karvellaka	Momordica charantia
64	Ketaki	Pandanus ororatissimus
65	Khadir	Acacia catechu
66	Ksiravidari	Ipomoea panniculata
67	Kutaja	Holarrhena antidysenterica
68	Kokodumbarica	Ficus hispida
69	Kusumbha	Carthamus tinctoris
70	Kulattha	Cassia absus
71	Lajjalu	Mimosa pudika
72	Langaii	Gloriosa superba
73	Madanphala	Randia dometorum
74	Madayantika	Lawsonia inermis
75	Madhuka	Madhuka longifolia
76	Mahanimba	Melia azedarach
77	Mamira	Coptis teeta

Agriculture in Rigveda: Seeds of India's Civilizational Prosperity

S.No	Sanskrit Name	Botanical Name
78	Mandukparni	Centella asiaflca
79	Matsyangj	Alternathera sessilis
80	Matulunga	Citrus medica
81	Masura	Lens culinaris
82	Mayaphala	Quercus infectoria
83	Mesasringi	Gymnema sylvestre
84	Muchkunda	Pterospermum aceri
85	Musta	Cyprus rotundus
86	Nagadamani	Crinum asiaticum
87	Nagakesar	Mesua ferrea
88	Narikela	Coccus nucifera
89	Nilini	Indigofera tinctoria
90	Nimba	Azadiracta indica
91	Palasa	Butea monospermum
92	Palandu	Allium cepa
93	Panasa	Artocarpus integrefolia
94	Patha	Cycleaburm anni
95	Padma	Nelumbo nucifera
96	Padmaka	Prunus cerasoides
97	Parijata	Nyctanthesarbortristis
98	Pippali	Piper longum
99	Prasarani	Ipomoea tridentata
100	Priyangu	Callicarpa macrophylla
101	RaktaChandan	Pterocarpus santalinus
102	Rasona	Allium sativum
103	Raktapamarga	Desmochaeta prostrate
104	Rohitak	Amora rohataka
105	Sahanchara	Nilgirianthus ciliatus
106	Sarala	Pinus roxburghaii
107	Sariva	Hemidesmus indicus
108	Saivala	Ceratophyllum xemersum

S.No	Sanskrit Name	Botanical Name
109	Saivala	Ceratophyllum demersum
110	Salmali	Bombax ceiba
111	Sallaki	Boswellia serrata
112	Sankhapuspi	Convolvulus pluricalis
113	Saptaparn	Alstonia scholaris
114	Sarsap	Brassica juncea
115	Satavari	Asparagus racemosus
116	Sathi	Hedychium coronareum
117	Shirish	Albizia lebbeck
118	Sigru	Moringa oleifera
119	Simsapa	Delbergia sissoo
120	Sihlaka	Liquidamber orientalis
121	Suchimallika	Jasminum auriculatum
122	Sunissna	Marselia quadrifolia
123	Suryamukhi	Helianthus anus
124	Snuhi	Euphorbia neriifolia
125	Somavalka	Acacia polyantha
126	Sthulela	Amomum subulatum
127	Svarnaksiri	Argemone mexicana
128	Tamalpatra	Cinnamomum tamala
129	Tambula	Piper betle
130	Tavaksiri	Maranla arndinacea
131	Tripadi	Desmodium triflorum
132	Trivrit	Operculina turpithum
133	Tuvaraka	Hydnocarpus taurifolia
134	Tulasi	Ocimum sanctum
135	Tvak	Cinnamomum zeylenica
136	Udumbara	Ficus racemose
137	Vacha	Acorus calamus
138	Vakula	Mimosops elengi

Agriculture in Rigveda: Seeds of India's Civilizational Prosperity

S.No	Sanskrit Name	Botanical Name
139	Vakuchi	Psoralea corylifolia
140	Vamsa	Bambusa arundinacea
141	Vatsnabha	Aconitum ferox
142	Vata	Ficus bengalensis
143	Varuna	Crataea nurvala
144	Vana-Haridra	Curauma aromatica
145	Vidari	Pueraria tuberosa
146	Vidanga	Embelia ribes
147	Vriddhadaruk	Argyreia nervosa
148	Vanbarbari	Oscimum americanum
149	Yastimadhu	Glycyrrhiza glabra

Source: Sing, et. al. (2002)

Appendix 4: Notes on India's Erstwhile Prosperity

In this Volume, we have argued that the seeds of India's original prosperity which lasted for thousands of years until just a few centuries ago, derived largely from the rich Rigvaidic agricultural principles which were woven into broader economic principles along with a very productive interface with industrial development, development of technologies, extensive provision of services such as health and education and growth of trade and commerce. In fact, it was the surplus produced by India's rich agricultural traditions that provided the foundation for prosperous, welfare-oriented and value-oriented society. The relatively large share of India's contribution to the global economy has been authentically documented by Madisson in his works entitled 'Monitoring the world economy' and 'Explaining the economic performance of nations' in 1995.

According to estimates provided by Maddison (2007), India's share in the global GDP in 1 A.D. was 32%. It progressively fell to 22.4% by 1600 A.D. and then increased again to 24.5% by 1700 A.D. After that, it kept falling sharply, reaching its lowest level at 3.2% in 1980. Since then, India's share in world GDP started to rise again, reaching a level of 6.7% by 2008. India's current share in world GDP is 6.8% (2021-22)[22]. In contrast, India's share in world population is 17.8%. This implies that India's per-capita GDP in US$ 1990 is only 38.2% of world per-capita GDP. In terms of pursuing economic development, India has a considerable gap to cover before it can provide for its average citizen, a level of prosperity comparable to world average. In 1000 AD, India's share in world population was just a little more than 28% which was only marginally

---

[22] Gross domestic product based on purchasing-power-parity (PPP) share of world total, sourced from IMF World Economic Outlook, April 2022.

Agriculture in Rigveda: Seeds of India's Civilizational Prosperity

higher than its share in world GDP implying that the per capita GDP at that point of time was close to the world per-capita GDP.

India's relative position in terms of its share in world GDP is also highlighted in Figure A4.1 and Table 4.1.

Figure A4.1: India's share in world GDP

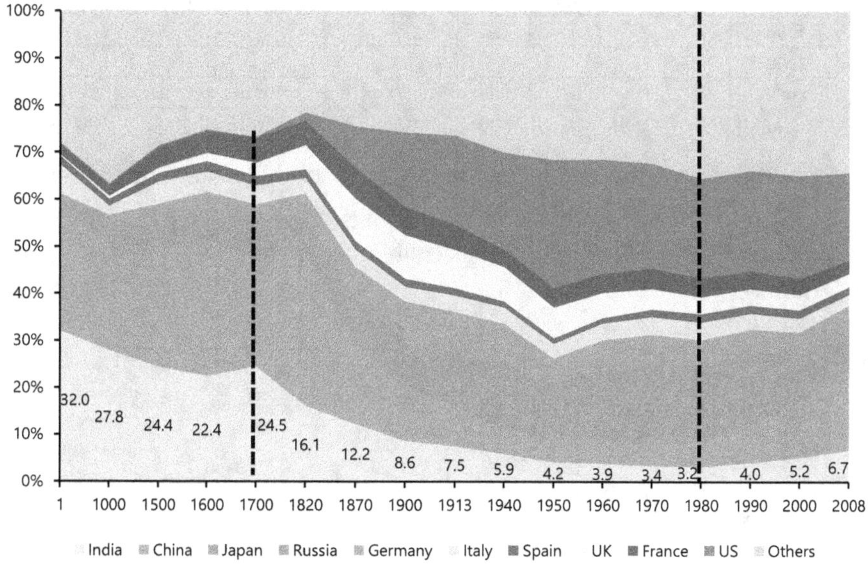

Source: http://www.ggdc.net/maddison/Historical_Statistics/vertical-file_02-2010.xls
Note: the figures pertain to percentage share of individual countries in world GDP. The original magnitudes are given in 1990 Geary Khamis international dollars. The relevant shares are also given in Appendix table A.

Table A4.1: India's share in world GDP: a long history

Year (A.D.)	India	China	Japan	Russia	Germany	Italy	Spain	UK	France	US	Others
1	32	25.4	1.1	1.5	1.2	6.1	1.8	0.3	2.2	0.3	28
1000	27.8	22.7	2.6	2.3	1.2	1.9	1.5	0.7	2.3	0.4	36.6
1500	24.4	24.9	3.1	3.4	3.3	4.7	1.8	1.1	4.4	0.3	28.6
1600	22.4	29	2.9	3.4	3.8	4.3	2.1	1.8	4.7	0.2	25.3
1700	24.5	22.3	4.1	4.4	3.7	3.9	2	2.9	5.3	0.1	26.8
1820	16.1	33	3	5.4	3.9	3.2	1.8	5.2	5.1	1.8	21.5
1870	12.2	17.1	2.3	7.5	6.5	3.8	1.8	9	6.5	8.9	24.5

Year (A.D.)	India	China	Japan	Russia	Germany	Italy	Spain	UK	France	US	Others
1900	8.6	11.1	2.6	7.8	8.2	3	1.7	9.4	5.9	15.8	25.7
1913	7.5	8.8	2.6	8.5	8.7	3.5	1.5	8.2	5.3	18.9	26.4
1940	5.9	5.4	4.7	9.3	8.4	3.5	1.2	7.3	3.7	20.6	30
1950	4.2	4.6	3	9.6	5	3.1	1.2	6.5	4.1	27.3	31.5
1960	3.9	5.2	4.4	10	6.6	3.5	1.1	5.4	4.1	24.3	31.4
1970	3.4	4.6	7.4	9.8	6.1	3.8	1.6	4.4	4.3	22.4	32.3
1980	3.2	5.2	7.8	8.5	5.5	3.7	1.7	3.6	4.1	21.1	35.5
1990	4	7.8	8.6	7.3	4.7	3.4	1.7	3.5	3.8	21.4	33.8
2000	5.2	11.8	7.2	3.5	4.2	3	1.7	3.3	3.4	21.9	34.9
2008	6.7	17.5	5.7	4.4	3.4	2.3	1.6	2.8	2.8	18.6	34.3

Source: http://www.ggdc.net/maddison/Historical_Statistics/vertical-file_02-2010.xls

Even this description of India's relative prosperity is starting only from 1 A.D. that is 1 C.E. (common era). But the seeds of India's real prosperity predate these years by several millennia as briefly discussed in this Volume.

Appendix 5: More on the Historicity of River Saraswati

In recent years considerable work has been done in India and elsewhere to establish the historicity of the Saraswati river beyond any doubt. The government of India also set up an expert committee consisting of various experts drawn from different fields who have been working on different aspects of the historicity of Saraswati especially that based on researches relating to its paleochannels. This committee has brought together all the available researches on the matter, collated these and has provided in its report an authentic review of these scientific works. A summary of the report of this expert committee is given below.

Summary of the Report of the Expert Committee on Saraswati's Paleochannels[23]

In the dry western part of the Indian sub-continent encompassing Haryana, southern Punjab, Rajasthan and Gujarat, numerous paleochannels have been identified and comprehensively investigated since early nineteenth century by geomorphologists, geologists, geophysists, geohydrologists, archaeologists and remote-sensing specialists using high-end techniques. Also, a large number of exploratory wells were dug along the paleochannels in these states to establish extensive networks of surface and buried paleochannels constituting potential water-bearing aquifers in multiple groups covering the entire plain of the drainage system. In this review their main findings are brought together.

---

[23] http://cgwb.gov.in/Ground-Water/Final%20print%20version_Palaeochannel%20Expert%20Committee_15thOct2016.pdf

The banks of Ghaggar-Hakra-Saraswati-Drishadvati river system are intimately associated with multiplicity of paleochannels dotted densely with ruins of settlements, including the largest ones such as Ganweriwala (>100 ha) in Cholistan (Pakistan) and Rakhigarhi (>150 ha) in Haryana and such medium to large cities as Kalibangan, Farmana, Karanpura, Baror, Banawail, Bhirrana, and Mitathal. These settlements belong to the Hakra, Pre/ Early Harappan, Harappan, Late Harappan, Painted Grey Ware and Rangmahal cultures. The middle course of the Ghaggar-Hakra paleochannels (Saraswati) is thus related with archaeological sites from the fourth millennium BCE to the historical period. However, there was perceptible dwindling, both quantitatively and qualitatively, in the settlement pattern during the second millennium BCE, which is attributed to the changing water regime. The river that supported these settlements finally disappeared in the late Holocene period.

In the Hakra reach, where among hundreds of settlements, the largest city of the Harappan civilization, Ganweriwala was located, the buried paleochannel yielded potable water dated 12,900 BP to 4,700 BP. Likewise the paleochannels in the Jaisalmer area have been supplying potable water. The water in the depth range of 30 to 50mts being 1,800 to 5,000 years old and in the 60 to 250mts deep aquifers dates 6,000 to 22,000 years old.

This review confirms the conclusion that in the northern Haryana, the Ghaggar-Patialiwali rivulets provided pathways to the western branch of the Himalayan born river (paleo Satluj) and through the former courses of the Markanda and hydraulically connected Sarsuti rivulets which flowed through the eastern branch of the Himalayan river (paleo Yamuna). The two branches combined 25 km south of Patiala, then flowed through the extraordinarily wide channel of the Ghaggar-Hakra-Nara and emptied itself into the Gulf of the Arabian Sea. In recent years, the Jodhpur based Regional Remote Sensing Centre of Indian Space Research Organization has carried out comprehensive and extensive integration of the paleochannels including that of the Ghaggar-Hakra-Nara studies in Haryana, Punjab and Rajasthan (Gupta et. al. 2004, 2008,

2011, Bhadra et. al., 2009, Sharma & Bhadra, 2012). They identified these paleochannel system with the River Saraswati. Chart A5.1 summarizes the latest available information on the Saraswati river system.

Figure A5.1: Paleochannels recognised in the Ghaggar-Hakara-Nara

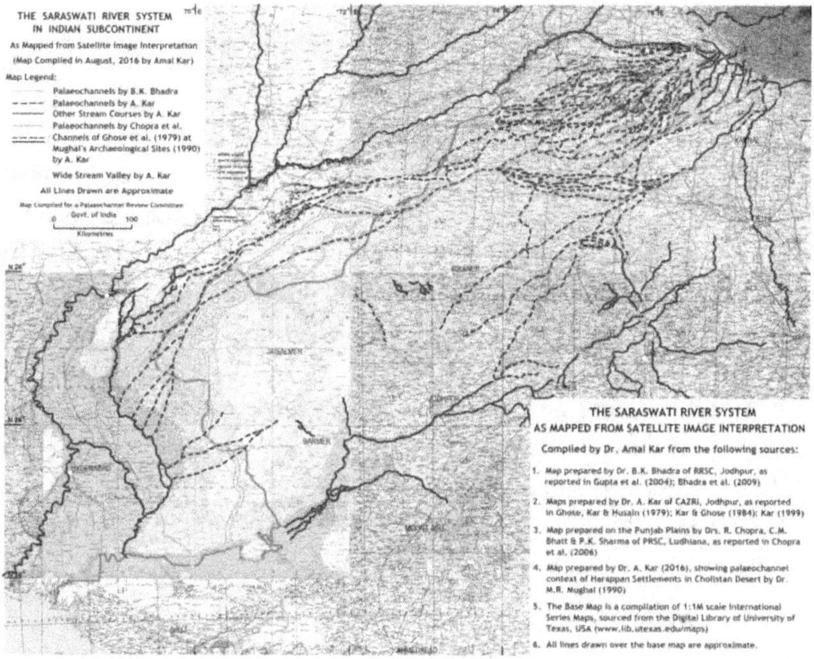

Palaeochannels recognised in the Ghaggar-Hakra-Nara, at the both basins, West of Aravalli Range (after A. Kar)

Source (basic data): Report of the Expert Committee to review available information on Paleochannels (2016)

The Sindhu and the Saraswati were the two major river systems with their network of their tributaries of north western India during the ancient period. Sridhar et al., (1999) have classified the rivers of Indo-Gangetic plains into four main groups (i) Indus (Sindhu) and its tributaries, Vitasta (Jhelum) and Askini (Chenab), (ii) Shatadru (Satluj) and its two major tributaries Vipasa (Beas) and Parasuni or Iravati (Ravi), (iii) Saraswati and its three tributaries Markanda, Ghaggar and Patialewali in its upper reaches and a major tributary in its middle course, (iv) Drishadvati and

Lavanavati. Sindhu shifted westwards up to 160 km, primarily as a consequence of the northward drifting Indian plate, which must have caused subsidence of the belt adjacent to the Kirthar-Sulaiman mountain front. The Sindhu also flowed through its many channels in different time periods as testified by its multiple paleochannels.

Sinha et al. (2013) utilized resistivity surveys and drill cores to confirm the presence of the buried paleochannel in the Ghaggar plains and to establish its upstream connectivity. Two transects for resistivity soundings mapped the sub-surface lithology of the region close to Kalibangan and Kunal across the large valley partially occupied by the Ghaggar river channel at present. The third transect, SRH, was located across the trace of a paleochannel near Sirhd in Punjab close to the Himalayan front. This paleochannel was originally identified by Yashpal et al. (1980) as a possible former course of the Satluj River. Although this area lies in the semi-humid region with an average annual rainfall of 690 mm per year, there is no major surface drainage in this region. The modern Satluj flows ~150 km west and the Yamuna flows ~150 km east of this transect. It has been suggested that the Satluj flowed through this region before moving west (Yashpal et al., 1980).

They also point out toward the existence of subsurface multilateral channel systems on the basis of apparent high widths and presence of silty clay and mixed sand layer fluvial bodies and later suggested three phases of fluvial activity (F-1, F-2 and F-3) as given in Figure A5.2.

Based on the review of available evidence the committee concluded that using the OSL dating of sediments in the Tohana–Ellenabad reach of the river that flowed through the Ghaggar basin, it is demonstrated that the river became sluggish in the period 4300 BP to 2900 BP (Saini et al., 2009). Further downstream in the Hakra reach this happened a little earlier where the river was active only until about 4500 BP as inferred from testimony of the U-Pb zircon dates (Clift et al., 2012). In this tract the fluvial sediments were covered by aeolian sediments dated 3356 BP (Giosan et al., 2012).

Figure A5.2: Phases of fluvial activity

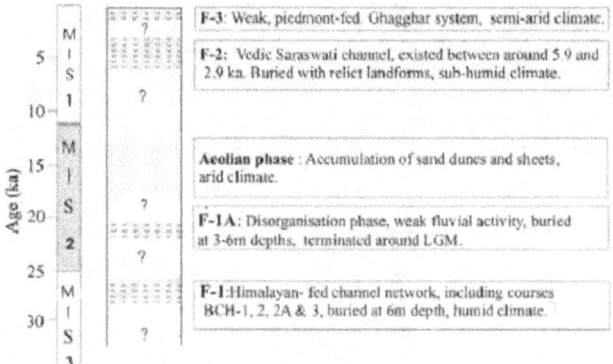

Summary diagram of the area showing three phases of fluvial activity (F-1 to F-3). F-1 and F-1A are buried, the F-2 is mappable as a relict landform on aerial photos and imagery and has subtle expression on the ground. The F-3 is represented by the present day Ghaggar River (From Saini et al., 2009).

Source (basic data): Report of the Expert Committee to review available information on Paleochannels (2016)

It is obvious that the discharge of the river had declined in the Later Holocene time. Alongside, there was a large-scale upstream exodus around 3750 BP of the Harappans (Thapar, 1975) as borne out by sudden appearance of a large number of Late Harappan (3900–3300 B.P) settlements in the upper reaches of the river in the belt south of the Siwalik Hills, and also in the north western parts of the Yamuna–Ganga interfluves in Uttar Pradesh (Dixit, 1981, 1993).

On the basis of detailed geological, geomorphological, geohydrological and archaeological studies backed strongly by comprehensive remote-sensing investigations using latest technology, carried out in the last six decades, it is concluded that the Himalayan-born Satluj of the past that flowed through the channels of the present-day Ghaggar-Patialiwali rivulets represent the western branch of the ancient River Saraswati. Further, the Markanda and the Sarsuti rivers provided pathways to the eastern branch of the Saraswati river, now known as the Tons-Yamuna rivers. These two branches joined at Shatrana, 25 km south of Patiala, and flowed as a large river through the wide channel of the Ghaggar-Hakra-Nara before emptying itself into the Rann of Kachchh.

Work on locating paleochannels relating to the Saraswati system has continued even after the Review Committee's work. More and more evidence is being gathered confirming the exact details of the different phases of Saraswati as it flowed in the historical period. One of the latest evidence relates to identifying a Saraswati river paleochannel in Kurukshetra's Baholi village. This finding was reported in the Times of India dated 24 April 2022[24].

According to Director CERSR, nearly all the paleochannels of the Saraswati river in Haryana and Rajasthan up to the India-Pakistan border in Anupgarh have been identified. The research findings have already been published in 2021 in peer-review Journal of Archaeological Prospection which is published in the United Kingdom.

According to the researchers, the typical light grey sand at Bohali matches very well with similar sand examined at Bushangarh and Bhaur Saidan villages in Kurukshetra district where a depositional history of the past 14,000 years of the Saraswati river has been documented in the sediment record. The walls of the channel show well developed laminations, current and cross-bedding, and other sedimentary structures which develop in fluviatile depositional environments.

According to Professor A R Chaudhri, Director, Centre for Excellence for Research on Saraswati River (CERSR), a site near Baholi village on Kurukshetra-Ladwa road has been identified where Saraswati river's thick sand deposits were encountered in a 10-meter deep trench which was specially dug "for establishing a reservoir". The Baholi site falls on the paleochannel which crosses the NH44 at Pipli near Kurukshetra. The width of the Saraswati river channel at Pipli is more than 3 km.

---

[24]http://timesofindia.indiatimes.com/articleshow/91034515.cms?utm_source=contentofinterest&utm_medium=text&utm_campaign=cppst

As per details provided by Professor Chaudhri, this site is a depression which is more than 400 meters long and is 100 meters wide and it is littered with fine clay and silt. The study team gathered evidence about the presence of a mega-river paleochannel after the removal of the top 4 meters of clay-rich topsoil. In this deep stratum, 24 different layers of varying sediment types were identified.

Index

Aditi *33, 50, 220*

Agni *33, 34, 49, 90, 91, 93, 158, 170, 171, 176, 182, 211, 212*

animals *34, 39, 56, 57, 60, 61, 65, 66, 74, 78, 84, 127, 152, 173, 174, 175, 179, 188, 192, 199, 206, 209, 211, 214, 215, 216, 219, 240, 242, 257, 259*

Anushtup *14, 15, 16, 38, 44, 53, 54, 55, 56, 57, 58, 59, 60, 67, 68, 73, 84, 88, 155, 156, 188, 189, 190, 191, 192, 193, 194, 195, 196, 197, 198, 199, 200, 201, 202, 203, 204, 205, 206, 208, 236*

Artha .... *ix, 12, 227*

Arthasastra .... *ix*

Ashwattha *19, 192, 193, 194*

Ashwavati *187, 195, 196, 210*

Ashwini Kumars *42, 43, 49, 77, 184*

Atharvan *161, 162, 188, 189, 190, 191, 192, 194, 195, 196, 197, 198, 199, 200, 201, 202, 203, 204, 205, 206, 208*

Atharvaveda *viii, xxvii, 2, 6, 12, 20, 41, 43, 44, 64, 65, 66, 67, 68, 69, 70, 72, 81, 161, 162,* *163, 173, 174, 188, 193, 194, 235*

Aushadhi ... *22, 73, 187, 188, 209*

axles *218, 219*

Bharadwaj *33, 45, 77, 78, 79, 80, 90, 91, 92, 93, 94, 95, 96, 97, 98, 99, 100, 101, 102, 103, 168, 180, 183, 184*

Bhishaj *188, 189, 190, 191, 192, 194, 195, 196, 197, 198, 199, 200, 201, 202, 203, 204, 205, 206, 208*

cattle *39, 40, 53, 54, 63, 74, 118, 152, 154, 155, 166, 167, 168, 169, 172, 173, 175, 182, 183, 185, 186, 192, 216, 223, 248*

Chanda *1, 14, 16, 24, 33, 38, 42, 45, 46, 47, 48, 49, 53, 54, 55, 56, 57, 58, 59, 60, 61, 62, 63, 77, 78, 79, 80, 81, 82, 84, 88, 89, 90, 91, 92, 93, 94, 95, 96, 97, 98, 99, 100, 101, 102, 103, 104, 105, 115, 116, 122, 149, 150, 151, 152, 153, 154, 155, 156, 157, 158, 159, 160, 161, 162, 167, 168, 169, 170, 171, 172, 174, 182, 183, 211, 212, 213, 214, 215, 216, 217, 218, 219, 220, 222*

chandas *18, 53*

chanting 2, 214

charioteer 117, 151

Clouds 83, 154, 237

cows 20, 23, 40, 63, 66, 72, 75, 108, 169, 175, 176, 177, 178, 179, 180, 181, 183, 184, 185, 186, 191, 192, 196, 198, 211, 214, 216, 217, 218, 257, 260

crop 39, 40, 43, 50, 59, 74, 140, 161, 169, 173, 213, 240, 241, 254, 255

Dashrajna Yuddha 186

Dasyus 47, 171

Datra 221, 255

Devarishis 193

Devi 22, 82, 87, 88, 89, 90, 91, 94, 97, 98, 101, 104, 105, 106, 122, 124, 132, 134, 191, 212

Devta x, 1, 4, 5, 15, 16, 20, 21, 22, 23, 33, 34, 38, 41, 44, 45, 46, 47, 48, 49, 50, 53, 54, 55, 56, 57, 58, 59, 60, 61, 62, 63, 64, 65, 66, 67, 68, 69, 70, 73, 74, 77, 78, 79, 80, 81, 82, 84, 88, 89, 90, 91, 92, 93, 94, 95, 96, 97, 98, 99, 100, 101, 102, 103, 104, 105, 107, 114, 115, 116, 117, 118, 119, 120, 121, 122, 123, 124, 125, 126, 127, 128, 129, 131, 132, 133, 134, 149, 150, 151, 152, 153, 154, 155, 156, 157, 159, 160, 161, 162, 163, 165, 166, 168, 169, 170, 171, 172, 174, 175, 176, 177, 178, 179, 180, 181, 182, 183, 184, 185, 193, 194, 202, 220, 222, 237

Devtas vi, vii, 1, 2, 3, 4, 5, 7, 11, 21, 22, 24, 33, 34, 35, 36, 39, 42, 43, 45, 46, 47, 48, 49, 50, 51, 53, 54, 55, 57, 58, 59, 60, 61, 62, 64, 65, 66, 67, 68, 69, 70, 71, 73, 74, 77, 81, 82, 84, 90, 91, 92, 93, 96, 101, 103, 115, 118, 123, 128, 129, 130, 132, 133, 147, 149, 153, 155, 156, 158, 160, 161, 163, 167, 168, 170, 171, 175, 177, 178, 179, 180, 182, 183, 184, 187, 188, 189, 191, 197, 198, 202, 203, 204, 205, 209, 210, 211, 212, 213, 214, 215, 216, 217, 218, 219, 220, 236, 238, 256

dhan 213

Dharma .... ix, 12

Dharma, ... ix, 12

disease-free 186, 189, 190, 194, 197, 198, 203, 248

diseases 155, 166, 175, 186, 188, 189, 190, 191, 195, 196, 197, 198, 199, 200, 202, 204, 208, 209, 250, 251, 252, 256

Dwaparyug 189

Dyulok *5, 46, 48, 49, 57, 58, 77, 78, 79, 80, 81, 101, 102, 123, 187, 203, 204, 209*

Earth *5, 13, 31, 34, 39, 42, 43, 44, 46, 48, 49, 57, 58, 59, 60, 65, 69, 74, 77, 78, 79, 80, 81, 82, 83, 84, 91, 101, 102, 106, 107, 108, 120, 123, 130, 133, 134, 151, 152, 153, 154, 155, 156, 157, 161, 162, 165, 166, 169, 171, 172, 176, 180, 182, 191, 194, 204, 205, 209, 210, 237, 247, 249, 260*

Economics *ix, 12, 13, 57, 225, 226, 227*

Efficiency *224*

farm *23, 60, 175*

field *49, 53, 54, 55, 56, 62, 63, 64, 65, 69, 71, 72, 73, 74, 141, 173, 213, 214, 216, 226, 240, 242, 255*

fruits *58, 70, 78, 187, 190, 191, 202, 209, 240, 250, 252, 253, 260*

Gandharvas *193*

grain *39, 42, 43, 61, 65, 156, 175, 185, 213, 216, 219, 221, 223, 224, 240*

Guru .... *viii, 11, 225*

harmony *13, 61, 165, 212, 259, 260*

heaven *5, 49, 57, 69, 78, 79, 80, 81, 101, 119, 123, 133, 134, 153, 154, 155, 157, 158, 182*

herbs *34, 39, 55, 56, 72, 85, 116, 170, 187, 188, 189, 190, 191, 192, 194, 195, 196, 197, 198, 199, 200, 201, 202, 203, 204, 205, 206, 208, 209, 210, 233, 262*

Hindi *2, 7, 42, 57, 116*

horses *23, 34, 39, 53, 54, 66, 111, 112, 116, 151, 153, 154, 167, 172, 175, 179, 181, 182, 183, 184, 185, 191, 211, 216, 223, 257*

implements *39, 50, 56, 57, 61, 68, 74, 211, 213, 218, 223, 240, 254*

Indra *16, 25, 34, 35, 46, 47, 48, 50, 51, 57, 59, 60, 67, 71, 77, 93, 97, 113, 114, 115, 118, 128, 147, 149, 158, 160, 161, 168, 171, 172, 174, 177, 179, 180, 181, 182, 183, 184, 185, 211, 212, 220, 221, 237, 238*

industry *ix, x, 12, 127, 147, 211, 222, 223, 227*

interrelationship *147, 211*

Jagati *14, 15, 16, 38, 61, 77, 78, 79, 80, 94, 95, 96, 102, 106, 107, 108, 109, 110, 111, 112, 113, 128, 150, 151*

Kakup 172

Kama .... ix, 12

Kanda 64, 65, 66, 67, 68, 69, 72, 81, 193

Kanva... 25, 33, 42, 169, 172, 182

Kapil Muni 193

Khal 221

kings 21, 195

Krishi 42, 53

Kshetrapati 53, 54, 55, 56, 57, 71, 72, 73, 172

land vii, 5, 11, 23, 39, 40, 43, 47, 53, 54, 57, 58, 59, 60, 67, 68, 69, 70, 81, 84, 85, 89, 103, 111, 113, 114, 123, 140, 146, 147, 154, 161, 162, 163, 167, 168, 169, 172, 173, 185, 186, 187, 203, 209, 214, 237, 239, 245, 247, 248, 250, 254, 257

Madhuchanda 32, 33, 104

Mandals 7, 25, 26

mankind v, vi, vii, viii, 3, 11, 13, 37, 39, 40, 42, 43, 50, 73, 74, 81, 83, 84, 91, 96, 115, 147, 152, 158, 159, 160, 161, 165, 166, 175, 180, 181, 182, 184, 185, 186, 187, 189, 190, 191, 192, 194, 196, 197, 198, 199, 202, 203, 204, 205, 206, 208, 209, 210, 236, 238, 247, 249, 256

Mantras vi, viii, xxvii, 1, 2, 5, 11, 12, 17, 19, 22, 23, 24, 25, 26, 31, 33, 38, 64, 72, 187, 188, 193, 196, 200, 209, 210, 218, 232, 238, 241, 259

Maruts 46, 123, 124, 149, 153, 156, 171

medicinal 22, 34, 55, 56, 73, 116, 170, 187, 188, 189, 190, 191, 192, 195, 196, 197, 198, 199, 200, 201, 203, 205, 206, 208, 209, 210, 249, 250, 258, 262

medicinal plants 73, 188, 191, 196, 197, 198, 199, 206, 208, 209

men vii, 11, 21, 34, 39, 45, 48, 50, 56, 57, 61, 64, 65, 68, 71, 74, 79, 81, 88, 90, 91, 92, 93, 96, 97, 100, 101, 103, 115, 118, 119, 120, 121, 123, 124, 129, 132, 133, 150, 151, 152, 155, 156, 159, 161, 163, 170, 171, 177, 178, 179, 180, 183, 185, 188, 190, 192, 194, 199, 200, 209, 212, 216, 219, 220, 222, 223, 252, 259

metals 13, 101

Metre 1, 14, 15, 24, 44, 47, 64, 65, 66, 67, 68, 69, 70, 106, 107, 108, 109, 110, 111, 112, 113, 117, 118, 119, 120, 121, 122, 123, 124, 125, 126, 128, 129, 131, 132, 133, 134, 175, 176, 177, 178, 179, 180, 181, 183,

184, 185, 188, 189, 190, 191, 192, 193, 194, 195, 196, 197, 198, 199, 200, 201, 202, 203, 204, 205, 206, 208, 211

Mitra 16, 34, 47, 49, 50, 51, 71, 82, 116, 128, 167, 168, 184, 185

Moksha .... ix, 12

mother 20, 65, 80, 81, 88, 89, 127, 140, 189, 190, 191, 197, 222, 260

Narad 193

nation 13, 22, 127, 130, 211, 223

Oak 28, 31

organic 20, 23, 39, 72, 257, 259, 260

oxen 23, 56, 60, 61, 64, 65, 67, 68, 75, 169, 170, 173, 185, 186, 214, 216, 218, 219, 223, 240, 241, 248, 255, 257

Palasha 187, 192, 210

Pankti 14, 15, 16, 38, 103, 154, 156, 179

Parjanya 22, 44, 60, 77, 93, 147, 149, 150, 151, 152, 153, 154, 155, 156, 163, 165, 166, 176

Peepal 19, 187, 192, 193, 194, 210

plants 11, 22, 23, 34, 55, 56, 60, 68, 72, 73, 74, 75, 78, 85, 93, 111, 141, 149, 151, 152, 153, 154, 156, 157, 183, 186, 187, 188, 189, 190, 191, 192, 194, 195, 196, 197, 198, 199, 200, 201, 202, 203, 204, 205, 206, 208, 209, 210, 240, 250, 253, 259, 262

plough 13, 42, 43, 47, 51, 56, 57, 59, 60, 64, 65, 66, 67, 68, 169, 173, 213, 241, 242, 243, 244, 255

prayer 74, 191, 201, 206, 213

products 13, 39, 173, 177, 211

purport 44, 55, 56, 58, 59, 60, 65, 66, 68, 70, 88, 97, 100, 101, 121, 125, 133, 151, 154, 156, 157, 158, 160, 169, 174, 177, 179, 194, 195, 197, 198, 201, 202, 206, 209, 214, 218, 219, 220, 222, 236, 240

Purusha 193, 194

Pusha 16, 45, 98, 169

rainfall 22, 23, 39, 41, 42, 56, 58, 73, 77, 83, 93, 146, 147, 149, 159, 161, 163, 164, 165, 166, 174, 236, 237, 238, 239, 245, 274

Richa vi, ix, 1, 8, 12, 24, 26, 32, 33, 34, 41, 42, 43, 45, 46, 47, 48, 49, 53, 54, 55, 56, 57, 58, 59, 60, 61, 62, 63, 77, 78, 79, 80, 81, 82, 83, 84, 87, 88, 89, 90, 91, 92, 93, 94, 95, 96, 97, 98, 99, 100, 101, 102, 103, 104,

105, 106, 107, 108, 109, 110, 111, 112, 113, 114, 115, 116, 149, 150, 151, 152, 153, 154, 155, 156, 157, 158, 159, 160, 161, 167, 168, 169, 170, 174, 175, 176, 177, 178, 179, 180, 181, 182, 183, 184, 185, 188, 211, 212, 213, 214, 215, 216, 217, 218, 219, 220, 221, 222

Rigveda *i, v, vi, vii, viii, ix, x, xix,* 1, 2, 4, 5, 6, 7, 8, 11, 12, 13, 14, 15, 18, 19, 20, 21, 22, 23, 24, 25, 26, 27, 28, 31, 32, 33, 34, 37, 38, 39, 40, 41, 42, 43, 44, 46, 49, 50, 53, 57, 61, 64, 68, 71, 72, 73, 74, 77, 83, 84, 85, 86, 87, 93, 102, 112, 113, 117, 126, 135, 137, 145, 147, 149, 150, 151, 153, 154, 155, 156, 157, 161, 163, 165, 167, 172, 173, 174, 179, 187, 188, 204, 209, 221, 222, 223, 224, 230, 233, 235, 237, 262

Rishi *vi,* 1, 2, 22, 24, 25, 32, 33, 37, 38, 42, 43, 44, 45, 46, 47, 48, 49, 50, 53, 54, 55, 56, 57, 58, 59, 60, 61, 62, 63, 64, 65, 66, 67, 68, 69, 70, 77, 78, 79, 80, 81, 82, 84, 88, 89, 90, 91, 92, 93, 94, 95, 96, 97, 98, 99, 100, 101, 102, 103, 104, 105, 106, 107, 108, 109, 110, 111, 112, 113, 115, 116, 117, 118, 119, 120, 121, 122, 123, 124, 125, 126, 128, 129, 131, 132, 133, 134, 149, 150, 151, 152, 153

154, 155, 156, 157, 158, 160, 161, 162, 167, 168, 169, 170, 171, 172, 174, 175, 176, 177, 178, 179, 180, 181, 182, 183, 184, 185, 188, 189, 190, 191, 192, 193, 194, 195, 196, 197, 198, 199, 200, 201, 202, 203, 204, 205, 206, 208, 211, 212, 213, 214, 215, 216, 217, 218, 219, 220, 222, 235, 237, 238, 241

Rishis *viii,* 11, 12, 17, 24, 25, 26, 37, 46, 77, 95, 146, 149, 159

Samhita 1, 24, 26, 27, 255

Samveda, ... *viii,* 2, 12

Sanskrit *viii,* 1, 7, 17, 42, 43, 108, 175, 235

Saraswati 23, 40, 85, 87, 88, 89, 90, 91, 92, 93, 94, 95, 96, 97, 98, 99, 100, 101, 102, 103, 104, 105, 106, 109, 111, 112, 114

Satyug 189

seas 153, 154, 181, 223, 224

Shimyus 171

ships 13, 40, 85, 211, 212, 223, 224

Soma 25, 61, 62, 129, 158, 160, 169, 172, 177, 181, 187, 204, 205, 208, 209, 210, 218, 219, 262

Somaras 5, 26, 61, 66, 161, 169, 218, 219, 220

Somavati 187, 195, 196, 210

Soop 221

Sri Krishna v, 2, 3, 71, 72, 163, 192, 193, 247

Sukta 1, 24, 26, 32, 41, 42, 49, 53, 61, 78, 79, 82, 87, 93, 106, 149, 150, 151, 152, 153, 154, 155, 156, 157, 158, 159, 160, 169, 175, 211

Taitariya Samhita 35, 170, 172

taxation .... ix, 13

trade viii, ix, 12, 23, 24, 40, 85, 127, 147, 211, 223, 224, 255, 268

Tretayug 189

Trishtup 14, 15, 16, 38, 47, 53, 62, 65, 73, 81, 82, 90, 91, 92, 93, 113, 115, 117, 118, 119, 120, 121, 128, 129, 131, 132, 133, 134, 149, 150, 151, 152, 153, 154, 156, 157, 168, 171, 175, 176, 177, 178, 180, 183, 184, 185, 211, 212, 213, 215, 216, 217, 218, 219, 220, 222

Udojas 187, 195, 196, 210

universe v, vii, viii, 11, 12, 23, 48, 49, 101, 105, 106, 157, 182

universes 101

Urjayanti 187, 195, 196, 210

Vaidic viii, ix, x, 3, 8, 12, 13, 14, 15, 16, 17, 18, 19, 20, 33, 38, 39, 40, 41, 43, 77, 85, 135, 137, 139, 144, 162, 168, 173, 174, 185, 186, 187, 188, 209, 215, 222, 231, 235, 236, 241, 254, 255, 256, 257, 258, 259, 260

Varuna 16, 34, 47, 49, 50, 71, 77, 78, 82, 84, 107, 116, 128, 147, 157, 158, 159, 167, 168, 184, 185, 202, 203, 266

Vashishtha vi, 33, 82, 117, 118, 119, 122, 123, 124, 125, 126, 160, 184, 185

Vedam 31

Vedas .... viii, 12, 33, 170, 254

Vibhuti 193

Vishvedevas 211, 212, 213, 214, 215, 216, 217, 218, 219, 220

Viswamitra 32, 159

war 34, 97, 133, 151, 171, 186, 190, 220

water viii, x, 5, 13, 22, 23, 24, 39, 40, 46, 47, 48, 49, 50, 54, 55, 56, 57, 58, 59, 60, 67, 68, 69, 70, 71, 73, 74, 77, 78, 79, 80, 81, 82, 83, 84, 85, 90, 92, 93, 95, 96, 98, 99, 100, 102, 103, 112, 113, 114, 116, 117, 120, 122, 126, 127, 133, 139, 143, 145, 146, 147, 149, 150, 151, 152, 153, 154, 155, 156, 157,

159, 161, 165, 167, 168, 169, 171, 175, 176, 181, 182, 183, 186, 214, 215, 216, 217, 218, 223, 224, 229, 237, 238, 245, 247, 249, 250, 251, 252, 253, 254, 257, 271, 272

wealth *ix, 13, 23, 39, 44, 48, 49, 50, 54, 62, 63, 79, 80, 81, 97, 98, 101, 103, 104, 113, 114, 127, 129, 130, 158, 167, 172, 173, 174, 179, 181, 182, 184, 185, 186, 191, 196, 197, 241, 242, 257*

weapons *13, 21, 129, 212, 217, 220, 221*

wheels *13, 83, 98, 115, 219*

Yajna *2, 3, 4, 33, 41, 44, 48, 50, 65, 66, 69, 71, 74, 79, 80, 88, 97, 98, 106, 120, 121, 122, 129, 154, 163, 164, 165, 166, 168, 170, 176, 177, 180, 181, 212, 217, 218, 256*

Yajurveda .... *viii, 2, 12*

yava *213*

yoke... *56, 57, 173, 213, 214, 243*

www.ingramcontent.com/pod-product-compliance
Lightning Source LLC
Chambersburg PA
CBHW052342220526
45465CB00003BA/914